Long Distance Relationships:
The Complete Guide

Long Distance Relationships: The Complete Guide

Dr. Gregory T. Guldner

J$_F$Milne Publications

Corona, CA

www.jfmilne.com

Dedicated to my wife, Amy

First printing 2003, second printing 2004

ISBN 0-9721148-0-7

LCCN 2002094181

ATTENTION UNIVERSITIES, COLLEGES, LIBRARIES, CORPORATIONS AND PROFESSIONAL ORGANIZATIONS: JFMilne publications offers discounts for bulk orders of this book for distribution to students, employees, counselors, therapists, researchers, and other interested parties. For more information please write to JFMilne Publications 750 S. Lincoln Ave # 104–373, Corona, CA, 92882 or email inquiries to customerservice@jfmilne.com.

What People Are Saying About
Long Distance Relationships: The Complete Guide

This book puts a whole new meaning to Romeo's balcony soliloquy "Goodnight—goodnight! Parting is such sweet sorrow. That I shall say goodnight till it be morrow." To maintain a Long Distance Relationship for more than 24 hours—you'd be advised to read Gregory Guldner's book. Actually the advice could be a guide to enhance every relationship over a long period of time.

Sue Johanson, RN
Host of syndicated television's Talk Sex *and the* Sunday Night Sex Show

This wise, illuminating, and highly readable guide for how to successfully negotiate the challenges of living apart should be read by any couple living in or considering a long distance relationship, even for a few months. Based on the actual experiences of hundreds of couples, it provides a rich compendium of information, ideas, survival tips and resources, a framework for understanding the emotional stages of an LDR, and strategies and guidance for managing each stage.

Judith Meyers Avis, PhD
Award winning couples therapist
Professor of Couples Therapy

This very readable book is based on sound research and yet is also able to offer many practical tips on this important topic.

Steve Duck, PhD
Author of 36 books on interpersonal
relationships and founding editor of
Journal of Social and Personal Relationships; *Department of Communication Studies, University of Iowa*

LDDRs (long distance dating relationships) continue to increase in frequency and Dr. Guldner's guide provides a roadmap/safe way through this most difficult journey.

David Knox, PhD
Professor of Sociology
East Carolina State University

The most readable guide to long distance relationships. Loaded with tips and resources for separated couples.

Julie Ferman, Founder, CupidsCoach.com
Author, Marketing Yourself for Romance

. . . insightful, thoughtful, real world practical, and very highly recommended reading for anyone who must deal with a long range, long distance relationship.

The Midwest Book Review

This book gets right to the point and addresses all of the issues that couples in long distance relationships agonize over while they have to be apart.

Jan Price, Relationship communication consultant and author

Bang! Target . . . dead center! This book hits the mark! This book is the most complete book of little-known but critical "ground rules" for a happy and successful long distance relationship you will find.

Larry James, author How to Really Love the One You're With

Awesome! This book changed the way I looked at my long distance relationship. I started out worried that Mark and I might not make it. Now I'm sure we can do it.

Susan L. (Chicago, IL)

This book shatters so many myths about long distance relationships. Finally, something that relies on research instead of just opinions.

Ryan T. (Fort Meade, U.S. Army)

Table of Contents

Chapter 1

Welcome to the World of Long-Distance Relationships

John and Catherine

John and Catherine met during the summer between their sophomore and junior years at college, when John inadvertently careened his bicycle into Catherine while rushing across campus. After exchanging apologies, John offered to make up for his blunder over coffee; and thus began two years of what Catherine later told me was a "deliciously romantic affair."

As the end of their senior year approached the two found themselves applying for graduate positions at universities scattered throughout the country. John was looking for a position in chemical engineering, preferably in northern California, while Catherine was applying for a masters program in education in the Midwest. Ultimately, they both landed their top choices in graduate schools–placing them roughly 2,000 miles away from one another.

Both were very much committed to making the relationship work and decided to try a long-distance relationship (LDR). After roughly a year of monthly plane flights, escalating telephone bills, and lonely Saturday nights, Catherine spotted a flyer for a study of long-distance relationships, and she decided to come and share with me some of what she and John had learned.

John and Catherine belong to a growing number of couples who find themselves involved in long-distance relationships. That you've read this far suggests that you probably are either one of those many, or know someone who is. Assuming you are indeed in a long-distance relationship, rest assured that you are in a very large minority. We don't know exactly how many people consider themselves involved in an LDR, but estimates suggest that there are somewhere between 700,000 and one million of you in geographically separated marriages[1] and an additional one to one-and-a-half million in long-distance dating relationships.[2] And these numbers don't include the hundreds of thousands of you in the Armed Forces.

While the statistics may not be surprising, the lack of information and assistance for those in LDRs is. Make a quick browse through any bookstore and you'll

1

find several shelves of books on dating, marriage, and romance, yet very little about LDRs. In my extensive search over the last 10 years, I have found a few dozen articles, a couple of books meant for psychologists, and very few books meant for those in LDRs. Unfortunately, some of the suggestions made in a few of these books, although sound for most "normal" relationships, were in direct conflict with the results of recent studies done with couples in LDRs.

Over the past decade that I have studied LDRs I have realized that, while a fair amount of accurate information exists out there, no one has taken the time to put it together in a simple guide for those of you actually in long-distance relationships. This book fills that gap. It draws on several sources, the most detailed of which involves a study that I undertook during my clinical psychology training–a study that eventually became one of the largest projects examining LDRs ever completed.[3] As part of the study, we examined over 200 LDRs, personally interviewed dozens of couples, and followed almost a hundred couples over time to see how their relationships eventually turned out. Since that time, I have had the luxury of speaking with several hundred people in LDRs, learning what worked for them and why. I also draw upon my own experience, having been in a wonderful and fulfilling LDR myself for many years.

What you will learn in this book are the answers to the most common questions I'm asked about LDRs. You will also be provided with practical answers gleaned from the hundreds of those who shared their wisdom. Throughout the text I've illustrated certain points by introducing you to the true stories of various couples, like John and Catherine, who are in LDRs. I've changed the names and identifying situations of some couples, as they preferred to remain anonymous, but the rest of the information is accurate. I've also highlighted a number of survival tips in each chapter that provide practical advice to help make your experience as fulfilling and successful as possible.

While there are many opinions out there about LDRs, very few are anything but that–an opinion. This book will guide you along, with answers provided by both rigorous scientific study and the heartfelt passionate explorations of those who have traveled this path before. Because this book represents the first attempt to gather together all of the scientific information available on long-distance relationships, I've chosen to provide the specific reference for any claims or suggestions I make. The full description of any source cited in the text can be found in the bibliography at the end of the book.

Whatever type of LDR you have–dating or married, military or civilian, separated because of school or career–you'll find the secrets that have allowed others in your situation to triumph over the distance and keep that someone special close at heart.

Some of the many questions we'll answer include:

• Do long-distance relationships really work?
• How often should I visit?
• Is an LDR right for me?

- Are people in LDRs more likely to cheat on each other compared to those people in traditional relationships?
- How do I make it easier when we have to leave each other?
- I feel like I'm on a constant rollercoaster ride of emotions. Is this normal?
- Should we see other people while we're apart?
- How should we deal with arguments when we're apart?

LDRs can be a wonderful and exciting way to combine important career issues with a meaningful and committed relationship. They can and do work every day, and millions of us have tremendously fulfilling adventures with LDRs.

However, long-distance love has many pitfalls, and navigating through the ups and downs unique to these types of relationships often takes guidance and reassurance. As you begin your journey of discovery, I'll answer the most pressing question in the next chapter: Do long-distance relationships work? In Chapter 3, you can take the *Separation Inventory* by answering 25 questions in a brief survey designed to assess important areas of your personality, your support system, and your unique situation, all of which may affect your LDR. Then, we'll expand on your Separation Inventory by having you and your partner together complete a second questionnaire that is designed to pinpoint strengths and weaknesses within your relationship that may need attention. Then in Chapters 5 through 8, I'll discuss the results of these two tests and focus on how to distance-proof your relationship based on your own unique strengths and weaknesses.

Part II discusses specific issues common to long-distance relationships, and we'll discuss some very practical suggestions for your LDR. I'll show you the wonderful advantages that come from having a long-distance romance, and then discuss the emotional stages we all go through during separation: anger, depression, loneliness, emotional detachment, anxiety, guilt, and so forth. Building on these stages, I'll show you the 10 steps research has shown to help you stay emotionally healthy while apart from your loved one.

Chapter 12 discusses the secret to keeping your relationship as intimate as ever, even when you have to be so far apart. After this discussion, we'll tackle the question of how often you should visit, call, and write your partner. You can also peruse statistics from our study showing what the average couple in an LDR is doing in this regard.

I'll also tell you why using the telephone may not be the next best thing to being there. Research has shown six pitfalls of talking on the telephone, and we'll discuss how to avoid them.

Then in Chapter 15, we'll discuss the research that shows you may have a secret weapon for your LDR–writing letters! If you aren't writing to your partner, read this fascinating research and then get out your pen. In Chapter 16, we'll heat things up a bit and talk about sex and how the separation can make things wild or wobbly. We'll explore the various ways couples keep their sex lives hot even when they're a thousand miles apart. In keeping with this theme, we'll discuss the problem of sexual affairs. (Can you guess whether they are more common in LDRs?)

We'll also address the issue of whether you should date other people while you're apart, if this is something you're considering.

Finally, we'll explore the difficult process of saying goodbye, and I'll share some hints to make the parting a little easier. We'll look at problems that you're likely to encounter when you and your partner have the opportunity to get together. We'll also discuss the difficult issue of how to argue when you're apart, and we'll review some of the differences between men and women when it comes to separation.

While the vignettes I use to illustrate important concepts come from heterosexual relationships, I do not in any way mean to exclude those gay and lesbian couples in LDRs. The time I've spent with hundreds of couples in LDRs has led me to believe that the same fundamental principals apply to everyone in separated relationships regardless of their sexual orientation.

Before we begin I'd like to offer my congratulations and encouragement to you and your partner for caring enough about one another to embark on a long-distance relationship. The path may be turbulent, but the result is well worth the effort.

Chapter 2

Do LDRs Really Work?

Tara and Keith

Tara and Keith had been married only two years when Keith was offered a huge promotion that he'd been waiting for since he began working as a biotechnology consultant. He had assumed that Tara would approve of the 1200-mile move, even though Tara was working as an architect in her dream job. Keith was wrong. The couple began a two-week battle over whether Keith should take the promotion (although Keith had already begun to make the arrangements). Toward the end of the two weeks, they had come no closer to a decision, and Keith felt strongly that he needed to take the promotion in order to continue climbing the corporate ladder. Tara felt strongly that her career was well entrenched and that a move would significantly set her back. Each had a lot to lose.

A friend of Tara's finally suggested that they could compromise by having a temporary LDR. Keith would take the new job and move, and they could see one another about once every three weeks. Tara thought that their relationship was strong enough to survive an LDR and she set out to sell the idea to Keith. Keith was leery of this option but recognized that it did seem better than the alternatives. He began asking around his office, curious as to what his coworkers would think of the idea. The consensus: "You guys are going to try a long-distance relationship? They never work!"

Eventually Tara and Keith decided to give it a go, and I was able to talk with them after an eight-month separation. They had made a very difficult choice because they had heard from almost everyone that LDRs don't work. They believed that they were taking a serious risk with their relationship in order to further their careers.

Ask around yourself whether LDRs work and you'll find that most people have the same opinion. In my own studies I've found that you get two different answers. If you ask people who are not currently in an LDR they will say, "LDRs don't work." Of course, you get a slightly different story from those in separated relationships who, understandably, want to believe that everything will work out in the end. The truly sad part about these opposite camps is that those in LDRs often face daily bombardment from the naysayers, which for some couples makes them constantly reevaluate their choice.

Julie, a 20-year-old college student dating a Navy diver, asked me once, "Am I crazy for even trying this? Everyone tells me this will never work out." Julie wasn't having any particular difficulty with her LDR and told me she was quite satisfied with the relationship. Julie needed reassurance that what she was doing was normal and rational.

Let me assure you that LDRs are both normal–in the sense that a large majority of us have, at one time or another, been involved in an LDR–and rational, in that they do work, and often they are the best choice given the alternatives that we face. In one study of premarital couples, we found that nearly three-quarters had been involved in an LDR at some point and that around 25% were currently involved in an LDR.[3] Long-distance marriages are less common, but by no means rare.

So LDRs are everywhere, and everyone wants to know one thing: Do they work? Before answering this I need to define what it means for a relationship "to work." Most people are interested in whether or not the relationship can simply survive the separation. They want to know if trying a long-distance relationship means that they have a greater chance of breaking up than if they were in a geographically close relationship. The most accurate answer to this is that no one knows for sure. However, the majority of studies that have been done show no greater risk of an LDR breaking up than any other relationship.[2, 4–6]

Many people find this hard to believe, and I've heard scores of people scoff when I say this. They then quickly produce their own story of how their LDR didn't last. Let me make it clear that I'm not saying that every LDR will work, only that they work *as well as any other relationship.* When we followed premarital couples in LDRs and compared them to another group of couples in geographically close relationships, we found that around 40% of both groups eventually went their separate ways. Many relationships end, but we tend to remember those LDRs that did not work, more so than the geographically closer relationships that failed.

Studies have shown that whenever a close relationship ends we try to figure out why. People basically focus on four possibilities:

- There was something wrong with themselves. ("I was too clingy.")
- There was something wrong with their partner. ("He was a jerk!")
- There was simply an incompatibility. ("He's kind of an introvert and I like to party.")
- There was something external to the relationship. ("We just couldn't handle the distance.")

Interestingly, research has shown that women tend to find fault within the relationship, seeing the breakup as resulting from interpersonal problems ("We're just not right for each other"), while men are more likely to try to place the blame on something outside of the relationship, such as too much time apart.[7–9] While the studies have shown that LDRs stay together just as frequently (or infrequently) as other relationships, we often try to blame the distance when they do fail. Admittedly, it is easier to say, "Everything would have been fine had we lived closer," than to say that things didn't work out because of some issue with the relationship or ourselves. In fact, this tendency to blame the distance usually ends up in a more amicable breakup.[10] However, this also means that many people firmly believe that LDRs don't work. Fortunately, the research shows that this isn't true.

While this is good news, it's only part of the story. Staying together isn't always the best thing for a relationship, as we all know. Many relationships should end if those involved are unsatisfied or feel trapped. So another way of looking at whether LDRs, or any relationship, "work" is to examine the quality of the relationship. Conveniently, researchers have done just that. In our study we compared those in LDRs with those in geographically close relationships. We looked at relationship satisfaction, commitment, intimacy, and trust. We found that on all these measures the two groups were *identical.*[11] While our study was the largest and most detailed, several other studies have found the same thing.[5, 12–17, 176]

Survival Tip # 1

First and foremost, remember that despite anything people tell you to the contrary, studies have shown that LDRs have as much chance of making it as any other relationship.

Remember, these numbers compare one group to another. However, there are certainly individuals who have more or less difficulty in an LDR. So while it is true that, as a group, those in LDRs do as well as those in geographically close relationships, this does not mean that you personally will do as well. Many factors make some people better able to deal with the different advantages and disadvantages of LDRs. The next chapter examines the question, "How difficult will an LDR be *for me?*"

Part I

The Separation Inventory: Exploring Your Long-Distance Relationship

Chapter 3

The Separation Inventory: Part I

Jamie and Andrew

Jamie, a 27-year-old law student dating a graphic design artist who lived 300 miles away, came to talk with me about the difficulties she was having in the relationship. They had been dating for almost two years when Jamie moved to northern California for law school, and her partner, Andrew, had agreed that they should try a long-distance relationship. At the time Jamie was confident that she would have little difficulty with an LDR, although she admits to me now that she can't remember, "what possessed me to think that!"

After three weeks of being separated, she began having serious doubts about whether she and Andrew would make it in an LDR. When I asked her what things bothered her the most about the distance, she pulled out a list that she had already been preparing: "Number one, I'm lonely all the time. Number two, I really miss having him next to me when I sleep. Number three, I have absolutely no social life now without him around . . ." Jamie's list continued beyond number twenty. I sympathized for Jamie, as she was obviously struggling to make sense of her LDR.

She spent the next several weeks trying to decide what to do with her career and her relationship. Ultimately, she and Andrew decided that they would give the LDR six months and reassess the relationship at that time. After six months Jamie felt no different. After discussing the situation with Jamie, Andrew decided that he would move closer to Jamie and find a job in California. Jamie, a former psychology major, shared with me that while she believes that LDRs can work, she realizes that for some people the disadvantages of the separation far outweigh the advantages.

Jamie and Andrew were in a fortunate situation in that Andrew had enough flexibility to be able to relocate when they decided that the separation was simply too difficult. Many other couples do not have that opportunity, and the decision they have to make is often between a long-distance relationship and no relationship at all. Still others find themselves entertaining the possibility of starting a relationship-at-a-distance after having met someone special on a vacation, or on a business trip, or over the Internet. While no one can tell you for sure how easy or difficult the experience will be for you, there has been a fair amount of research that can help in evaluating how well or poorly you may do in an LDR.

I've developed a brief questionnaire that will help you determine how difficult an LDR will be for you, and will help pinpoint areas that may be particularly at risk. Remember that regardless of how difficult or easy an experience you may have, you can still enjoy a successful LDR. I've seen relationships survive when both people seem to hate being in an LDR, while other LDRs break up even though both people seem to prefer being separated. It's simply a matter of your satisfaction with the relationship compared to the costs of being in an LDR.

The Separation Inventory: Part I

The Separation Inventory consists of 25 items, each with three possible choices. (In the appendix, you will find additional answer sheets for the Separation Inventory.) Circle the choice that best fits you.

1. The distance separating you and your partner is/will be:
   a. Less than 150 miles.
   b. Between 150 and 900 miles.
   c. Over 900 miles.
2. How long do you expect to be in an LDR prior to being able to live closer to one another?
   a. Less than a year.
   b. Between a year and three years.
   c. More than three years or for an unknown amount of time.
3. How would you rank you and your partner's combined financial situation?
   a. We're on a tight budget.
   b. Not fantastic but we have enough spending money.
   c. No problem; we have plenty of extra cash.
4. Do you and your partner have easy access to email?
   a. No.
   b. Yes, but it's difficult to access it every day.
   c. Yes, and we can both access it every day.
5. If the LDR was simply too difficult for one of you, could you move closer to one another?
   a. Yes, either one of us could move to meet the other one.
   b. Yes, one of us could move.
   c. No, neither of us could move.
6. How *flexible* is your schedule with regard to being able to see one another?
   a. We both have great control over our schedules. Scheduling trips will be no problem.

b. We have some control over our schedules but not as much as we'd like.

c. We have very little control over our schedules. We'll find the time to see each other, but it will be quite difficult.

7. How *predictable* is your schedule with regard to being able to see one another and talk to one another on the telephone?

   a. We generally know exactly when we'll be able to see or talk to one another again.

   b. We often know when we'll be able to see or talk to one another again, but sometimes there are unexpected changes.

   c. We can rarely predict accurately when we'll be able to see or talk to one another again.

8. How would you describe your attitude toward talking on the telephone?

   a. I could (and do) spend hours on the telephone.

   b. I do okay for about 30 minutes or so, but then get tired.

   c. I rarely know what to say on the telephone and prefer to talk as little as possible.

9. In the past month how many cards or letters have you written to anyone?

   a. None.

   b. One.

   c. More than one.

10. Close your eyes and imagine that your partner is standing a few feet from you. Picture his or her face. Now imagine him or her saying how nice you look. Finally, imagine him or her giving you a warm hug. Do this now. Which of the following seemed most real (which was the easiest to imagine)?

    a. I could most easily *hear* my partner's voice.

    b. I could most easily *see* my partner's face.

    c. I could most easily *feel* my partner's hug.

11. How concerned are you that your partner may have an affair while you are separated?

    a. I think it's very likely that he/she could have an affair.

    b. I think it's possible but not very likely.

    c. I think it's virtually impossible.

12. How concerned are you that you may have an affair?

    a. I think it is very likely.

    b. It's possible but pretty unlikely.

    c. I'm not concerned at all.

13. Over the past week, how many days have you felt sad or blue?

    a. None or one.

    b. Two or three.

    c. More than three.

14. How would you describe the advantages of your LDR?

    a. An LDR, while difficult sometimes, is the best choice right now for my career/education.

    b. I think my LDR will help me focus on my career/education, but I probably could have done as well if my partner were living closer.

    c. I don't think an LDR will help my career/education in any way.

15. How would you rate your self-esteem?

    a. Better than most.

    b. About the same as most.

    c. Lower than most.

16. How often do you think about your partner?

    a. Constantly. I often find it difficult to concentrate on my work because I'm thinking about my partner.

    b. A lot, but it never seems to interrupt my work/study.

    c. Not very often. Probably several times a day.

17. How likely do you think it is that your relationship will survive the physical separation?

    a. 20% chance of making it.

    b. 80% chance of making it.

    c. 99.9% chance of making it.

18. Do you feel that your partner acknowledges and appreciates your efforts to maintain your long-distance relationship?

    a. My partner often does not realize how much effort I put into making the relationship work.

    b. My partner usually recognizes and appreciates my efforts but sometimes fails to realize how hard I work at it.

    c. My partner almost always acknowledges and appreciates my efforts to make this relationship work.

19. How do you view the physical separation between you and your partner?

    a. I see it as a potential crisis in our relationship that will take a great deal of work to maneuver through successfully.

    b. I see it as an obstacle that we'll overcome with our efforts to make it work.

    c. I see it as an opportunity for us to grow, both individually and as a couple.

20. Do you currently have a special friend (not including your partner) with whom you can discuss issues about your relationship?

    a. Yes, and this person is also in an LDR.

    b. Yes, but this person is not themselves involved in an LDR.

    c. No, I have no one with whom I can easily discuss these things.

21. How would you describe the support for your relationship from your *family?*

    a. They all seem to encourage me/us and think that an LDR is a good idea.

    b. Most encourage the LDR but several think we're crazy.

    c. Most think we're crazy for trying an LDR.

22. How would you describe the support network that you have (or will have) while separated?

    a. I have several friends who could take me to the airport, have lunch, go to a movie, chat about the relationship, etc.

    b. I have one or two friends who could do those things.

    c. I have no one who could help me out with those things.

23. How would you describe the support for your relationship from your *friends?*

    a. They all seem to encourage me/us and think that an LDR is a good idea.

    b. Most encourage the LDR but several think we're crazy.

    c. Most think we're crazy for trying an LDR.

24. How would you describe your relationship with your partner's friends?

    a. When we get together with each other we often find time to spend with friends.

    b. When we get together we usually spend time with just each other, although we could easily get together with friends if we wanted to.

    c. My partner's friends don't understand our relationship and we choose not to spend much time with them when we get together.

25. How often do you feel isolated from the activities of others in your community?

    a. I often find that I'm not included or not welcome in events where I live, and I feel socially isolated much of the time.

    b. I occasionally feel excluded or not welcome in events where I live, and sometimes feel socially isolated.

    c. I rarely feel excluded or not welcome in events where I live, and rarely feel socially isolated.

Scoring the Separation Inventory

The Separation Inventory: Part I gives you four scores: one overall score, that we'll discuss below, and three subscores that help pinpoint difficult areas, each of which are discussed in later chapters.

First, transfer your answers from the Separation Inventory answer sheet to the Separation Inventory scoring sheet found in the appendix. Now, add all of the point values together to get your total score. Then, add the points for each item in each subscale. This should give you four scores:

- A total score from 0–50
- A demographics score from 0–14
- A personality score from 0–24
- A support score from 0–12

Before I discuss the results, I would like to make an analogy that I've found helpful. Think of your LDR as a complicated aircraft, and you are the pilot. When the plane reaches its cruising altitude, you don't have to pay much attention. In fact you may have the autopilot doing most of the minute-to-minute changes. Yet during landing and takeoff you must focus intensely on what you're doing.

Most of the time is spent cruising and requires little effort. This represents the time away from each other when your attention is, for the most part, focused on issues other than the relationship, such as career and education. Every so often the air traffic controller chimes in with a suggestion, or the plane hits a bit of turbulence and the pilot needs to make a brief adjustment. The pilot must return his or her focus to the plane for a few moments.

Each time you call your partner or get an email or run to the store to find the right "I miss you" card, you are that pilot making some minor adjustments to help keep the relationship on course. Then comes the landing and takeoff, which are similar to the time you actually spend with your partner when you're very focused on the relationship. Unfortunately, for some, there are also the occasional times when the midair collision warning alarm starts screaming, and they find that they have to focus intensely on the relationship, usually with a good helping of butterflies in the stomach.

I mention this analogy to help bring into focus the meaning of your Separation Inventory. Each of the groups below needs to pilot their relationship a little differently.

If Your Total Score on Part I of the Separation Inventory Is Between 41–50

Long-distance relationships pose few difficulties for you. You'll find that while there will be some areas that will give you trouble, as a whole you have an excellent combination of personality, support system, and environment for a long-distance relationship. This is the group who pretty much fly on autopilot. It's unlikely that you'll have to make many adjustments, except for the occasional glance at the instruments and out the window. You won't feel like you'll need to put a great deal of energy into the flight.

If Your Total Score on Part I of the Separation Inventory Is Between 21–40

Most people in LDRs fall in this range, and they usually say that while they prefer the LDR to the other available alternatives they do have a difficult time with it. This is the group of people who can benefit the most from assessing their strengths and weaknesses and making an effort to bolster their LDR survival skills. Whether the relationship will flourish or wither with the distance is difficult to say with this group, and depends mostly on the effort of those involved. Use this information as simply a yellow warning light to signal that you need to be on guard for problems that come with most LDRs. You may need to change some things to make the relationship work. This group doesn't have the luxury of leaving things on autopilot. Keep your hands on the stick and your eyes on the gauges, but stay calm and comfortable. You'll likely have a relatively smooth and pleasant flight.

If Your Total Score on Part I of the Separation Inventory Is Between 0–20

Long-distance relationships pose some particularly difficult issues for you. By no means does this mean that your LDR is doomed to failure–it just may take more work than most. As I mentioned for the group above, you should consider this an early warning signal and prepare yourself for the challenge. Buckle your safety belts and wake up the copilot; you'll need to focus on the bumpy ride ahead. But take heart–sometimes the most enjoyable and fulfilling flights are the wild rides (once you've safely landed). You may consider attempting to cut short the flight if you can. Talk with your partner and plan on reevaluating the relationship every few months. Try to change what you can to make this relationship a little easier. Use the Separation Inventory to focus on the areas that seem to need the most help and to change those things that you can.

Incidentally, the copilot refers to your partner. Make sure they know that you need them awake and alert in the cockpit.

Using the Subscale Scores

The questionnaire you just completed looks at how your own personality and situation will affect your ability to handle the LDR. Chapters 5, 6, and 7 discuss how each of the subscale scores can be used to pinpoint specific areas in your LDR that may need more attention than others. The next chapter delves into Part II of your Separation Inventory, which consists of questions for you and your partner to take together. Part II assesses the relationship, compared to Part I, which looked more at your own personality and situation. While many tests are available to examine relationships, this quiz focuses specifically on the unique aspects of LDRs.

Chapter 4

Your Separation Inventory: Part II–Your Relationship

David and Sarah

David and Sarah had been married less than a year when Sarah decided to return to school for an MBA program that was about four hours away by car. They had dated for two years prior to marriage, and David felt like they knew one another quite well. But during the first month after Sarah moved into her new apartment, things began to fall apart.

"I expected that Sarah would be back each weekend," David told me. "I don't think it's that much to ask; it's only four hours away."

Sarah disagreed. She was busy with her studies and found that the weekend gave her a great opportunity to get work done, especially without needing to focus on David.

"Every time I call, she's out at one of their get-togethers and by the time she gets home I'm already asleep."

David felt threatened that Sarah spent so much time networking, even though he knew that socializing with other business students was important to her. Ultimately, it became clear that David and Sarah had very different ideas about the day-to-day maintenance of an LDR.

David wanted to talk to Sarah daily and see her every weekend. Sarah was busy enjoying her new life as a graduate student and felt comfortable seeing David once or twice a month. Sarah felt that David was insecure, while David felt Sarah didn't care. Both of their feelings are understandable, and neither more valid than the other. They needed to discuss these issues directly and agree upon a plan of action, which they did. They agreed to have "telephone dates" on Tuesday, Thursday, and Friday and to visit each other three weekends a month. They would reevaluate this plan after six months, with both agreeing to change if the other felt the current plan wasn't working.

Unfortunately, David and Sarah could not agree on how much time to spend together, and the issue remained a difficult one for their relationship. Their dilemma is a common one, especially among those who have no experience with

LDRs, and therefore don't know how comfortable they are with various aspects unique to this kind of relationship. Part II of the Separation Inventory is designed to see how well you and your partner's preferences match.

There are no right or wrong answers in Part II. Your score as a couple is calculated by looking at the differences between your answer and your partner's answer. The overall score will help decide if this is an area you'll both need to work on. Individual items on which you differ should stimulate discussion between the two of you. One of the themes that will come up again and again in long-distance relationships is that it doesn't matter so much what you decide, as long as you discuss it openly and come to an agreement. Later chapters will help guide you and your partner in making several of these decisions, but realize that these decisions differ for every couple.

You should first answer the questions in Part II yourself. Then, have your partner answer the questions either by email, fax, regular mail, or telephone. Be very careful not to influence your partner's answers if you do this over the telephone. Have them silently write down their answer for each item as they go.

The appendix contains several answer sheets for Part II of the Separation Inventory.

The Separation Inventory–Part II: Your Relationship

1. Over the next six months, how often, on average, will you visit one another face-to-face?
   a. Weekly.
   b. Twice a month.
   c. Monthly.
   d. Every other month.
   e. Once every four months or less.
2. Over the next six months, how often, on average, will you speak to one another on the telephone?
   a. Daily.
   b. Every other day.
   c. Twice a week.
   d. Once a week.
   e. Less than once a week.
3. If you were leaving your partner to return home, which of the following would you prefer? (Assume you had to fly.)
   a. Saying goodbye at his/her place and taking a taxi or shuttle to the airport.
   b. Having him/her drive me to the airport, and saying goodbye in the car. (He/she doesn't get out of the car.)
   c. Having him/her drive me to the airport, and saying goodbye at the curb. (He/she gets out of the car.)
   d. Having him/her drive me to the airport and stay with me as long as possible before saying goodbye.

4. One night you're watching a program on TV you've been waiting to see all week. The telephone rings right at the most interesting part of the show. You're pretty sure it's your partner calling. (Consider the VCR broken for this question.) You:

   a. Don't answer the telephone. You'll check your messages after the show.

   b. Answer the telephone, tell him/her you want to finish watching the show, and you'll call back when it's done.

   c. Answer the telephone, talk to your partner, and watch TV at the same time.

   d. Answer the telephone and talk to your partner, missing the rest of the TV show.

5. How long will your geographical separation last before you'll be able to live closer to one another? Your best guess would be:

   a. Less than 6 months.

   b. Six months to 1 year.

   c. Between 1 year and 18 months.

   d. Between 18 months and 2 years.

   e. Between 2 and 3 years.

   f. Between 3 and 4 years.

   g. More than 4 years.

6. Your partner calls and casually mentions that she/he had dinner yesterday night with a new friend who turns out to be single and just your partner's type. (Your partner doesn't say this, but you know him or her pretty well.) How do you feel about this?

   a. I think it's a major mistake to have dinner with someone like this, even casually. I would prefer my partner have nothing to do with this person.

   b. It worries me a lot. I'd prefer my partner only be around this person if they are in a group. Doing things with this person alone is a mistake.

   c. It worries me. I'd prefer my partner not be having dinner with this person, though a business lunch alone with them is probably okay.

   d. It worries me a little. I'm comfortable with my partner having dinner alone with this person, but I'd like to know that they're not spending too much time together.

   e. It doesn't worry me at all. I'm glad my partner has found a friend.

7. You and your partner have not seen one another for four weeks when you get together for a three-day weekend. During this three-day weekend, how much of your time should you spend apart from your partner (for instance, how much time alone or with friends other than your partner)?

   a. I'd prefer that we be together the entire weekend. I'm alone enough most of the time.

   b. I'd like to spend the vast majority of my time with my partner but an hour or two out of the weekend I might spend by myself.

    c. I'd spend most of the time together, but I'd probably take one evening or so (out of three) to spend without my partner.

    d. I enjoy spending time with my partner, but I also need time for myself. I'd probably spend about half of the time without my partner.

8. You and your partner have been away from one another for four weeks. How soon after you reunite would you like to have sex? (If you and your partner are in a relationship that does not yet include sex, answer the question as if sex was part of your relationship.)

    a. In the airport if we could get away with it.

    b. We'd head home and take care of a couple of necessities (hanging up clothes that don't do well in a suitcase, etc.), but definitely within the hour.

    c. I'd like to have a nice dinner out with my partner, and then head home after a couple of hours.

    d. I need some time to get to know my partner again before sex; probably several hours of talking about what's been happening in our lives, but almost certainly we'd make love the first night.

    e. I need a little longer to become emotionally close to my partner after we've been away. We'd definitely make love at some point but probably not the first night.

    f. Sex is not that important to our relationship. If it happens, great. Otherwise, it's not a big loss.

9. We all face the struggle of balancing our needs for intimacy and autonomy. Both are very important, but we each value them differently. Which statement sounds most like you?

    a. Autonomy is clearly more important, but intimacy is necessary as well.

    b. They are almost equal, but autonomy is probably more important.

    c. They are almost equal, but intimacy is probably more important.

    d. Intimacy is clearly more important, but autonomy is necessary as well.

10. You and your partner have been separated for four weeks when you get together for only a single day. You will have to part again tomorrow for three weeks. Which of the following itineraries for the day best suits you?

    a. Drive to a motel, order room service, and hide away from the rest of the world.

    b. Just the two of you go for a walk around the city, have dinner at a fancy restaurant, catch a movie, and then head back home.

    c. Join a couple who are good friends with both you and your partner, have dinner and a movie with them, and then you and your partner head back home.

    d. Call up a group of your friends and go out as a group, catch dinner and a movie as a group, and then head back home.

11. Some couples like to use the telephone and the mail to enhance their sex life while physically separated. What is your opinion about telephone sex

and erotic letters? (Note: telephone sex refers to fantasizing with your partner over the telephone, *not* the 1–900 numbers.)

   a. I'm very comfortable with the idea and plan on frequent telephone sex and the occasional erotic letter.
   b. I'm a little uncomfortable with the idea, but I'd be willing to try it if my partner was.
   c. I could send erotic letters without much difficulty, but I don't think telephone sex is for me.
   d. I don't think either telephone sex or erotic letters would work for me.

12. Some people place more importance on writing and receiving letters than do others. Which statement best fits you?
   a. I write several letters a week and expect to receive at least a letter a week from my partner.
   b. I enjoy letters and hope to write and receive at least one a month.
   c. I'm not a letter writer, but I'll probably send a card once in a while and expect the same from my partner.
   d. I much prefer the telephone and will only send a card or letter on special occasions.

13. You are flying in to see your partner after a four-week separation. Your flight arrives at rush hour, and getting to the airport, as well as trying to park, is rather difficult. Which of the following would you prefer?
   a. I'd just as soon catch a shuttle or taxi home so that my partner doesn't have the hassle of traffic and parking.
   b. I'd have my partner pick me up at the curbside of the airport so that they don't have to hassle with parking.
   c. I'd prefer my partner meet me inside the terminal. I'd do the same for them.

14. How often would you like to discuss issues or problems that come up in the relationship?
   a. I want to have routine planned discussions, even if there aren't any obvious issues or problems, so that nothing big surprises us.
   b. I want to have daily or weekly discussions if there is an ongoing issue that we're trying to resolve.
   c. I want to have at least monthly discussions if there is an ongoing issue that we're trying to resolve.
   d. I want to have a discussion about once every three to four months, but the rest of the time things will work themselves out.
   e. I don't want any planned discussions; things will just work themselves out.

Scoring Part II of the Separation Inventory

Part II is simple to score. A score sheet can be found in the appendix. Assign each of the letters a numerical value: a = 1, b = 2, c = 3, d = 4, e = 5, f = 6. Then, compare your partner's and your own answer for each question, and subtract the smaller number from the larger. If you both answered the question the same, then the score for that question is 0. For example, if you answered "a" and your partner answered "c" your score for that question would be 2 ($3 - 1 = 2$.) Add the score for each of the 14 items. This will give you a subtotal of between 0 and 50. Now subtract this subtotal from 50 for your final score for Part II.

Interpreting Your Score on Parts I and II of the Separation Inventory

You now should have the three subscores of Part I: *Demographics, Personality,* and *Support,* along with your score for Part II that looks at *Relationship* aspects. In the appendix, you'll find the *Separation Inventory Scoring Circle,* a circle divided into four quadrants, representing each of the four areas mentioned. Place an X on the dotted line in each quadrant corresponding to your score on that section of the Separation Inventory. Now draw a circle that connects the Xs. You should note that the circles for you and your partner will be different, because Part I of the inventory should be taken separately by each of you. However, your relationship score will be the same for both of you.

The larger your circle, the less difficult the LDR will be for you. Conversely, if your circle is very small, you'll need to work harder on this relationship than you might have expected. Most people find that they do not have a perfectly round circle, but that some areas are more collapsed than others. The areas where the circle tightens toward the center are the areas on which you need to concentrate the most. You may find that more than one area needs work.

By adding all four of your scores (personality, demographics, social support, and relationship) you will have a number between 0 and 100. This is your total score for the Separation Inventory. You can use this number as a more global measure of where your LDR stands. By taking the Separation Inventory every few months you can determine if your relationship is heading in the right direction (increasing score) or if it needs more focused effort (decreasing score).

The next four chapters will discuss each of the areas of the circle and direct you to the specific chapters that will give you tips on how to make your experience in an LDR even better.

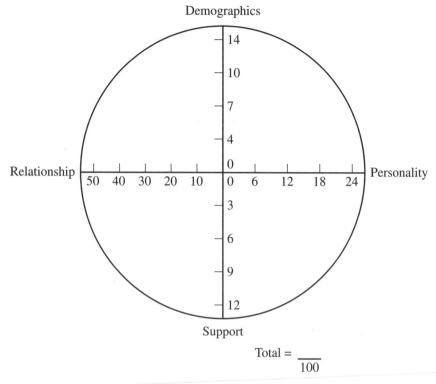

Figure 1. The Separation Inventory Scoring Circle

Chapter 5

Exploring Your Separation Inventory: Demographics– How Far Is Too Far and How Long Is Too Long?

Michelle and George

Michelle and George have been in a long-distance relationship for nearly two years. Michelle teaches third grade at a school in Indiana, while George is a Navy officer stationed in Japan. They have managed to see one another less than five times over the last two years, and yet they both say that they have a fantastic, loving relationship. Michelle told me that she has always preferred relationships that were a little more emotionally distant.

"I always felt like I was losing myself in other relationships. My boyfriends always wanted to spend so much time with me, but I've always enjoyed my time alone and with friends."

Fortunately, Michelle has a great group of friends, many of whom are also in LDRs or have experience with them. They have encouraged and supported her throughout the separation. Early on, she and George had their difficulties deciding on some ground rules about the relationship (primarily involving some of Michelle's male friends), but eventually they were able to discuss these difficulties and come to an agreement. Michelle's circle is shown on page 28, and as you can see, she does pretty well in every area except for demographics. Because George is in the Navy, they have very little control over some aspects of their relationship.

In this chapter, and the three chapters that follow, we'll take a closer look at the results from your Separation Inventory, with the goal of beginning to focus on those areas of your relationship that may need more attention.

You've already calculated your total score from the Separation Inventory, so you should have a general idea of how easy the LDR will be for you. You also should have plotted the results of the questionnaire on the Separation Inventory Scoring Circle. You will likely want to read about each of the four areas of the circle:

- Demographics
- Personality

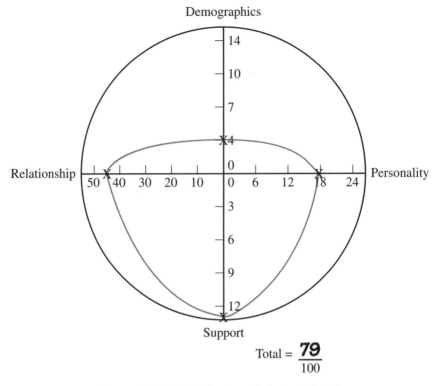

Figure 2. The LDR Scoring Circle for Michelle

• Support
• Relationship

Also, you will want to focus particular attention on the area, or areas, that need the most work. The next chapters look at personality, social support, and the relationship itself. This chapter addresses demographics–the easily quantifiable parts of your relationship, such as the distance between you and your partner, the amount of time you'll have to be separated, and the financial resources that you and your partner have at your disposal. The bad news about demographics is that, like George and Michelle, you're often not able to make significant changes in these areas of your relationship. The good news is that research has shown that, of the four factors on the Separation Inventory Circle, demographics have the least impact on how successful your LDR will be.[3, 11, 18] This often surprises people, as it sometimes goes against our common sense. I've heard well-meaning friends insist that LDRs only work if those involved live within a four-hour drive. I wish it were that easy. Fortunately for those of you in *longer* distance LDRs, this isn't the case.

The Distance Between You

In our study of nearly 200 LDRs we were surprised to find absolutely no connection between the quality of the relationship (including whether or not the couple stayed together) and the distance between the couple.[3] As we all know, the farther away your partner lives, the fewer opportunities you'll have to visit them and the larger your telephone bill will be. Common sense would suggest that those couples that can visit one another more often would have more satisfying relationships. However, this isn't true. Amazingly, we found no connection between how often couples visited their partner and how successful and fulfilling their relationships were. In Chapter 13, we'll return to this point and we'll discuss this issue in a little more detail.

One note worth mentioning: The average distance between couples in our study was about 320 miles. Although there were a few couples living over 5000 miles from one another, they were uncommon enough that we were unable to gather much information about them. If you're in that situation, don't panic. I'm not suggesting your relationship is doomed, only that we can't say for sure if these large distances play a role in the outcome of the relationship. You may just have to work a little harder.

If distance plays such a minor role in the quality of the LDR, why was it on the LDR Separation Inventory? While it is true that the amount of distance doesn't change relationship outcome or quality, shorter distances do make it easier to cope. Returning to the airplane analogy, whether we're flying on a 300-mile trip or a 3000-mile trip, we can all make it through the flight. It's just a lot more comfortable being on the plane for only one hour instead of eight. Whether you live an hour away or a full day's flight away, your relationship can make it. It just may take slightly more effort and patience.

Survival Tip # 2

Remember that the distance between you and your partner makes very little difference on whether or not your relationship will survive. Those factors over which you have more control play a larger role.

Short or Long: The Duration of Your Separation

Gwen and Harold

Gwen and Harold met in medical school and married in the spring prior to beginning their residencies. Gwen chose general surgery and began her training in California, while Harold began a program in dermatology in Boston. They both realized that there was little hope of living closer to one another for the next five years. Even worse, they could barely find time between their busy schedules to see one another more than four times a year. Yet they both told me that they actually preferred being in an LDR.

"I have virtually no life outside of the hospital," Gwen shared with me. "It's much easier not having to try to work around Harold's schedule. I just focus on what I need to do."

Harold agreed. "When something comes up and I need some support, I page her and just hearing her voice for a couple of minutes works for me. Then I can get back to work. We both have such little time to be together, and this way we don't have any expectations that can't be met."

I'm happy to report that Gwen and Harold both finished their residencies and are still happily married. They managed to carry on a long-distance relationship for over five years, and they say they would do it again if it were necessary.

Gwen and Harold are rather extraordinary. Most couples choose not to stay apart for quite so long. In our study, we found that the longer the couples thought they would have to be apart, the less happy they were with the relationship, and the more difficulty they had dealing with the separation.[3] We also found that as time went by, the couples tended to shorten how long they thought they would be apart. Earlier in the separation couples expected to be apart for an average of about two-and-a-half years. About six months later, they had shortened this by a full year.

Unfortunately, many of us feel that we have little control over the length of time we'll be separated. In reality, however, most of us have a lot of control over the situation, but the cost of moving closer is simply too high.

Survival Tip # 3

The more control you perceive over your LDR, the less difficult it will seem. Realize that for most of you, while it would be costly in terms of education or career to close the distance, you could do it if you *made the choice*. Most of you will choose to stay in the LDR rather than move closer. But simply recognizing that you could make the choice, if necessary, puts the control in your own hands rather then feeling like you are at the mercy of your environment.

After having spoken with hundreds of couples in LDRs, I have found that virtually everyone looks at the separation as temporary. No couple believed that they would always be in a long-distance relationship. Just as our formal research had shown, many of the couples I spoke with had repeatedly changed their expectations about how long the separation would last.

John and Catherine

John and Catherine, you'll recall, had separated after graduation, with John beginning a program in chemical engineering in California and Catherine a program in education in the Midwest. Both of them would finish their degrees in two years. When they first began their LDR, they agreed that after they completed their education, Catherine would move to California. After just six months apart, Catherine was finding the separation much more difficult than she anticipated.

"Weekends are the worst," she told me. "During the weekdays I'm busy and I don't miss him as much, but Friday and Saturday nights are horrible. For the first time in my life I prefer Monday to Friday."

Over Christmas break John and Catherine discussed their plan and thought about one or the other moving closer. "We discussed the possibility of me transferring to a program at a location nearer to John after a year." Ultimately, they agreed that they would continue to work on the LDR over the next six months and then reassess the relationship again. They would talk more often on the weekends and Catherine would become more involved with some of her friends, which would make Friday nights more bearable. They decided on what Catherine called their "six-month plan." Every six months Catherine and John reviewed the prior six months and made a plan for the next six.

John and Catherine changed plans several times during their separation, wavering between a year apart and two years. Eventually time caught up with them, and they both finished their two-year programs while apart. Catherine's six-month plan allowed them to focus on a smaller, more manageable amount of time than trying to look at the entire two years.

When I was in medical school, I recall with unpleasant memories that my least favorite rotation was surgery. I'd arrive at 4:30 A.M. and leave by 8:00 P.M., with every third night on call (meaning a straight 38 hours without sleep). These horrid hours were punctuated with 10-hour long procedures in the OR. As a medical student, I would stand for hours, bored half asleep holding a retractor, and often unable to see anything of what the surgeons were doing.

After the first few days of this, I could not even fathom finishing the remaining eight weeks. The only way I managed to complete the two months was by focusing not on the months, weeks, or even days ahead, but rather I focused on getting through that very hour. I survived that rotation relatively unscathed, primarily because I broke it up into very small segments, organized my thoughts and actions around completing each segment, and then moved on to the next. Looking at the entirety of the rotation would have paralyzed me emotionally.

LDRs have the same potential effect on some couples. Don't focus on the thought of trying to accomplish the separation for a period of two or three years–focus on smaller intervals such as six months.

Survival Tip # 4

Make a six-month plan. Remind yourself that your separation is temporary, and simply focus on the next six months. Decide on what strategies have
been working for you during the prior six months and what things need to be
changed. Try to set a formal date to discuss this with your partner and to set
an agenda for the next six months.

Then There's the Telephone Bill

Ted and Amanda

*Ted and Amanda had been married for six years when the steel refinery where
Ted had worked was finally shut down. Ted was one of the fortunate employees
who was offered another job, but it was at a refinery 190 miles to the north. More-
over, the new position came with a substantial pay cut, and they were already in
trouble financially.*

*Amanda had a two-year-old and a five-year-old at home, both of whom
needed constant attention, and she did not want to take a part-time job. Ted began
to work overtime whenever possible, but the cost of his new apartment, which he
shared with two other workers, used up most of the extra cash. The first month they
talked every other day, sometimes for over an hour. When the first telephone bill
came to over $200, they knew something had to change. They decided that it was
more important to be able to talk for about an hour uninterrupted than it was to
talk every day. So they planned to talk twice a week. To make up for the lack of
daily contact, Ted and Amanda devised a cheap way to say, "I'm thinking of you."
They would call, let the telephone ring once and then hang up.*

*"I know it sounds silly," Ted explained, "but it was enough for me to know
that she was thinking about me and that she missed me."*

One of the most common complaints I hear about LDRs is that they're so expensive. Yet, in our study when we asked about money problems, we found that
the 200 couples in LDRs had no more financial difficulties than the 200 couples
in geographically close relationships.[2] It seems that while LDRs have telephone
bills and transportation costs, they do not have the day-to-day expenses of closer
relationships: going out to dinner, movies, etc. Much of the expense depends on
telephone bills, which vary greatly among couples in LDRs. In our study the average telephone bill was around $60 a month, but for some it was as high as $385
a month. Airline ticket prices also vary greatly depending on the route, the time of
year, and the distance.

Fortunately, your relationship depends more on you and your partner than on
your financial reserves. While it may be much easier for those who can talk nightly

for hours than for those of you stuck on tight budgets, your relationship can work out just as well.

Survival Tip # 5

When your budget is tight and the telephone bills have been way too high, try the "I'm thinking of you" telephone ring. Call your partner, letting the telephone ring only once before hanging up. You'll be surprised how nice it is to hear that ring on a lonely evening.

Email

Steven and Jessica

Steven and Jessica live 100 miles apart; Steven at Indiana University, Jessica at Purdue (also in Indiana). Jessica confided in me that the worst part about her LDR is that she couldn't afford to talk to Steven every day.

"I want to be able to share with him the little day-to-day things that affect me. We talk on the telephone twice a week, and I try to remember all of the neat things that have happened to me that week, but they aren't as exciting three days after the fact. I also write him once or twice a month, but I don't write about the little things.

"Email is a great way for me to tell him about my day. We write to one another twice a day. In the morning I send him a message about my plans for the day, and then in the late afternoon or evening I send another telling him how my day actually went. I'm sure it's all pretty boring, but this way we feel like we know what's going on in each other's lives."

Perhaps the best innovation for those in LDRs, email provides an inexpensive way of communicating with their partners day-to-day. No one knows for sure how many have access to email, but virtually every couple I've encountered has discovered the joys of the Internet. Email has some distinct advantages over other forms of communication, most notably the low cost and speed of transmission.

This brings us to one of the more important discoveries about long-distance relationships. While sharing your feelings about one another is important, even more central to the relationship is sharing day-to-day events. Social psychologists who study romantic relationships have found that it is the sharing of these day-to-day experiences that makes us feel connected to our partners.[20, 21] Imagine for a moment calling your partner tonight and discussing whatever you'd like, except that you cannot mention anything about the events of your day. If you were to extend this for weeks, and then months, the two of you would begin to feel very out of touch with each other, regardless of how easily you can share your feelings.

We've found that couples in LDRs seem to be better suited than their geographically closer counterparts at sharing their feelings and expressing their affection toward one another.[3, 16] As wonderful as that is, it must happen within the framework of sharing your everyday experiences.

Survival Tip # 6

Make every effort to share your daily events with your partner, whether it's over the telephone or by email. Don't feel that you need to make every conversation special. It's more important that as a couple you become involved in each other's day-to-day lives.

While the telephone provides the fastest means of connecting with your partner, it has several drawbacks including expense, timing, and availability. Expense is obvious to anyone trying to call cross-country during the middle of a weekday. The timing drawback has to do with busy schedules that most of you keep daily. Trying to match both schedules for a telephone call can be tricky. Email solves that problem by allowing both parties the convenience of sending or checking their mail whenever they prefer. Finally, many people do not work by a telephone, and reaching them during the day isn't always feasible. I'll admit that while I loved talking to my partner in the evenings (once I had settled down and finished my errands), I preferred email during the day. Like most people, I looked forward to logging on and getting the "You have mail" message. I could do this at my convenience several times a day.

If you don't have email and can afford the computer and Internet cost, I would say it's probably one of the best values toward making the separation a little easier.

Survival Tip # 7

Try your best to have access to email. The cost for an Internet hook-up is well worth the advantages that email has for long-distance relationships. Try to send a message once or twice daily. Make sure you share your daily agenda and experiences. Consider sending one message in the morning discussing what you plan on doing that day, and another message in the evening sharing how your day actually ended up. The connection you can create with your partner is one of the most important keys to a successful LDR–becoming involved in their daily lives.

Control over Your Schedule

Todd and Lynn

Todd and Lynn met in Phoenix on New Year's Eve. Todd worked as a resident physician at a hospital in California while Lynn was an attorney in Phoenix. Both had very tight schedules with very little time available to see one another. Early on in their long-distance romance they found that, when they had to leave one another after a brief visit, they had a great deal of difficulty.

"I hated not knowing when I'd see her again," Todd complained. Eventually, they worked out a plan that helped make the transition easier.

"We had a ritual. Toward the end of each trip, we would get out our calendars and start searching ahead until we found a time that the two of us could get together again, no matter how far ahead it was. Then we purchased the airline tickets, then and there, at the airport right before she left. I'm not sure why, but having the tickets in my hands made it a little more bearable. At least I knew for sure that I'd see her at a set time. If something came up that let us get together earlier–great! But I always had the next sure get-together in my hands."

As I mentioned earlier, one of the most important elements to making the LDR run smoothly is a sense of control over the relationship. The more control you have, the better you feel. If you cannot control the events in the relationship, the next best thing is to predict them. Todd's schedule as a resident is fixed for the entire year. While this doesn't afford them much control, they do know exactly when his vacations will be, and they can make the best of that knowledge by purchasing tickets well in advance.

Compare calendars with your partner and come up with several times when you may be able to get together. If you settle on a definite time, then purchase your tickets early. Once you have the reservation made, the upcoming trip feels more real than if you simply assumed you'd get together some time soon.

Also, as soon as you agree on a date, mark it on your calendar. If you decide on a date together and then have to cancel, it will feel like a loss of control. If at all possible, protect the time you've scheduled to be with your partner from the other obligations you may have.

Survival Tip # 8

Do as much as you can to maintain control over your schedule. Predict, as best as possible, times you can get together and mark them on your calendar. Make reservations so the upcoming trip feels more real. Protect the time you've scheduled to be with your partner from your other obligations.

How Often Should We Visit?

Amazingly, studies have shown that it doesn't matter very much how often you visit one another. In our study of 200 LDRs, we could find no connection between how often couples saw one another face-to-face and any of our measures of the quality of their relationships.[11] Even when we followed couples over time, those that saw each other more often did no better than those who could only see one another every few months.[3]

I'll admit that this shocked us, so we did some additional studies. We looked at 123 relationships that in the past had been long-distance. Some of these couples had ended their relationships while apart. Other couples had made it through the separation, reunited, and continued to date one another. When we compared these two groups (the one that had survived the LDR with the one that had not), we again could find no difference in how often they visited one another.[3] I'm convinced that it simply is not a critical element.

Once again, factors such as your personality, social support, and the quality of your relationship play a much more significant role. In Chapter 13, I'll discuss this point again and I'll provide tips on deciding the frequency of face-to-face visits that is right for you and your partner. But for now, remember that how often you visit is a choice the two of you can make without much concern about how often is the "right" amount.

Survival Tip # 9

Don't listen to people who tell you that you must visit each other a certain amount "or it will never work." Several studies have shown that it does not matter. Your personality, support system, and the quality of your relationship has much more to do with the success of your long-distance relationship.

Chapter 6

Exploring Your Separation Inventory: Your Personality

Chapter 5 discussed the various demographics of your LDR. I mentioned that, in general, demographics such as the distance between you and your partner have little to do with making it work. In this chapter, I'll explore differences in personality that make it easier, or more difficult, to deal with the separation.

Of the four factors (demographics, personality, support, and your relationship) your personality plays the biggest role in determining how difficult the separation will be *for you*. While you can't easily change your personality, you can change the way you think and the things you do.

David and Sarah

David and Sarah, as you recall, are a newlywed couple separated by about 200 miles while Sarah finishes an MBA program. After they finished the LDR Separation Inventory, David realized that the most difficult area for him was his personality and how it affected the separation. David considered himself a very visual person. He enjoyed the visual arts and took great pleasure in simply seeing the world. Talking on the telephone tended to bore him, and he wasn't much of a letter writer. He also saw little personal advantage in the separation. After all, it was Sarah "who decided to leave to get her MBA." Although David told me that he really did trust Sarah to be faithful, he simply couldn't help thinking about all of the men she was meeting at her MBA get-togethers.

I've shown the results of David's Separation Inventory on page 38. As you can see, he does pretty well in most of the categories except for personality. If your results are similar, you'll want to pay special attention to this chapter. Remember that personality, along with support, plays a big role in your ability to make it through the separation. Yet, regardless of your score on this section, your relationship can thrive and grow at a distance; it just may be more of a strain on you than on others.

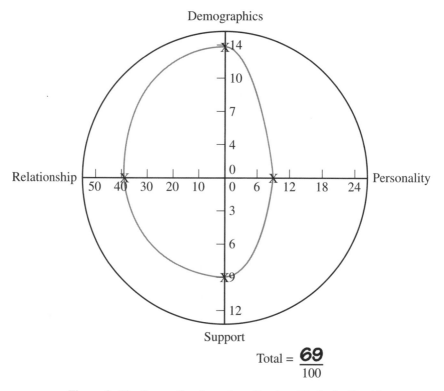

Figure 3. The Separation Inventory Scoring Circle for David

Eyes, Ears, or Skin?

Learning theorists have shown that people organize the world in distinctly different ways: visually, verbally, or kinesthetically (through touch).[22] While all of our senses play important roles in the way we memorize and retrieve information, most of us have one sense that dominates over the others. For example, some people memorize a telephone number by the way it looks, while others memorize it by saying it over and over again, and still others memorize it by writing it repeatedly so that they can focus on the actual feeling of their hand during this process. When asked to recall the number, these same people either attempt to see the number in their mind's eye, hear themselves saying it, or try to write it to recall the feeling of their hand when they first memorized it. The easiest way to determine what style of learning you prefer involves imagery. In your own mind, try to bring forth a picture of the Statue of Liberty. Hold it in your thoughts and rotate around it, as if you're in a circling airplane. Can you easily bring the picture to mind, keep it clear, and then manipulate it at will? If so, you have a strong visual component to your learning framework.

Visualizers

A slight majority of people arrange the world visually; they recall information by forming pictures in their minds. When asked how to spell a word, for example, they form a picture of the word in their minds. They tend to excel at, and enjoy, the visual arts. If you're a visually oriented person, when you took the Separation Inventory you likely were able to create an image of your partner much more easily and in more detail than you could imagine his or her voice or hug. For you, the inability to *see* your partner on a daily basis likely has the biggest impact. You will have an easier time than those who organize through touch, but not as easy as those verbalizers who can use the telephone for their primary sense.

To make your LDR a little easier, you must focus on visual cues and images.

Survival Tip # 10

Use plenty of pictures to help bring you closer to your partner. Try to send a new picture a week. The easiest way to do this is with a digital camera with images sent over the Internet. Alternatively, a Polaroid camera can develop a single image at a time, rather than having to wait until the whole roll is exposed. Polaroid cameras are surprisingly cheap. (It's the film that can get expensive.) Digital cameras have become relatively inexpensive as well. It's well worth the effort to have a friend snap a picture of you in day-to-day activities to slip into an envelope once a week or upload on the Internet.

Verbalizers

Verbalizers tend to have the least difficulty with LDRs. These people organize the world through auditory connections.

Return to the imagery exercise and try to focus now on hearing the national anthem in your own mind. First sung, then played by trumpets, then by piano. Can you easily hear the notes and hear the transition to the instruments? If so, you likely have a strong component of verbal organization as a style of learning. If you pictured the instruments in your mind more easily than you heard them, you're probably visually oriented.

When asked how to spell a word, verbalizers recall the sound of the word in their head. They thoroughly enjoy music and are quick to identify celebrity voices on the radio. If you're a verbalizer, you likely have no difficulty imagining the sound of your partner's voice. Fortunately, verbalizers have the distinct advantage of being able to access their primary sense by telephone, even when their partners are distant. However, for some couples the telephone isn't available (such as with military separations) or becomes too expensive to use repeatedly.

During the Vietnam conflict, many LDRs relied on tape-recorded messages that were mailed to one another. Obviously they could have simply written a letter, but the importance of hearing a voice made the tape recorder preferred by some couples. Today, I can find few people in LDRs that use tape-recorded messages, except for those in military deployments. Still, for those of you who are verbalizers, and have only rare access to the telephone, it's a good alternative.

Survival Tip # 11

If you and your partner don't have daily access to a telephone, try sending tape-recorded messages to one another. I suggest purchasing the small dictation tape recorders that use the microcassettes. They're handy enough to keep with you during the day. Spend a day imagining your partner is with you, and simply talk to them (through the recorder) whenever something comes up. As I've mentioned before, sharing in the seemingly insignificant day-to-day events is what bonds the relationship together. The microcassettes are light and can be sent in a regular envelope, usually without additional postage.

Another ingenious invention that I've found helpful for verbalizers is the digitally encoding voice memo machines, many of which are very inexpensive.

Survival Tip # 12

Consider buying a small voice memo digital recorder. (I personally had a small one on my key chain.) These recorders use a computer chip rather than magnetic tape to record short messages. Have your partner say a few words into the recorder each time you visit. Being a verbalizer myself, I found it comforting to press a button and hear my partner's voice anytime I chose.

Recently, the Internet has become another inexpensive way of talking with your partner. Several providers now have digital voice messages sent in real time. Essentially, this creates a telephone connection to your partner, but the caller only has to dial locally to the Internet provider. Your voice is digitally encoded and sent over the Internet. This technology has the potential for tremendous financial savings, especially for those who want to spend hours at a time talking with one another.

Touchers

Those who organize the world by tactile sensation are the least common. They usually enjoy using their hands and often make great dancers. When asked how to spell a word, they tend to write it out a few times, not so much to see which version *looks* right, but rather to determine which *feels* right. If you're a toucher, you likely could imagine in more detail the feel of your partner as they hugged you than you could imagine their appearance or voice. Unfortunately, unlike the verbalizers and visualizers, touchers don't have easy ways of satisfying their primary sense when separated. No matter how much you hug that huge pillow, it still doesn't feel like your partner. However, I'll share with you what one couple discovered.

Kelly and Tom

Kelly and Tom met when Tom took a break from working on his doctoral thesis to watch a dance recital that happened to feature Kelly. Following the performance, there was a wine and cheese mixer at which Tom and Kelly bumped elbows and started to flirt. As you can guess, they seemed right for one another and began dating.

Tom finished his doctoral program three months later and managed to land a wonderful professorship at a university two states away. They agreed to try the "long-distance thing." While Tom was a visualizer, Kelly was a toucher.

"I really miss holding hands or curling up next to him on the couch. I miss feeling him next to me."

For Kelly's birthday, Tom had managed to schedule a visit and bought tickets for a ballet that he knew Kelly would enjoy. During the performance Tom took Kelly's hand, palm up, and began to write with his finger the letters "I-L-O-V-E-Y-O-U." Kelly, being a toucher, remembers the sensation vividly. She told me during our interview that now, when she really misses Tom, she uses her own finger to write the same letters on her palm while imagining that it is Tom's finger. When she does this, it reminds her of that night and how important Tom is to her.

Kelly discovered that she could trigger a feeling of connection with Tom simply by replicating his touch on her palm. While this doesn't work well for everyone, it certainly worked for Kelly and it may work for you.

Survival Tip # 13

If you're a toucher, try developing a special connection between you and your partner using touch. Spell the words "I love you" on each other's palms with your finger. Close your eyes while you feel each letter being drawn. When you're again separated, you can help your mind create a connection by reenacting the same touch with your own finger.

Self-Esteem

Clinical psychologists have long realized that self-esteem plays a central role in many types of emotional and psychological difficulties. Good self-esteem provides a buffer that helps protect us from all of the day-to-day indignities that the world hurls upon us. While self-esteem clearly impacts our intimate relationships, research has shown that it seems to play an even more important role in long-distance relationships.[23–27]

As expected, our own study of LDRs found that people with less self-esteem reported greater psychological difficulties with the separation. What was not as expected, however, was that those with less self-esteem also said that their relationships were less satisfying and intimate. Interestingly, when we looked at people in geographically close relationships there was no connection between self-esteem and the quality of their relationships.[3] Apparently, the combination of low self-esteem and physical separation act together to undermine our intimate bonds.

If you find that your own level of self-esteem is not as well developed as you'd like, I encourage you to take advantage of whatever professional or self-help services are available to you. The huge field of self-esteem building is far beyond the scope of this book. Fortunately, there have been many fine works written on self-esteem. You should have no trouble locating them in any bookstore. Also, most psychotherapists have experience in helping people explore these issues, and I know of many people in LDRs who have been smart enough to take advantage of their services.

Survival Tip # 14

Research has shown that successful LDRs usually require high levels of self-esteem. Self-esteem not only affects your own personal emotional health during the separation, but it actually affects the intimacy of your relationship. If you feel that your self-esteem could use a boost, don't hesitate to work on it either with self-help books or, better yet, with a trained therapist. The most emotionally healthy people are often those who can make honest self-assessments and then have the courage to work on areas they would like to change.

Independence

Not surprisingly, independence ranks high on the list of desirable characteristics for those in an LDR. We all struggle with the balance between autonomy and intimacy. On the one hand, we yearn for freedom and independence: the ability to choose what we do based solely on our own preferences and needs. No need to check with someone else, to obtain permission, or to be constantly checking the clock to make sure you're home on time. On the other hand, we also crave intimacy: feeling loved and cared for, caring for and loving someone else, and the feeling of sharing your life with another.

Often these two wonderful experiences–intimacy and autonomy–form a sort of emotional teeter-totter. As intimacy goes up, autonomy goes down and vice versa. Once we have plenty of intimacy, we often find ourselves desiring a little more autonomy. Too much autonomy and we crave intimacy. For some, the teeter-totter can eventually be abandoned, and intimacy and autonomy can both flourish without forcing the other into remission.

But we all have our intimacy/autonomy thermostats; that is, we all have an idea of how emotionally hot or cool we'd like to keep the relationship. We develop a feeling of just the right warmth, and we strive to keep the relationship at that level. However, a relationship is like a room with two separate thermostats: yours and your partner's. Just how comfortable each of you feels depends on how close, or far apart, the two of you set your thermostats. If you both like it hot, great. If you both like to keep things pretty cool, wonderful. When one of you likes it hot and the other cool, things get tricky.

Because it's a little easier to cool things down while in a long-distance relationship, those of you who prefer a little more autonomy in lieu of a little bit of intimacy tend to do somewhat better.[25, 28, 29] But there is a trade off. Research suggests that while you do better during your time apart, you may find things a little more difficult to deal with once you move closer together, as you then have to surrender a little bit of the independence you've learned to enjoy.[23]

If you're the type who likes to keep things cooking (that is, you prefer to be a little more intimate at the expense of a little autonomy), take heart. Not only has research shown that your LDR will help you further develop your independence,[14, 30–33] but you may have an easier time of it when you and your partner finally do close the distance. You'll have less difficulty adjusting to the change in intimacy and autonomy. While it may be slightly more difficult during the separation, think of your relationship as undergoing some earthquake proofing. A little inconvenience now will help when you shake things up with your reunion.

Survival Tip # 15

If you consider yourself a very independent person, you'll likely have an easier time with your separation. If not, focus on learning new skills or activities that your partner has traditionally done for you. Ultimately, becoming more independent will be an important advantage for both your relationship and your life in general.

Optimism

During our study of LDRs, we asked nearly a hundred people to detail the things they did to cope with the separation. When we analyzed the results, we found that those who had the least trouble with the separation, and had the best relationships, had one thing in common: They viewed the relationship optimistically.[3] They all believed that their long-distance relationship was the right thing to do, that their relationship was as intimate, trusting, and caring as any other, and that, in the end, their separation would make their relationship even stronger.

There are many advantages to LDRs, and of course, a few disadvantages. You will hear about the disadvantages from many people, but you need to constantly remind yourself of the good things. (A little later, we will discuss some of these rewards that come from an LDR.) I'm not asking you to be unrealistic. Many relationships never make it. But, as I discussed in Chapter 2, your long-distance relationship is as likely to make it as any other.

Survival Tip # 16

The best way of coping with the separation is to stay optimistic. Couples who believe in their chances and focus on the advantages of being in an LDR have less emotional difficulties and stronger relationships. Fortunately, you don't have to lie to yourself. Remember, studies have shown that your LDR has *as much chance as any other relationship.*

Trust

I've talked with hundreds of people about LDRs and almost universally the first question they ask is, "Do they work?" The next one is frequently, "Don't they cheat on each other more?" The answer is no, but this is such a common concern that I'll discuss it in more detail later.

The fact that couples ask this question so frequently highlights the degree of concern that many people in LDRs have over issues of infidelity. Whether or not those in LDRs cheat on each other more frequently than those in geographically close relationships, they definitely *worry about it more* than couples who live close to one another.[3, 34] Couples in geographically close relationships feel a sense of security because they can visually monitor their partner much of the time. Those with a little less trust in their partner can make up for this by more diligent monitoring. Those of us in LDRs don't have this option.

Some people are trusting by nature, while others feel that their trust must be earned. Obviously, the former will have an easier time with LDRs. Trust is such an important component of all relationships, and even more so in LDRs, that I've set a rule: If you want your LDR to fail miserably and be agonizingly painful while it does so, do something to break your partner's trust.

Sarah and David

Sarah, pursuing an MBA while apart from David, spent Thursday nights with a group of fellow students. These scheduled evenings involved networking with others that always included alcohol, bars, and late nights out. Sarah felt very uncomfortable revealing the true nature of these weekly events to David and decided to cover up the truth to protect him.

"I told David that on Thursday nights we had a study group meeting. I know how paranoid he gets about social activities that [the MBA students] plan and I didn't want him to be worrying about me."

Sarah meant well, but unfortunately during one of their visits a friend of Sarah's mentioned their "wild Thursday nights," and Sarah's attempt to protect David backfired.

"I know she wasn't sleeping around or anything," David explained. "I just felt very hurt that she lied to me. I keep wondering what else she may have lied about."

Fortunately, David and Sarah worked things out, but it took many months for David to relax his guard again.

No matter how unlikely it is that your partner will discover a little white lie, don't create stories to protect him or her. First, each little fabrication can make you feel less intimate with your partner and, if discovered, can whittle away at the trust that forms a critical foundation in LDRs. Second, by protecting your partner from events in your life, you surrender an important opportunity to strengthen your LDR.

Conflict serves a critical role in relationships by pointing out areas that need attention. Think of it this way: The pain you have when you step on a tack isn't fun, but it draws your attention to the problem before it gets out of hand. People with diabetes often lose the sensation of pain in their feet, and the little tack can cause them to lose their entire leg from infection. Similarly, couples who cannot, or will not, communicate potentially painful information risk having a small incident develop into an issue that can end the relationship.

Survival Tip # 17

Research shows us that trust plays an even more important role in LDRs than in geographically close relationships. Never do anything to undermine your partner's trust once it's established. Don't use little white lies on the telephone to protect your partner. They threaten your intimacy and if discovered (and believe me, they often are), they can cause much more pain in the long run.

Feeling Down

When our research on LDRs began, one of our central questions involved the relationship between depression and separation. Numerous early studies of separated military families showed a tremendous amount of clinical depression,[12, 35-38] and we were interested in finding out if the same was true of civilian LDRs.

While we didn't find a great deal of clinical depression (which by definition is very severe), we did find that those in LDRs reported more difficulties with minor depression compared to those in geographically close relationships.[2] Feeling a little down is so common in LDRs that I'll discuss it in more detail in Chapters 10 and 11. I'll also discuss ways of dealing with feelings of depression and its emotional cousin, loneliness. For now, realize that if you have a tendency toward feeling down, LDRs will likely worsen the problem slightly.

Telephone and Letter Habits

In discussing LDRs with other couples, I've found a surprising range of comfort with using the telephone and writing letters. Some people shared that they could spend half the day on the telephone, while for others 10 minutes felt like an eternity. Obviously, these traits play only a minor role in the relationships of geographically close couples, while for LDRs they can take on great significance.

Sandra and Hiren

Sandra complained bitterly about her boyfriend's lack of joy for the telephone. At her insistence, they talked nightly but he never seemed interested. After about 20 minutes, Hiren would quickly bring the conversation to a close and hang up.

"I've never been a telephone person," Hiren told me. "I like talking to her, and I write long letters by email, but I get bored on the telephone."

How much you enjoy talking on the telephone is probably already ingrained in your personality and difficult to change. If you find chatting on the telephone entertaining, then you'll likely have fewer problems than those of us who don't. Fortunately, there are a few things you can do to make your time on the telephone more enjoyable, and I'll discuss these in more detail later.

The same holds true for your tendency to write letters. Some couples wrote two or three times a week, while others had been separated for years without even so much as a greeting card. While it's easy to focus on visits and telephone calls, don't underestimate the importance of letters. Some very provocative research shows that couples who wrote letters to one another had a significantly better chance of staying together throughout their LDR than those who did not.

Chapter 7

Exploring Your Separation Inventory: Support from Friends and Family

The last chapter discussed how various personality traits could affect the difficulty or ease with which you manage your separation. As mentioned earlier, your personality has one of the largest impacts on emotional and psychological difficulties during a long-distance relationship, much more so than demographic factors such as distance and time apart. The next most important factor in determining how difficult you'll find the separation is the degree of support you and your relationship receive from friends and family.

Steven and Jessica

Steven and Jessica, as you'll recall, live 100 miles apart, both working on degrees at different universities. Looking back on their LDR, Jessica rates the relationship as A+. Both she and Steven have great personalities for their lifestyle. Both are independent, self-confident, and optimistic about the relationship. Both believe it's the best choice for them at this time.

Steven has had little difficulty with the separation, partly due to the fantastic social support he enjoys at Indiana University. He has a large group of friends that he spends time with on weekend nights, and his friends and family all support him in his choice of an LDR. One of his roommates even has his own long-distance relationship, and the two of them often discuss the advantages and disadvantages that come with the separation.

Jessica has had a more difficult time. She lives alone and unfortunately for her, most of her colleagues are older and married. Her best friend Tammy is single and Jessica enjoys spending time with her. But Tammy's agenda usually sets a high priority for mingling with eligible men, something in which Jessica is much less interested.

"I don't seem to fit in whenever we go out. I don't have a date with me, but I'm definitely taken. I feel awkward and I think everyone else feels awkward, too."

47

Jessica found herself retreating more and more into her work and gradually lost contact with many of her friends. The result of Jessica's Separation Inventory is shown below.

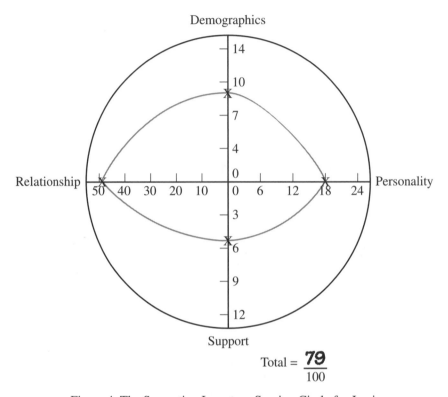

Total = $\dfrac{\textbf{79}}{100}$

Figure 4. The Separation Inventory Scoring Circle for Jessica

After talking with Jessica and Steven, I realized that they both had very similar personalities but were having very different experiences with the separation. Steven had wonderful social support and friends who encouraged his LDR. Jessica was gradually retreating away from her few friends. Her somewhat ambiguous status (not a couple, but not available) made her feel uncomfortable and gave her an excuse to withdraw even further. Jessica's worsening experience resulted from inadequate social support, both for herself and for her relationship.

Many studies have shown that one of the best ways of dealing with separation is to seek out your friends and family for support.[25, 27, 36, 39–45] Sociologists have described four types of support:

- Emotional
- Appraisal

- Informational
- Instrumental[46]

Emotional support involves those things that make you feel respected and esteemed. When a friend listens to your problems and sends the message "I care about you," you are receiving emotional support. *Appraisal support* consists of your friends and family providing feedback on your own behavior, viewpoints, and values. This occurs, for example, when your friends tell you that you're doing the right thing in staying together with your partner despite the distance. While emotional support provides the hugs and pats on the back, appraisal support provides honest opinions about your own thoughts and actions. *Informational support* occurs when others provide information that you need to problem solve. Reading this book is an example of informational support. Finally, *instrumental support* occurs when others provide tangible assistance, such as a ride to the airport, money, or someone to watch the dog when you're gone.

Each of these types of support plays an important role in LDRs, and you need to nurture each type. Emotional support comes primarily from your partner. Generally, most loving relationships provide strong emotional support for one another. Other sources of emotional support include friends, family, mentors, and professional coworkers–the people who make you feel good about yourself as a person.

Appraisal support can be more difficult to find. For those in LDRs this requires finding someone with whom you can discuss your opinions, your values, and the strategies you use to help your relationship. Ideally, this would require someone who knows about LDRs, but this can be challenging. Sometimes, people who are less optimistic or less knowledgeable about separated relationships will not be supportive. When asked about their opinion you may find that they give answers that undermine your efforts. Be alert for individuals you believe cannot or do not provide appraisal support for your separation. They may still have wonderful qualities that make them fun to be around, but avoid asking opinions or discussing strategies about your LDR with them.

Instead, seek out people who you believe share your optimism for your relationship and who have some knowledge about LDRs that they can use to help guide you. Friends involved in their own LDRs are a typical resource. Other sources include Internet sites dedicated to LDRs (see the chapter on *Resources*), support groups for LDRs (if there's not one near you, consider starting one yourself), and books or articles on the topic.

Be a little careful of the last suggestion. The few works on the topic can provide some appraisal support by providing you a collection of the values, behaviors, and opinions of others involved in LDRs. However, some of these make claims that the research does not seem to support. Suppose you can only see your partner every six weeks, and you read a book that says you have to see one another at least every month to make the relationship work. This can significantly undermine a relationship. Accordingly, be careful taking anything too seriously that you read about LDRs, including in this book. People are unique and everyone's situation is different.

The last type of support, instrumental, often receives the least attention. It somehow seems less important than the other types of support. However, instrumental support can significantly assist your LDR. Occasionally during my research, I would find someone who had no one to assist with the day-to-day necessities of an LDR, such as driving them to and from the airport, taking care of their house or apartment, and so forth. While these people still managed to maintain their LDR, they had much more difficulty and stress with their separation.

Survival Tip # 18

Find and maintain relationships with people who can assist you in each of the four types of support: emotional, appraisal, informational, and instrumental. Once a month take a minute to review your support network and determine if any of these types of support are missing. Work hard to build support in any area that seems lacking.

Despite the apparent necessity of support from friends and family, many studies of LDRs have found that separated couples report significant isolation from these very people.[14, 30, 34, 47, 48–52] Often they found themselves in situations where their unclear status alienated them from both the singles crowd and the married couples.[29] Some even reported that they felt lonelier when they were out with friends, so they chose to withdraw from their support networks all together. Our own study found something similar. Early in the separation people tended to feel more isolated from their friends and from society in general. As they learned to better cope with the separation, they reentered the social scene and reconnected with friends and colleagues.[3]

Survival Tip # 19

Many people in LDRs find themselves socially isolated. Sometimes they choose to focus on work to avoid the loneliness, and end up withdrawing from friends. Others find that they can no longer relate easily to their friends, who are either single or in geographically close relationships. The unclear role (physically alone but romantically unavailable) makes many people feel uncomfortable and worsens their tendency to withdraw or be excluded. Actively fight this tendency by working hard to maintain friendships, both when you and your partner are apart and when you are together. Don't withdraw from the support system that research shows can play a pivotal role in your LDR.

Not only do you personally need support, but your relationship also needs the support of friends and family. Social psychologists have studied a phenomenon called the *labeling effect*. Essentially this refers to a self-fulfilling prophecy. If you allow yourself or your friends to label your relationship "doomed from the start," then it may well be.[53] While most couples I talk with have optimistic projections for their relationship, many constantly put up with friends or family members bombarding them with lines like: "Long-distance relationships never work;" "You're going to be lonely and miserable, and then it's going to fall apart anyway;" "He's going to cheat on you. They always do when you're apart like that."

I've already alluded to the importance of optimism. Now let me assure you that you must educate your friends and family so they can join you in your positive thinking. Don't simply ignore negative references–challenge them.

Survival Tip # 20

Don't let friends or family undermine your confidence in your LDR. Not only do you need to be optimistic, but so do the people whose opinions you value. Work on educating them about the success rate of LDRs. Focus on the advantages of being separated. Above all, don't allow them to make negative predictions about the relationship without challenging them. Few people would tolerate a friend telling them how their geographically close relationship was doomed. You should expect the same degree of respect and encouragement for your LDR.

One last point: in our study we found that not only did social support help prevent emotional and psychological difficulties, but it seemed to help the relationship itself.[3] We examined couples in LDRs who reported low levels of intimacy to discover what factors seemed to play a role in this deficit. We found that less intimate couples had less social support and less support for their relationship from friends and family. Additionally, they reported more problems in their relationships with friends. Therefore, focusing on your support system not only helps you, it helps your relationship as well.

Chapter 8

Exploring Your Separation Inventory: Your Relationship

The previous three chapters have focused on the demographics of your relationship, your personality, and your degree of social support. These three elements play an important role in the amount of emotional difficulty you may experience during the separation. This chapter examines the compatibility between you and your partner when it comes to issues unique to LDRs. Additionally, we'll discuss the general overall quality of your relationship and how it relates to the separation.

Chris and Cindy

Chris and Cindy had dated for two years when Cindy graduated with a degree in biology. She had hoped to find a job in her field but after searching for several months, she came up empty-handed and became discouraged. She reevaluated her interest in biology and branched out in her career search, ultimately responding to an advertisement for flight attendants. When the airline offered her a position, she discussed it with Chris. His main concern was that the two-month training course was held in Indianapolis, a two-hour drive away. Cindy also expressed concern, and she shared with me her pessimism.

"For the last six months or so we've begun to fight more often and the really good times together seem fewer and fewer. Chris doesn't know it, but I've thought a lot about whether I even want to try to make the relationship work. I don't know what effect a separation will have."

Without sharing her concerns with Chris, she ultimately accepted the position and they began a brief LDR. Within the first month, the relationship started to feel the stress. Chris had hoped for daily telephone calls and weekly visits. Cindy was enjoying her freedom and used the time to evaluate the relationship and "catch my breath."

When I talked to them about their expectations for their LDR, two difficulties became apparent. First, they differed greatly on practical aspects such as how often to call and visit one another. Second, although they both realized this discordance, they had never discussed it–both were uncomfortable raising the issue.

Although they agreed to keep working on their LDR, it lasted only another three weeks before Cindy ended the relationship. The difficulties they already faced, combined with the new issues that the separation had unearthed, were too much for her to handle.

Looking back on the relationship, Chris attributes the break-up to the distance. He agrees that the relationship was on shaky ground well before the separation but believes that everything could have been worked out had they lived closer to one another. Cindy disagrees. She sees the distance as merely having given her time to think about and prepare for the ending of the relationship.

Obviously, they'll never know for sure what effect the separation had on their relationship. Would it have ended regardless of the distance? I like to make this point whenever I hear someone claim, "LDRs don't work," usually followed by an anecdote illustrating their point. While it's convenient to attribute the breakup to the distance, it's probably not accurate. As I've mentioned before, the data simply doesn't support the claim that distance *causes* relationships to fail. Long-distance relationships fail for essentially the same reasons other relationships fail.

What research suggests, however, is that separation can have an interesting effect on the *timing* of relationship changes. The first weeks to months after a relationship becomes long-distance represents a period of rapid change. The direction of this change depends almost entirely on which direction the relationship was heading prior to the separation. Relationships that were already doing rather poorly tend to deteriorate quickly. Relationships that were reporting excellent intimacy, communication, and commitment prior to the LDR tend to strengthen during the early part of the separation.[7]

Yet this period of rapid change lasts only a few weeks, and eventually separation slows the overall progression of the relationship.[3] When we examined dating couples over time, we found that, compared to geographically close relationships, the separated couples progressed toward marriage at a slower rate. This doesn't imply that their relationships were in any way worse than those geographically closer together–remember that our study showed no difference in their reported intimacy, satisfaction, commitment, or trust. Simply put, the separation slowed everything down. Similarly, relationships that will ultimately break up will take longer to do so once they survive those first few weeks of rapid change. Separation allows us to tolerate much more dissatisfaction because we tend to think, "They'll be gone in a couple of days anyway."

Communication

What all this means for you is that the better your relationship, the easier and more successful the separation will be.[34, 36] While this shouldn't surprise anyone, it's worth discussing some of the finer points that relate more specifically to LDRs. First, your communication style plays a more important role in LDRs than in other relationships. LDRs generally have a reduced quantity of communication between partners, which amplifies the importance of the quality of each interaction. The old adage about quality time applies wholeheartedly to separated relationships. Poor communication, coupled with infrequent communication, quickly leads to trouble. Additionally, the communication that does take place often is handicapped by the use of the telephone. Studies have shown that people have significantly more difficulty making judgments about people's values, opinions, and emotions when talking with them on the telephone as compared to face-to-face.[55] Without the visual cues you normally perceive, you can have difficulty deciding on appropriate responses to vague comments made over the telephone.

Another impediment to communication comes in the form of greater tolerance of one's partner. In our study of LDRs we found that, compared to geographically close couples, those in LDRs reported significantly fewer arguments with their significant others.[2] Primarily this effect was due to their ability to exit the situation rather than challenge their partner. David demonstrated this well when he told me, "Whenever I found myself annoyed at Sarah, rather than bring it up and risk starting a fight, I'd say to myself, 'Let it go, I don't see her that much, and I'll be leaving in two days.'"

Couples who see one another day-to-day face a situation where they must either accept the behavior, or struggle to change it. Physically exiting the situation is not generally considered an option. But those of us in LDRs often shy away from confrontation because we don't want to risk spoiling the weekend, and escape is usually only a few days around the corner. While this strategy works well on occasion, in the long run it short circuits the relationship warning signals.[56] As I've mentioned before, conflict serves a very important function in relationships, and avoiding conflict simply prolongs the dysfunctional components of your interactions. Thus, as with geographically close relationships, couples who quickly raise issues and thoroughly discuss them to a mutually acceptable conclusion tend ultimately to find their LDRs more satisfying.

Survival Tip # 21

Realize that LDRs require you to become a master at communication. You're faced with two difficulties while separated. First, you'll need to communicate more than usual, as issues unique to the separation unfold. Second, you'll find communication difficult as the lack of time, the pitfalls of telephone talk, and the growing telephone bill conspire against you.

Also, it's easy to avoid talking about things that aggravate you while you're together. You'll tolerate more because you'll be leaving soon, and no one likes to spoil a weekend together with a fight. But ultimately failing to deal with issues that arise will undermine the relationship.

Expectations

If you have managed an LDR for several months or even years, you have developed a good sense of shared expectations about issues unique to LDRs: how often to call, how often to visit, what's important in terms of dropping off and picking up one another, how much time to spend together during reunions, what kind of socializing is acceptable while apart, and so forth.

Ultimately many of these preferences are rooted in one's value judgments about the importance of intimacy versus autonomy. Couples who share very similar values on this dimension usually have a much easier time agreeing on the practicalities of the separation. In contrast, couples who differ significantly can have serious problems. When one member of the LDR places intimacy well above autonomy, they usually prefer very frequent telephone calls and visits, enjoy longer and more emotional "hellos" and "goodbyes," prefer to spend the vast majority of their time together during reunions, and have stricter rules about socializing while apart. The opposite is true of those placing autonomy above intimacy. Both positions are perfectly normal and can lead to wonderful relationships, assuming that both partners feel the same.

Survival Tip # 22

Everyone varies as to the importance of autonomy and intimacy in their lives. In LDRs this means that everyone also varies as to their preferences for telephone calls, visits, and many other practical aspects of the separation. Ultimately, your relationship will enter a balance between your preferences and those of your partner. Help the relationship to obtain this balance by explicitly discussing the issues unique to LDRs. Review the questions in Part II of the LDR Separation Inventory with your partner and try to come to a consensus on the issues raised. Remember that everything is renegotiable, so each of you must be somewhat flexible.

Relationships That Began (and Remain) at a Distance

Many couples have shared with me that their relationship was never geographically close. These couples met one another over the Internet, or while one person was visiting relatives, or traveling to a conference. Their short time together convinced them that they wanted to try to continue the relationship via telephone and the occasional face-to-face visit. If you're in this situation, I have good news.

Common sense would suggest that the longer couples had been together prior to the separation, the more likely they were to survive an LDR. However, much like the other demographic factors, the amount of time that a couple spends dating one another prior to separating has shown little impact on the success or failure of the LDR.[3, 16, 45, 57] Once again this means that you, rather than the numbers, are in control of your relationship's destiny.

Survival Tip # 23

If your relationship began at a distance, you're not alone. Fortunately, studies show that couples who have never lived near one another did no worse, nor better, than couples who once lived close together prior to beginning an LDR.

Part II

Strategies for
Separated Couples

Chapter 9

The Advantages of LDRs

Maria and Chuck

"When we first began the LDR, I thought we were crazy," began Maria, a neurology resident in California dating a surgery resident in Boston. "But now I can honestly say that it has been the best choice for Chuck and I. We both have such little free time that if we lived closer we'd just be disappointing one another all the time. This way we both put 100% into our work when we're apart, and we put 100% into the relationship when we're together."

While LDRs do have their trials and tribulations, they also have some very distinct advantages over the alternatives. Don't get me wrong. I certainly would have preferred that my partner and I lived closer together if our career paths had so allowed. But to focus on the negatives, without giving proper credit to the positives, will only make the experience a miserable one. Many people find it relatively easy to obsess over how much they miss their partner or how lonely they are. Yet they rarely make the effort to acknowledge the good things that come from the separation: the amount of time they have to focus on work, the time to explore friendships, the time to be alone and grow as a person, the excitement of rediscovering their significant other after a long time apart. These are not trivial gifts, and I believe that for many of us the LDR grants us a wonderful opportunity to foster our careers, our personal growth, and our intimate relationships.

Career or Educational Advancement

The number one advantage of most LDRs is the opportunity for career or educational advancement. With the exception of relationships separated as a result of incarceration or military deployments, the vast majority separate to allow one or both members to grow in their career field. Researchers have shown clearly that those in LDRs do experience significant opportunity for career or educational growth.[3, 16]

In part of our study, we asked hundreds of college students in LDRs and in geographically close relationships how much they had been bothered by some common college hassles. Included in this list were questions related to difficulties in meeting academic standards. We found that those in geographically close relationships reported significantly more difficulty with several aspects of their education, compared to those in LDRs. They found the courses more demanding and less interesting, and they had too little time for work. They also reported their schoolwork was interrupted more frequently. While it's possible that those in LDRs were simply more intelligent, I think that's unlikely. Clearly those in LDRs were able to use the time that others spent on relationships to focus more intently on their educational growth. This advantage holds true for most LDRs: The time away allows us to accomplish something important in our lives while also holding on to an important relationship.

Free Time

Paula and Mark

"Two years ago, after I married Paula, I began to realize how I had gradually stopped hanging out with my friends. I spent the day at work, and then Paula and I had become accustomed to spending the evening alone as a couple. One Monday morning I found out that the old gang had gotten together for a game of basketball and hadn't invited me. 'We didn't think you'd come,' was their excuse. It hit me how much I missed their friendship.

"Then Paula left to go to Japan for a year, which certainly was difficult for us both. But I reconnected with my buddies, and even now that Paula's returned, I feel like I have brought a better balance to my life. Paula and I have a wonderful marriage, and the guys now invite me for the Saturday afternoon game."

Mark and Paula used their time away from one another to help develop other areas of their lives. Paula advanced her career as a civil engineer by working in Japan on some projects related to her expertise. While their separation did not particularly benefit Mark's career, he used the time to focus on reuniting with his friends and developing relationships that continue to enrich his life.

The free time that comes with most LDRs provides a framework that we must choose to fill with either loneliness or personal growth. Some people with whom I've spoken have had a great deal of difficulty with the separation, and they sit morbidly at home spending their time watching TV and waiting for the telephone to ring. Obviously, this is not a great way of making it through the LDR. Others have used the free time in a wonderful variety of ways: exercising, canvas painting, adult education classes, winemaking, working on relationships with friends or family, writing a book, building model trains, or learning to crochet. The list is endless.

Survival Tip # 24

Most LDRs allow us to have more free time to focus on areas of our lives that interest us. The free time can be either a blessing or a curse, and only you can decide which it will become. Use the free time to develop and grow as a person. Think about taking a class, or working on a hobby, or spending more time with friends and family. Actively work on using the time to your advantage. You'll find that the more you do, the more positively you'll view the separation, which is very important to a successful LDR.

Novelty

Michelle and George

Michelle and George, you'll recall, have a very long-distance relationship, with George in the Navy in Japan and Michelle teaching school in Indiana. While she'd prefer to be closer, Michelle has found that the separation has prevented their relationship from becoming too routine.

"I only get to see George every three or four months, and we can't talk all that often on the telephone. So when we do meet, it's like we're falling in love all over again. You know that giddy feeling you get when you first start to fall for someone? Well, I get that every time we get together. I go through a period of rediscovery where I realize again how special he is and how much he means to me. I don't think we ever take each other for granted anymore."

I remember as a child going to an amusement park and riding the rollercoaster in an endless process of standing in line, hopping onto the ride for the 30-second thrill, and then running down the exit ramp to assume my position again at the end of the line. This entertained me exactly four times before the novelty wore off. While routine plays an important role in stabilizing our relationships, it also tends to dull things down. Much like the interplay between autonomy and intimacy, novelty and routine work against one another, and each of us must find the balance that works for us in each particular relationship.

Geographically close couples have the advantage of seeing one another daily. Yet that level of familiarity sometimes creeps beyond routine and into boredom. Many of these couples struggle to bring novelty to their relationship. LDRs have novelty thrust upon them. Most couples in LDRs report a honeymoon period whenever they get together, with each partner paying special attention to the other.

As Michelle mentioned previously, the feelings unearthed during this period are likened to falling in love all over again.

Survival Tip # 25

Most couples in LDRs describe an enjoyable honeymoon during the first few hours to days of a reunion. This time together allows for a mutual rediscovery of each other and of the relationship. For many people the emotional excitement of seeing their partner begins even before they actually get together. Just planning and preparing for reunion can bring out the exhilaration. Try to enjoy the experience and recognize it as another gift that your LDR affords.

As mentioned earlier, we already know that LDRs do not break up any more frequently than geographically close relationships. What we don't know is what exactly prevents them from breaking up, given all of the disadvantages that come with separation. One interesting theory comes from one of the best-researched branches of psychology known as behavioral psychology. Studies have shown that we are much more likely to keep doing something when we get rewards only every so often rather than all the time. Continual rewards seem to cause us to lose interest as soon as the reward is stopped, even if only temporarily.

The owners of the casinos know this very well. The slot machines are designed to pay out only every so often, so that people don't lose interest. If they paid out a little every time someone pulled the lever, people would still play, but they would get really bored. If the machine then stopped paying out, even for a short time, people would rapidly move to other machines. However, if the machines pay out just often enough, people find themselves excited, and they will continue to play for long after the machine stops paying them back.

If we equate the payoff from a slot machine with the fun we get when we interact with our partner, we see some similarities. Those who receive constant payoffs by being in a geographically close relationship reap many benefits but often become bored. If those payoffs suddenly stop, for example during a period of conflict, these couples may quickly lose interest in one another. However, those of us in LDRs receiving only occasional payoffs will tend to "keep playing" even when the rewards stop for a while. It's only speculation at this point, but I certainly believe that for many people the thrill of seeing their partner after a long break helps offset some of the disadvantages of being in an LDR.

One last point about novelty: Many couples told me that when they do finally get together, they tend to plan exciting activities to make the most of the weekend. Picnics, woodland hikes, camping, skydiving, canoeing–the list goes on. While there's no need to overschedule your time together, you may want to plan some fun activities that you ordinarily wouldn't give yourself the time to enjoy.

Survival Tip # 26

Research shows that couples in LDRs enjoy more exciting outdoor activities than couples who live closer to one another.[3] Take advantage of the times when you do get together to plan some novel adventures–rollerblading, skydiving, camping–whatever the two of you might enjoy. This extra benefit of being in an LDR will help offset the occasional disadvantages.

A Chance to Grow

Donna and Ed

Donna and Ed are not the traditional couple in an LDR. They have been married for nearly 21 years and both are in their early fifties. Donna works part-time at a local library while Ed helps manage one of the major national computing firms. Two years ago, Ed's company asked him to move to help supervise a new project in California. Unfortunately, Donna's mother, who lived only a few miles away, was in poor health and Donna chose to stay nearby.

For the past year and a half, Donna and Ed have managed to see one another almost every other weekend. For Donna, the separation has allowed her to reconnect with a part of herself that she had let slip away nearly three decades ago.

"For a long time I've relied on Ed to take care of things: the checkbook, car repairs, planning our time together, deciding what we'd watch on TV. The first month after he left was quite a shock. I didn't have him around to balance the checkbook. I thought I'd wait until he came home, but finally I sat down and worked it out. Now I take care of most of the business around the house and I feel like I've reasserted myself. My sense of independence and self-reliance has grown tremendously."

As I mentioned before, LDRs require greater self-esteem than geographically close relationships. Fortunately, they also provide an opportunity to bring out the very activities that help build self-esteem.

As children we begin to learn our own self-worth and our own abilities by asserting our independence and trying things on our own. However, children require a reliable support (mom and dad) to fall back on should they fail. In many ways, the LDR provides us a similar opportunity to begin to explore our self-reliance while maintaining an important supportive connection (our partner) should we need the help.

Survival Tip # 27

Self-esteem flourishes in an environment that requires self-reliance, but also provides a secure relationship to fall back on when times get tough. For many people the LDR provides the perfect blend of independence and support to nourish self-esteem and personal growth.

LDRs as a Learning Experience
for the Future

Judy and Lane

"Our relationship is definitely different than most," began Judy. *"I don't think that on my wedding day I could have envisioned spending nearly a decade in a long-distance marriage. Now, looking back, I must say that it has brought more intimacy, personal growth, and family prosperity than I could possibly have imagined when Lane and I first reluctantly decided to work in two different cities."*

Judy and Lane have been married for 31 years. For the past 10 years of their relationship, they have lived in an LDR, though the distance and structure has varied during those years. Both Judy and Lane are professors. Following their marriage, Judy took time to complete her master's degree before they started their family. After they had two children, Judy stayed home until all the children were in school. She then returned to the university and completed her PhD. During that time, she started teaching in the anthropology department. She liked that arrangement and on completion of her degree she was offered a teaching position at a university 120 miles away.

They purchased a small second home there, where Judy would live four days a week, returning to the family home for three days. Lane took responsibility for the children during the week. The couple felt it was beneficial for all in the family because each could have their unique time with the children as well as with each other. This arrangement lasted for four years until Judy was offered a teaching position at her former university and agreed to take it. Just as she was moving back home, Lane was offered a very prestigious position in a city some 350 miles away. Again, the couple made the decision to take both positions and continue their LDR. This next phase lasted six years, during which Lane purchased a home in his new city. Judy and the children continued to live in the original home, while Lane spent every other weekend with the family. He also spent holidays and parts of his sabbatical year at home. Judy and the children spent holidays with Lane in what they called "dad's house."

After six years, the children were grown and out of the family home, and Judy was offered a new position at a university 50 miles from Lane. The couple felt it was still too far to attempt a commute. Lane kept his home and they bought a new family home in Judy's city.

The couple has come to terms with their separation and togetherness, and they value both blocks of time. They have both developed very successful careers and find that their separate time enables them to continue to enhance their careers. They also have much in common, and find that their time together is rich and fulfilling and gives them a lot to go on when alone. As Judy and Lane reflect back on their years together, both agree that they would not have undertaken their LDR if not for these advantages. Their children agree that it created unique relationships for them with each parent, as well as time together as a family, which they valued.

When Judy and Lane started their LDR, it was a very unusual lifestyle. However, now their story is only one example of many couples who are living a large portion of their lives through an LDR. Many couples are finding that the unique job that they want may not be in the same location as their partner.

With the transfer of Hong Kong back to China, a number of Hong Kong couples have made the choice to live out LDRs. One member of the couple has moved to another country to take up residence to apply for citizenship. This was viewed as a safety precaution should they decide to leave Hong Kong following China's takeover. For several years now, these couples have been living with one in Hong Kong and the other in their new country. The distance between Hong Kong and the new country of residence is always several hours by flight, so their time together has been minimal. The majority of these relationships have maintained their stability despite the distance and the time apart. Coping with an LDR enables these couples to manage a transition that was not of their own making, but rather part of a larger cultural upheaval.

Many couples, where one partner is in a diplomatic career, find that it is important to structure their relationship as an LDR so that the other partner's career and personal goals can be fulfilled at the same time as the one on diplomatic assignment. In the past, it was expected that the partner would go along with the overseas assignment. Today, it is more common that the couple choose to live this stage of their relationship as an LDR, rather than to jeopardize the future of the non-diplomatic mate. As we become a global economy and a more global community, the location of jobs tend to take on a worldwide scope. One never knows when they may be asked to spend at least a part of their job time in some distant location. To maintain a secure job, most individuals take a long and very serious look at this request.

As I have discussed in earlier chapters, when this request to fulfill a job at a distant location is within a limited time structure, most couples find ways of managing the transition. A temporary separation may secure a more enriched future not only in terms of financial and job security, but also in terms of personal enhancement and relationship enrichment.

Futurists predict that individuals who live comfortably and creatively with rapid and spontaneous personal and relational adjustments will adapt best to the fast-paced lifestyle of the new millennium. Given all these points, another benefit of a temporary LDR is that it provides good preparation for the future. While we have been learning how to manage our LDR, we have been learning coping and adapting methods that enhance our ability to adjust to an ever-changing world.

Chapter 10

The Emotional Stages
of Separation

David and Sarah

Sarah

"The one thing I've noticed about being apart is the incredible range of emotions I experience. While I'm away from David, I often feel lonely and depressed, especially on the weekends. As it comes closer to seeing him again, I get excited and even a little nervous. After we're together for a few hours, I settle back into the way we were before we had to separate. Then I notice that about a day or so before I have to leave again, I begin to refocus on all the work I have to do back home, and I begin to distance myself emotionally from David."

David

"I've always felt that Sarah has had an easier time with the separation than I have. Partly I think it helped her to be the one who moved away. She has such a new and different life, and her studies keep her busy. I'm the one who's always around all of the places we used to go for dinner, and the park we used to go for picnics. I think I'm reminded of her more because of that.

"She mentioned that she begins to pull away before she leaves. I've noticed that, and it's a bit of a problem because I tend to want to hold onto her even more tightly as I know she'll be leaving soon. When she does leave, I'll admit that I spend a few hours fighting back some anger. I know we both decided that this was the best thing for us, but I still get frustrated. If it becomes too obvious, and she notices that I'm acting upset at her, then the guilt sets in. I've heard people use the term 'emotional rollercoaster,' and I think that it fits my situation pretty well."

David and Sarah shared with me their own experiences of the separation. While they differ from one another on a few issues, such as their reactions toward

69

an impending separation, they share many of the emotions that most people experience while in LDRs. Fortunately, every one of us will travel through our separation with a slightly different emotional reaction. But researchers have discovered that separation evokes some very common patterns of emotions, patterns that I hear over and over when talking with couples in LDRs.

Some of the most detailed research on separation has examined the reactions of puppies temporarily isolated from their mothers.[58] Although it's difficult to apply conclusions from research done on animals to the emotions described in humans, I've found that the reactions of the pups are strikingly similar to the reactions of many of those in LDRs.

When the researchers removed the mother dog from the kennel, the pups began to protest. They cried and ran around the kennel sometimes for hours and even days. Eventually the pups stopped protesting, but they began to behave as if they were depressed. They slept poorly, they lost their appetites, they stopped playing with toys in the kennel, they lost weight, and they withdrew from other dogs.

Once mom returned, the dogs reacted in a variety of ways. Some dogs immediately leapt up and scrambled back to be close to their mother. They spent the next several hours to days within a few feet of their mother, never venturing out of her sight. Other dogs seemed almost angry. They initially looked excited and then seemed to ignore their mother, staying at some distance for a time. Still other pups showed a compromise between these styles, with an initial excitement and a few hours close by mom's side, and then they resumed their usual frolicking around the kennel.

For most of the pups, when mom began to distance herself as if to leave again, they began to appear anxious, pacing around and beginning to protest. Some pups, subjected to repeated separations, began to distance themselves from mom. They eventually appeared disinterested, and they stopped protesting when mom left. Unfortunately, they also failed to benefit from the guidance that mom had to offer as they matured.

This pattern of protesting the separation, then behaving depressed, then developing some emotional distance, seemed to represent the usual reaction of the pups to separation. Because these reactions occur very early in the lives of the pups, there is good reason to believe that the sequence of emotions may even be programmed to help them survive.[58] You can imagine how important the mother dog is to the survival of these pups had they been born in the wild. Should the mom begin to wander off, the pups' protests may help keep her and her offspring together where they are safe. However, if the mother leaves despite the cries of the pups, the energy required to keep up such a protest puts the pups in danger because they already have limited food-gathering skills. Thus, a safeguard is built in to end a futile protest.

This safeguard resembles depression. Researchers speculate that the sequence of separation, protest, depression, and detachment may reflect an almost automatic protective reflex in many mammals. How much of this reflex remains in us humans we don't know, but I think it unlikely that we have managed to escape it entirely. More likely, the emotional reactions remain, but we have learned to change the behavior they evoke. Instead of crying for days after a loved one leaves, we may cry a few minutes, or not at all. But the emotional triggers that cause the pups to cry for days, and us to feel saddened by our partner's departure, remain deeply ingrained.

Switching now to studies of couples in LDRs, researchers have found that in general, the same sequence of reactions occurs: *protest, depression,* and *detachment.* The intensity and the expression of each of these vary greatly, of course, but the vast majority of couples describe emotions that roughly fit into this pattern.

Protest

The *protest* phase begins when you first start to focus on the impending separation. The intensity of the emotions that follow can range from mild sorrow to absolute panic. Obviously, those who find themselves closer to the panic side might find LDRs less than ideal. Most of us have learned to accept the need for the separation and actual protests are few and far between. (I'm personally guilty of trying to convince my partner to extend her stay "just another day.")

Some people feel angry with their partner at this stage. One couple, Craig and Molly, were finding that they began to fight with each other as the time to leave approached. Neither could pinpoint why they were irritated at one another, until Molly one day realized that she was just plain angry at Craig for leaving. She knew that the LDR was their best alternative, but she couldn't help being angry. Molly was protesting Craig's departure. It just happened that her way of protesting was more along the lines of yelling at Craig rather than begging him to stay. Neither approach is particularly constructive, but both stem from our natural need to maintain a close connection to someone we care about.

Molly and Craig's case highlights another important point. Because the emotions stem directly from the separation itself, they can cause a great deal of confusion when we try to identify their source. Typically when we're angry, sad, or depressed, we begin to search back, trying to find out why we're feeling this way. Anger in particular seems to call for an explanation. Unfortunately, the best explanation in many situations may be simply that what we're feeling is a normal and natural response to being separated.

Survival Tip # 28

Research has shown us that whenever we are separated from someone we care about, we experience a very normal range of emotions. Anger, guilt, depression, anxiety, and many others stem directly from the separation. Realize that sometimes when you're feeling these emotions they may be caused simply by the separation rather than by something more complex.

Depression

The second stage of separation has traditionally been called depression, a term that I hesitate to use because it means many different things. Clinical psychologists usually use the term to refer to something called *major depression*. This describes a situation in which someone is significantly depressed, to the point that they have difficulty going to work and doing the day-to-day things that we all need to do to survive in today's society. They may be so depressed that they have thoughts of hurting or killing themselves. This degree of depression calls for professional help, either in the form of medication, psychotherapy, or both.

Some of the earliest studies of separation focused on the wives of soldiers fighting in World War II.[35, 45] These studies found a significant level of major depression, but their situation is much different than that of most modern day LDRs. Our study of LDRs found that separation did not appear to increase the risk of major depression.[2] So while I'll use the term "depression" to describe this stage of separation, realize that I'm referring to a relatively mild amount of depression, not major depression. If you think that you may have major depression, I urge you not to see it as simply part of the normal reaction to an LDR. Separation does not, by itself, cause that degree of depression. Because major depression has effective treatments, seek professional help if you're in this situation.

If you find that you do feel a little blue or down while you're separated, you're not alone. I reviewed 25 studies of separated relationships, and in every one the participants described feeling slightly depressed while apart.[3] In our own study we used a pencil and paper test that is used by therapists to screen for depression,[59] and we compared people in LDRs to people in geographically close relationships. I've already mentioned that we did not find any difference in the rates of major depression. But we did find that those in LDRs reported more symptoms of mild depression: feeling blue, difficulty sleeping, feeling uninterested in things, difficulty making decisions, and difficulty concentrating. These symptoms weren't severe enough to disrupt their day-to-day functioning (in fact, recall that those in LDRs had *less* difficulty with work than those in geographically closer relationships), but they were significant enough for most people to mention them as a disadvantage of LDRs. What causes these symptoms? Again, just a normal reaction to being separated.

One of the fascinating, but unfortunate, aspects of this mild depression is that it does indeed behave much like a reflex. We found that no matter how long couples had been separated, they still reported the same amount of mild depression. Couples separated for one month, and couples separated for three years, had roughly the same difficulty with feeling down.[2] Several other researchers have found the same thing.[27, 35, 36] A large study conducted by the U.S. Army of almost a thousand separated couples also found that more experience with separations did not seem to make these symptoms any easier.[44] Oddly enough, the puppy study I already mentioned showed the exact same thing.[58] Older puppies with more separation experience had as much difficulty with being separated as younger puppies.

Like any other reflex, it takes a very long time to change or eliminate the response, if it can be done at all. That is not to say that *dealing* with the emotions doesn't get easier; it does. It means that you need to take control of how you plan on coping with loneliness and depression rather than simply waiting for these feelings to go away with time. (Chapter 11 will discuss some of the best ways of taking control and staying emotionally healthy while separated.)

Survival Tip # 29

Feeling blue while you're apart is a common complaint in LDRs and, unfortunately, it often doesn't get any better with time. Create a plan to help deal with your loneliness and depression early on in your separation.

Detachment

The last stage of separation, *detachment,* sounds unpleasant but represents a worthwhile coping mechanism.[60]

Returning to the puppy studies, remember that protest helps prevent separation when possible. Depression helps prevent the wasting of energy on futile protests, while detachment helps prevent the lack of productivity associated with depression. Some degree of emotional detachment allows the puppies, and us, to continue with our lives while we have to be apart from the ones we care about.

As in the other two stages, the degree to which each of us detaches from our partner varies tremendously. At one extreme are those who barely detach at all. They spend most of their time stuck in the depression stage and sit around obsessing about their partner and the separation. The pain associated with constantly focusing on the distance often leads these LDRs to abandon the distance, either by moving closer or by simply ending the relationship. On the other extreme are those who detach so quickly and completely that they have trouble maintaining any intimacy while apart. When reunited, these people remain emotionally distant in order to avoid the pain of ultimately having to separate once again. While this strategy may help you to avoid pain, it obviously deprives you of the wonderful gifts that intimacy provides. Thus, a healthy level of detachment is one sufficient to propel you past any separation-related depression without being so intense that you lose the ability to connect intimately when you're together.

Another aspect of detachment that Molly and David faced involved what some have called *anticipatory distancing.*[28, 61] Many couples I spoke with described a situation in which one or both of them would begin to pull away from the other as the time to separate grew near. If this sounds familiar to you, recognize it as a normal way of trying to protect yourself from the pain of separation. Often the more someone cares about their partner, the more they feel the need to begin to pull away, even before the actual "goodbye."

The real difficulty comes when both partners respond to the actual departure in different ways. David preferred to hold on tighter until the very last minute, while Sarah chose to distance herself in advance. Negotiating this issue takes some compromise on the part of both partners.

Anxiety

Many people I spoke with described feeling nervous or anxious during their separation. For some people, the anxiety begins just prior to separation and probably results from the same reflex that leads to the protest stage. Anxiety represents your body's way of saying, *"Do something!"* Whether that something is running from a hungry bear or trying to prevent your loved one from leaving, the type of reaction is similar. It is usually the magnitude of the anxiety that differs.

Other people mostly reported being anxious when their partners were already away. Some were primarily concerned about sexual infidelity or that the relationship itself was disintegrating. This response isn't all that different from the anxiety involved in protesting the separation. Both are concerned with preventing the loss of a loved one. It's helpful to realize that the most important function of anxiety is to warn you that something may be wrong and to prompt you to take action.

Deciding what exactly is "wrong" can be frustrating. Remember that the mere act of separation generates emotions reflexively, and the only thing creating the anxiety may be the separation itself. In other situations the issue may be one of distrust or fear that the relationship will end. In any case, deciding what to do to help diminish the anxiety isn't particularly easy. Some people pay outrageous airline fares to fly back to their partner, simply because their anxiety grows to the point where the only action they can take is to temporarily reunite. Certainly there are situations that necessarily prompt an urgent flight to see your loved one, but because anxiety can be an intrinsic part of separation, this approach can prove quite expensive.

Survival Tip # 30

Anxiety often is a reflex emotion resulting from any separation from a loved one. When you find yourself anxious it may be due simply to this reflex or it may be due to specific thoughts about your relationship. If you can identify any thoughts that are making you fearful, challenge their validity. For example, if you're afraid of the relationship ending remember that LDRs don't breakup any more frequently than geographically close relationships. If you can't find any specific thoughts that are making you anxious, consider some general relaxation techniques such as meditation, breathing exercises, massage, yoga, or exercise.

Guilt

Unfortunately, guilt does play a role in LDRs, and it comes up in many different ways.

First, our society has decided that intimate relationships *should* be geographically close. Because of this, when we choose to try an LDR there can be a definite feeling of guilt associated with the separation. Guilt stems from the concern that we are violating social norms.[47-49] Second, if your LDR resulted from one of you having to move away for career reasons, that person may feel guilty and feel as though they had been overly selfish. Guilt can also creep up when you begin to judge yourself over the emotions that are naturally a part of separation.

The most common situations I've seen involve either anger (the protest stage) or crying (the depression stage). As David discussed in the opening quote for this chapter, he commonly finds himself angry with Sarah for no particular reason. His reason is simply that he doesn't want to be apart. Unfortunately, he then judges himself and thinks, "I shouldn't be angry at Sarah," and he begins to feel guilty about feeling angry. Michelle (who, you'll recall, is dating George, deployed with the Navy) sums up the other common situation.

George and Michelle

"When George leaves, it's a big affair. All of the girlfriends and wives come out to the dock, and there's lots of hugging and crying. I always try not to cry. I don't want to ruin our last few minutes together and I don't want George's last image of me to be one of me sobbing my eyes out. But I always cry, and I hate myself for not being able to hold it back."

Michelle's reaction to the separation is completely healthy, natural, and normal. Yet she has decided that crying somehow ruins their experience of being together, and so she floods herself with guilt. In reality, Michelle had never discussed this with George, and when it finally did come up he said that her crying showed him how much she cared. Had she ever been able to hold back the tears when he left, he would have been hurt by what he would have seen as her lack of caring.

Survival Tip # 31

Many people in LDRs experience guilt over the normal and natural emotions that come with separation. Allow yourself to feel anger when you don't want to part and to cry when you're sad. These are normal and healthy feelings.

Chapter 11

Ten Steps to Staying Emotionally Healthy While You Have to Be Apart

Angela and Tim

Angela and Tim met during a seminar sponsored by the computer company for which they both worked; Angela in the Colorado office, and Tim in the California office. After several two-hour telephone calls, Tim flew out to visit Angela. After having a wonderful weekend together, they decided to try to make the relationship work, even though they were several hours apart by plane. Angela spent some time talking with me about the difficulties she had during the separation and some of the tricks she used to help make things a little easier.

"First and foremost is the loneliness," she began. "Not all the time, but particularly on the weekends, or whenever I go out with friends and see them having a great time with their dates. When I'm in an environment that is geared toward socializing, I notice that I miss Tim a lot more. Then there are times when the loneliness creeps into a depression. Luckily these aren't very often, and Tim is great about helping me pull myself out of a slump.

"Early on, right after we met and decided to keep seeing each other, I spent several weekends wondering what he was doing. Was he out at bars picking up other women or on a date with someone else? We both had implicitly agreed that we would be monogamous, but we had never said anything directly. Finally, we had a long telephone call and discussed what was and wasn't okay for each of us. That seemed to help me with some of the anxiety. It wasn't that I didn't trust him. I wasn't sure we were on the same page before, and now that we've spelled everything out I know."

Angela described three very common reactions to separation: loneliness, depression, and anxiety. In the last chapter, I discussed these in more detail. In this chapter, I'll outline ways of dealing with these feelings.

First, remember that these emotions and many more are a normal and natural response to being separated from someone you care about. In fact, the least healthy response is to have no reaction whatsoever to separation. Obviously, if these feelings are so intense that they interfere with getting things done during the day, then you may have gone beyond the usual reaction to separation and you may need to seek some professional advice. But for most of us in LDRs, the loneliness, depression, anger, and guilt are a nuisance rather than a crippling reaction, even if it is a rather unpleasant nuisance.

Ten Steps to Staying Sane While Separated.

Step 1. Maintain a satisfying and intimate relationship.

I admit this sounds rather obvious. But it is worth discussing. The single most important step in staying emotionally healthy is forming and maintaining a healthy relationship with your partner. Numerous studies have shown that intimate and satisfying romantic relationships help buffer us from the usual stresses that the world hurls at us every day.[63, 64] One study in particular looked at separated couples and found that the quality of their relationship, more than any other factor, predicted the degree of emotional difficulty each would have with the separation. Fortunately, as I've already mentioned, LDRs, as a group, report just as satisfying and intimate relationships as geographically close couples.

Step 2. Socialize.

Loneliness comes with the territory for those of us in LDRs. As Angela mentioned, there are usually certain times when we feel lonelier. The usual culprits include being around other couples[47, 65] and doing activities by yourself that you would usually think of as something couples should do; for example, going to a movie, going out to eat,[62, 34] or watching a favorite television show on a Friday or Saturday night.[14, 61] For others, there are specific rituals that they developed with their partner, prior to their separation, that trigger the loneliness. Tina, an airline pilot, told me of how she and her husband always snuggled together on the couch to watch a particular TV show. Now, whenever that show comes on, it reminds her of his absence and the loneliness sets in.

Unfortunately, there is no simple trick to get rid of the loneliness we feel when away from our partners. Psychologists who specialize in loneliness describe two types: emotional and social.[66] *Emotional loneliness* occurs whenever we feel an unanswered need for intimacy. This is the type of loneliness most people in LDRs experience, and it's specific for one particular person. However, even geographically close couples experience this when their relationship begins to deteriorate and the intimacy disappears. The second type of loneliness, *social loneliness,* results when we isolate ourselves from society. It is a yearning for casual relationships with others. Unfortunately, many people in LDRs also experience this type of loneliness.[23, 29, 34, 50, 52, 67]

Sarah noticed this isolation early on in her separation from David. Recall that Sarah is working on an MBA at a university located four hours away from her husband. For the first few months, she would return to see David every weekend.

After she decided to spend many of her weekends at school, she found that no one in her program thought to invite her along for the weekend events, even though she was now available. Her early absence from their group resulted in a persistent assumption that she did not want to participate, even after her schedule changed.

Eventually Sarah took charge and managed to get more involved in the social activities. Yet her first few evenings out went rather poorly. She noticed the same feelings Angela described: She missed David more when she was out than if she stayed home and worked. She also had a distinctly unpleasant interaction with a man who assumed that, because she lived apart from her husband, she was fair game. Sarah eventually decided it wasn't worth going out, and she pulled further away from her friends.

Some of us have to deal with both social and emotional loneliness. Emotional loneliness is virtually impossible to eliminate without actually having your partner at your side. And, as researchers learned, you can't completely do away with one type of loneliness by dealing with the other type.[68] You can have the best social network in the city and still feel emotionally lonely. You can have the most wonderfully intimate connection with your partner and still feel socially isolated. But there is some crossover between the two types of loneliness that those of us in LDRs can use to our advantage.

Minimizing the amount of social isolation will lessen (but not eliminate) your feelings of emotional loneliness. Several studies on separated couples have confirmed the importance of getting out and spending time with friends.[25, 40–42] Companionship with friends helps strengthen your relationship and reduces the loneliness and depression reported by those in LDRs.

While it may feel awkward being out with friends on a Friday or Saturday night, you should make every effort to join the group. Consider it your contribution to keeping yourself sane and keeping your LDR strong. Be proactive in forming bonds with colleagues. Realize that your ambiguous status (not single but not with a date) may make others feel uncomfortable,[29, 61] and they may choose not to invite you along. Generally, once you voice a preference to be included, others will involve you in their social circle.

Step 3. Find a confidant.

One study of relationships found that people who had a confidant–someone they could easily talk with about personal problems–were 10 times less likely to be depressed or lonely than those without one.[69] That's a tremendous effect that even modern anti-depressant medications can't match. Other studies have shown a similarly powerful effect.[70] The ability to simply share both our fun times and our difficulties with someone we trust is a power you must use to your advantage. Let me say early on that the confidant is *not* your romantic partner. The importance of that relationship has already been stressed. This confidant must be someone else, preferably someone geographically closer to you. Usually people tend to choose someone of the same gender, although men sometimes share their feelings more easily with women than with other men. Ideally, this confidant is in a long-distance relationship as well, so the two of you can share ideas and experiences. This not only provides you someone to go out with, but also a companion who understands and shares your dating status.

One creative young law student, Tracy, placed a personal advertisement in the school newspaper, suggesting that anyone in an LDR meet for pizza and beer at the campus union to share their insights. She had roughly a dozen people attend, and she managed to meet several companions who routinely would get together on weekend nights to socialize. Included in this group was Meg, a sociology graduate student, who hit it off well with Tracy, and they spent the next two years supporting each other through their mutual LDRs. (Tracy eventually married her long-distance sweetheart with Meg as a bridesmaid.)

If Tracy's idea isn't for you and you're having trouble finding a confidant, you might consider paying for occasional time with a therapist. While the thought of seeing a therapist turns off many people, I assure you that generally the least healthy people are the ones who refuse to see a psychologist or other professional when they need to. Seeking someone to listen intently to the important issues in your life is anything but crazy. The advantage of paying this person is that you don't have the obligation to listen to his or her own problems. Additionally, professionals often have constructive insights and perspectives that you and your partner may not have considered when looking at the situation from within your own context.

Step 4. Touching.

One of the wonderful advantages of an intimate union that those in geographically close relationships often take for granted is the gift of human contact. Touch is a powerful force and has some amazing effects on the body that we don't fully understand. Touch has been shown to slow the heart rate, lower blood pressure, reduce the frequency of cardiac arrhythmias, and even help premature babies gain weight.[19, 71, 72] Exactly how it accomplishes these feats is a mystery.

Unfortunately, while we're separated from our loved one we may find that the amount of touch we experience drops significantly. This lack of touch may even be partially responsible for the persistent blues that many of us report throughout the separation. The good news is that pretty much any touch helps reverse this deficit. While it would be wonderful if we could receive this touch from our partners, it's not always possible.

One way of increasing physical touch is to seek out nonsexual contact from friends and colleagues. This is where having a confidant who lives nearby can be very helpful. A simple hug can make a great emotional Band-Aid.

Women typically are more comfortable hugging their friends than are men. It's unfortunate that in our society men aren't supposed to show that much affection, because it removes a wonderful source of touch. Other ways of touching that are more acceptable to men involve sports. Football, basketball, soccer, and baseball all can incorporate some amount of nonsexual touch. Personally, I work out with weights with two friends and we often support each other's elbows for safety reasons when we lift. Even this level of touch is much better than none at all. And for those of us who can afford it, a massage is perhaps the most lavish (and very effective) way of reducing stress and gaining the benefits of touch.

Another alternative is to get yourself a pet. The therapeutic effects of petting a dog or cat have already been shown in nursing home studies. If your situation lends itself to a furry friend, and you have the support system to help take care of him or her while you're away, a pet can do wonders for your spirit.

Step 5. Take control.

One of the most celebrated theories of depression called the *learned helplessness model,* focuses on the importance of control.[73] In this model many of the unpleasant emotions we experience, including anxiety and depression, result from the often incorrect belief that nothing we can do will make things different. When researchers were first exploring this model, they placed dogs into a room that was split in half with a little door between the two sides.[74] After the dogs were placed in one side of the room, a mild electric shock was administered. If the dogs ran through the door into the other side of the room, the shock was stopped. The dogs soon learned that to escape the shock they simply had to run into the other room. The dogs learned that they had control over this unpleasant event.

Next, a new set of dogs was put into the room. The researchers then administered shocks that could not be avoided by jumping through the door. These dogs learned that they could not escape the shock and were therefore helpless. However, when the researchers returned to the earlier strategy of stopping the shocks when the dogs jumped to the other side of the room, these new dogs couldn't seem to learn what to do. Their earlier episodes of learned helplessness prevented them from taking control of their destiny, even when a method to do so existed. Instead, these dogs simply stood around neither eating well nor playing. Essentially, the dogs were showing signs of depression.

Although I'm not a fan of shocking dogs in the name of science, this study did provide important insights into the nature of mood disorders. The implication from this research is that depression and anxiety result, in part, from our feelings of being out of control.

Imagine for an instant that you had access to a transporter machine that would allow you to step in and immediately materialize in your partner's room. It's a pretty nice fantasy, right? The transporter simply represents a level of control, albeit one that none of us will obtain. But each small step toward recognizing the control we do have helps quell those jittery feelings.

How do you establish control? First, you need to recognize that you have a choice in your decision to separate. Granted, some of you don't have much choice (such as military separations and those in prison), but the vast majority of us do. While it may be terribly expensive to close the distance, in either monetary or career terms, it's still possible and you have control over that choice. In my own

LDR, I realized that I made the decision every day to: 1) continue in the relationship with my partner, and 2) continue the relationship as an LDR rather than give up my career goals and move closer to her. While it would have been costly for me to simply pull up roots and move, I *could* have done it if I so chose. I had ultimate control over that decision.

The next way of feeling in control is to more explicitly define the parameters of the relationship. At the beginning of the chapter, Angela mentioned how helpful it was for her to openly discuss where she and Tim stood in terms of dating others. They also discussed how often they should talk on the telephone, how often they would try to visit one another, and what their eventual plans were for closing the distance. I realize how difficult it can be to discuss these issues, and working through them while separated seems even harder. In fact, couples in LDRs may indeed have more difficulty discussing issues about the relationship than do couples in geographically close relationships.[75] Unfortunately, couples in LDRs require this sort of discussion more so than other relationships.

Try working through these issues when you're together. Being able to watch your partner's body language greatly increases your ability to understand and connect with your partner.

Once you've decided on how often you will talk on the telephone, consider setting up *telephone dates.* A telephone date is an agreed upon specific time in which you and your partner will get together by telephone. Protect that time as you would a face-to-face date. Knowing in advance when exactly you'll be talking with your partner helps remove some of the uncertainty and helps regain some control. The same is true of face-to-face visits. When you purchase tickets in advance, as suggested before, not a single day of uncertainty has to pass.

Both of these strategies–telephone dates and making reservations early–help by creating structure to the separation, and providing some degree of control.

Step 6. Positive thinking.

During World War II, many thousands of couples were separated from loved ones as our men and women shipped out. During the separation, an Army sociologist studied the situation in detail, hoping to uncover the dynamics of separation to better support families during wartime.[45] One of the most important findings he uncovered was that the degree of difficulty families experienced depended primarily on whether they viewed the separation as a crisis. Those families who believed that the separation was a dreadful event that would result in great hardship, and in all likelihood the breakup of the relationship, found the LDR most difficult. Families that saw the separation as a challenge that they could overcome together reported much less difficulty.

The actual time away from one another was exactly the same for both groups of families; only the meanings that they gave to the separation differed. Once again, this research shows that a large amount of control rests in your hands, rather than in the factors that are less easily manipulated, such as the time apart and the frequency of visits. Simply redefining the separation as an opportunity to grow, rather than as a relationship crisis, may be one of the most powerful strategies to maintain a healthy union while apart.

Our own study of civilian LDRs showed very similar results.[3] When we attempted to uncover the best coping strategy for dealing with the separation, only one approach clearly stood out. Those who focused on the positive aspects of the separation were more likely to stay together and less likely to report personal difficulty dealing with distance. Other studies have found similar results.[26, 34, 42, 61, 76] If you're having difficulty seeing the positive points of your LDR, turn back to Chapter 9 and review some of the advantages of LDRs.

Step 7. View the separation as temporary.

When we first asked couples in LDRs how long they anticipated being apart, their answer was 26 months, on average. Barely five months later, when they should have had 21 months left, their estimate was only 15 months.[3] What happened to the extra six months? Had events changed that allowed these couples to reunite sooner than they originally anticipated?

Actually, very few of them had any real change in the reasons they had separated or in the possibilities of reuniting. But what did happen was that these couples identified times when they could consider closing the distance. These same opportunities existed all along, but the couples began to view the separation in shorter blocks of time. Rather than assume that the separation would last the entire 26 months as they had originally planned, they decided that it could end in a total of 15 months if need be. This allowed them to see the time apart in smaller blocks. In the future they could reevaluate and decide either to continue at a distance or close the gap. Viewing the separation as temporary, and focusing on managing small blocks of time apart rather than large ones, helped couples cope with the separation.[14, 29, 42, 52]

As I mentioned earlier in the book, many couples with whom I spoke used a six-month plan to help ease them through the separation. Every six months they discussed how the relationship was progressing, how often they needed to see one another or call each other, and whether there needed to be any other change in the mechanics of their separation. Setting a date for each six-month block allowed them to focus on simply getting through those six months, rather than trying to swallow the enormity of being separated for more than two or three years. One variant of this is the one-month plan that some of the couples used. In this strategy, people broke the LDR down into even smaller blocks, focusing on the separation from reunion to reunion. In any case, no one I interviewed felt the separation would be permanent; almost everyone sees it as temporary.

Step 8. Acknowledge each other's contributions.

We've all experienced a time when we went to great lengths to do something special for our partner, only to feel like he or she didn't fully appreciate the effort.

While this happens in both geographically close relationships as well as LDRs, it seems to affect the latter to a greater extent.[2] LDRs require special investments that often don't occur in other relationships. We take the time to write letters, we send little packages in the mail, we work around our schedules to catch airline flights, we drive four, five, or even six hours to spend the weekend. These events often take a fair amount of effort that can easily be overlooked when we're on the receiving end. I'll admit that I've not given my partner credit for the effort it takes to drive six hours to spend some time together. While this may seem like a small thing, our study showed that for some it was quite important. For example, men, compared to women, were more likely to complain about their partner ignoring their efforts. Why this difference? Perhaps men are simply more likely to expect thanks and recognition, or they fail to appreciate it when it's offered. In any case be aware of the time and effort each of you put into the relationship, and try to genuinely show your appreciation.

Step 9. Fuzzy poles.

Back in the 1950s, researchers conducted a fascinating study of separation using young monkeys.[77] The monkeys were separated from their mother and placed in an area that had two artificial mothers. Both mothers were manufactured from wire mesh poles shaped to look like adult female monkeys. One of these poles was left as is–just bare metal. The other was covered in a fuzzy material to make it feel soft and warm. Then the researchers placed a milk bottle in either the bare metal mother or the fuzzy mother. To their amazement they found that regardless of which mother fed the monkeys, the monkeys spent the vast majority of their time clinging to the fuzzy mother. This observation seemed to run contrary to the prevailing theory that the monkeys would spend more time with the mother that gave them food.

However, the monkeys chose to spend time with the mother that had fur, as it apparently provided comfort and reassurance. The fur on the pole acted as a *transitional object* for the monkeys. Although mom wasn't around, the feeling of the fur provided some sort of connection to her. In LDRs, transitional objects amount to anything to which you give special meaning because it connects you to your partner. It may be a stuffed animal, a picture, a letter, a piece of jewelry, and so on.

Many of us have our own fuzzy pole. I carried pictures in my wallet that I glanced at every time I opened it. Others wear necklaces or bracelets. Even wedding rings can function as transitional objects. Stuffed animals can make good companions at bedtime, as do those full-length body pillows. But transforming a simple gift from your partner into a fuzzy pole takes a little effort. First, try to have something unique about the object. My partner had a stuffed bear that wore a sweatshirt from my medical school. Anything that will set the object apart from others will do.

Next, take advantage of your partner's brain. The limbic system is a connection of nerve pathways in the brain that is probably one of the most primitive in humans. There are two fascinating oddities about the limbic system. First, it holds the power of emotion. The vast majority of our feelings–love, anger, sorrow, rage–seem to come from the limbic system. Second, our sense of smell plugs directly into this system. In fact, smell is the only sense that doesn't go through the processing station of the thalamus, another little bundle in the brain, prior to reaching our awareness. Smell can play a pivotal role in emotion, and I recommend tapping into that power. If your partner wears a certain perfume or cologne, dab a little on your fuzzy pole. I'm always amazed at how quickly images of my partner come to mind when someone passes by wearing the same perfume. You'll never have more direct access to the love center of your partner's brain, so use it to your advantage.

Finally, tap into your partner's voice. As I mentioned in an earlier chapter, I have an inexpensive digital voice memo key chain on which I have about 20 seconds of my partner's voice. When I found myself working late at night, I would occasionally hit the play button while running down a hallway, and her voice always picked me up. I know of one woman who has two voice memo recorders: one she carries with her and one she keeps on her nightstand. She has purchased one of the long sleeping pillows that substitutes for her husband (complete with cologne) and the voice memo has his personal "Goodnight, I love you" prerecorded.

Fuzzy poles can work for you. Virtually everyone has something that works as a transitional object, but you can (and should) work on creating the best connection possible.

Step 10. Keeping a healthy sex life while apart.

It probably comes as no surprise that sex can play an important role in our mental (and even physical) health. Studies show that orgasm has many of the same effects as morphine on pulse, blood pressure, pain, and stress, but without the adverse effects.[78] Unfortunately, for some of us in LDRs the lack of opportunity makes our sex life less than stellar. Some people choose not to involve sexual intercourse in their relationship, and I respect that decision. But if sex plays a role in your relationship, you may want to spend some time actively developing your skills as a long-distance lover.

Sexual intimacy seems to play a more important role for men in LDRs than for women.[3, 79] In our study, men who reported great sexual intimacy with their partners reported fewer episodes of loneliness and depression while apart. The connection between the two was less apparent for women, but undoubtedly exists.

How to become a first-rate long-distance lover is a question I've been asked many times. Because it's such an important issue we'll discuss it in detail in Chapter 16.

Survival Tip # 32

Staying emotionally healthy while separated requires many types of coping strategies. Work hard to include as many approaches as possible. Each month, review your separation strategies and make sure that you are taking advantage of each of the 10 strategies just discussed: 1) keep your relationship strong and healthy, 2) get out and socialize with others, 3) find a confidant, 4) increase your exposure to touch, 5) maximize your control over your separation, 6) constantly focus on the good things about the separation, 7) break the separation up into smaller blocks and develop a six-month plan, 8) remember to dole out lots of praise to your partner when they contribute to the relationship, 9) develop lots of transitional objects (fuzzy poles), and 10) develop a great sex life.

Chapter 12

Secrets to Long-Distance Intimacy

Sandra and Joseph

Sandra and Joseph's LDR was anything but typical. They met as undergraduates in Indiana and enjoyed a very close and caring relationship for two years. Then Joseph, a Mormon, embarked on a two-year mission to Africa. During this time he and Sandra agreed to have virtually no contact (no visits, no telephone calls) as he felt that he needed to focus entirely on his religious duties. He would write to her every two or three months. It was after the first three months that Sandra came to talk with me about their relationship.

"I love Joseph and I understand that he needs to do this for his faith. But it's very hard for me to pretend that we actually have a relationship anymore. I know lots of people with long-distance relationships, but they talk to each other a few times a week and visit on weekends. They seem involved in each other's lives. I have such little contact with Joseph that I don't sense a connection anymore."

Sandra was struggling with one of the fundamental difficulties of LDRs: How can two people separated by great distances be involved in one another's lives in a way that fosters an intimate connection? Sandra had observed that her relationship with Joseph differed from those of her friends who also were involved in LDRs.

"My roommate is seeing a guy who lives a couple hundred miles away," she explained. "They talk almost daily, and they see each other a couple of times a month. She's always telling me about things that are going on in his life. She's involved in what he's doing. I think they're pretty close, emotionally I mean, even though they live so far away. I don't feel that closeness with Joseph."

Sandra and Joseph's relationship represented a statistical *outlier* in our study. A much greater distance separated them, and they had such little contact compared to the vast majority of the relationships we studied, that they clearly represented a special situation. In talking with Sandra and the few other participants who had *very* long-distance relationships, we began to understand why some couples were able to maintain a sense of involvement, while others felt none whatsoever.

Couples in very long-distance relationships spent a great deal of energy sharing how much they cared for one another. Precious moments on intercontinental telephone calls were generally reserved for important things, which seemed to mean conveying one's feelings for the other and confirming that the relationship was still okay. Similarly, letters or greeting cards were fairly common in these very long-distance relationships, but again consisted mostly of "I love you."

"The one letter I received from Joseph was about a page long," Sandra told me. "It began with a few words about how his mission was going, and then he began writing about how much he missed me and how much he loved me. He ended with a whole discussion about how great it would be when we got back together. I remember feeling somewhat odd after reading it. Imagine having heard nothing for three months and then hearing how much he loved me. I think I felt a little guilty because my own feelings for Joseph were changing, and not in the same direction as his seemed to be."

Sandra had begun to realize that intimacy involves something more than simply sharing "I love you." Being emotionally honest and open with your partner is certainly an important component of any romance. Some relationship experts even suggest that those in LDRs may share their loving feelings more openly than those in geographically close relationships.[20] Perhaps the uncertainty inherent in the separation makes us a little more in need of explicit confirmation of how our partner feels and how the relationship stands. Yet letter after letter of deep emotional revelations can still leave one feeling distant, as Sandra discovered. What Joseph and Sandra lacked was simply the feeling that they were part of one another's lives in a day-to-day manner.

Intimacy requires at least two conditions: emotional sharing and what sociologists call *interrelatedness*. The first condition is what most of us think about when we use the term "intimate." Yet the second condition is just as important, and is often taken for granted when the relationship is geographically close. Interrelatedness simply means that you and your partner's lives are intertwined. This comes very naturally and almost imperceptibly in geographically close relationships because you're sharing lunch, going shopping, talking about the day-to-day trivia of your lives, or arguing over control of the TV remote. Every small interaction slowly creates the interrelatedness that forms a foundation for intimacy.

Focus on the Mundane

Probably the most effective way of creating and maintaining intimacy while apart is simply sharing with your partner what happened in your day. Couples in geographically close relationships do this all the time instinctively. In an LDR you need to make a conscious effort.

There are several ways that those in LDRs can bring their day-to-day life in contact with that of their partner. The most common method is using the telephone. The telephone has several advantages, the most important of which is the lack of any time delay. Unlike letters, you can discuss your day in real time, rather than having your partner read about activities that took place last week. Using the telephone to help establish intimacy takes effort because there are barriers inherent in voice-only interactions. (Some methods you can use to help make your conversations more fulfilling are discussed in Chapter 14.)

First, whatever else you plan on talking about over the telephone, you must allow time to share the mundane things that happened to you during the last day, week, or month. People in LDRs often don't want to waste time talking about the trivial details of their lives and they focus on what they perceive as more important issues. Don't be fooled by this. The only way to be intertwined with your partner's life is to share the mundane details of yours.

Second, keep track of the little things that come up during the day that you'd like to share with your partner. Several people with whom I spoke kept a little note card that they would use to keep a list of things to talk about. For those who spoke daily, the note card wasn't always necessary, as they could remember the day's events without difficulty. But most couples talked on the telephone less than once a day, and for them writing down interesting little things that occurred during the days since their last conversation helped them to share these details. After two or three days, the day-to-day issues that were once important often vanish from our memories or lose their significance. A written record can provide a roadmap of the last few days of our lives that we can share with our partners.

Similarly, some of us are less adept than others at recalling the small things that are going on in our partner's lives from day-to-day. These memory lapses are usually overlooked in geographically close relationships, as those couples can create interrelatedness in other ways. But for LDRs, failing to follow the little issues that are a part of our partner's lives removes one of the few means we have to maintain intimacy. Personally, my memory was often too cluttered with details from work to be a big help in this regard. So I kept a little record book by the telephone that I used to keep track of the things going on in my partner's life. I made it a point to ask about events from the last time we talked so I could get an update. This kept both my partner and I involved in each other's lives in a way that helped to create a feeling of intimacy.

For those with personal digital assistants (PDAs) or pocket personal computers, the memo pad function can be used to help keep track of both your partner's events and those that occurred during your own day.

Survival Tip # 33

Intimacy requires being involved in the mundane, day-to-day events of one another's lives. Develop some method to keep track of your daily events and your partner's. Pretend that your partner is waiting for you back at your home at the end of the day. What things would you want to tell them? Write these down and share them with your partner.

While the telephone is a great way to keep track of events from day-to-day, it can be expensive. Email is the next best method. Email allows almost instantaneous transmission that you can't get with traditional mail. Most providers allow for real-time chats between you and your partner called *instant messaging*. Many people have shared with me that real-time email conversations, although lacking in the comfort of hearing one's partner's voice, allow a feeling of connection that isn't present with normal mail. Email is relatively inexpensive, particularly if you have an affiliation with a business or university that has an Internet connection. Because of its speed and low cost, many people choose email to relay the mundane day-to-day issues to their partners, and reserve the more expensive telephone time for other activities.

Survival Tip # 34

Find an email system that allows instant messaging. You and your partner can hold real-time conversations with very little expense. These are great ways of sharing your day-to-day excitements. Most Internet providers will allow unlimited access for a single monthly fee. This allows a fantastic and inexpensive method of developing a strong foundation of intimacy.

A third way to communicate the events in your life is by traditional mail. While letters have some truly amazing advantages for LDRs, they lack the speed that helps promote the feeling of day-to-day involvement in your partner's life. Nonetheless, for some people letters represent the only means of communication available, either due to budgetary constraints or the lack of availability of telephones (such as in the military). Fortunately, a few tricks can help make letters a useful tool in sharing your day-to-day life.

Heidi, a 28-year-old graduate student dating a Navy officer, Gary, who was serving aboard a nuclear submarine, explained the best method I came across. Gary routinely was unavailable by telephone or email for weeks to months at a time, but mail was delivered fairly routinely.

Gary and Heidi

"I wanted Gary to feel like he was part of my life. So I always carried this little memo pad with me, and throughout the day I'd start writing to him about whatever was happening. By the end of the week, I'd have a seven-page letter with each page and entry dated and timed. When I'd reread the letter before mailing it, a lot of the entries sounded silly and boring. But Gary says he enjoys reading each day as if he was with me. Some days he would only read one day's worth of

my letter so he would feel in step with my life. He was always about two weeks be-
hind in my real life, but to him he was keeping on top of things back here."

Essentially, Heidi was keeping a diary and then sending it to Gary so he could feel involved. Letter writing, more than any other form of communication, can lull you into believing that only important things should make it into your letters. The effort involved in writing and mailing letters, along with the time lag between writing and receiving, often seems to encourage people to focus only on the big picture. If you routinely use other forms of contact such as the telephone or email, then using letters and cards only to say "I love you" probably works well. But if you have very little time on the telephone and no email access, make sure to use letters to connect with your partner about day-to-day events.

One other method that Heidi and Gary explored occurred to them after Heidi began a new job as a civil engineer. Although she tried to explain to Gary all the details of what she did day-to-day, he never quite understood. He never was able to picture the construction site where she worked. One day Heidi needed to film portions of the construction with a video camera, and she decided to slip in a tape of her own and tape record a few minutes of her working on the job while narrating for Gary. Although it took a few weeks to reach him, Gary loved seeing where Heidi worked and being able to watch what she did day-to-day. Eventually, Heidi rented a video camera for a day and taped about 30 minutes worth of several brief shots showing her usual day. Gary watched the video "until it began to wear out." Unfortunately, when Gary wanted to send a tape to Heidi, he found out that the captain of the submarine wasn't very receptive to having the insides of the ship videotaped.

Renting a video camera for a day is quite inexpensive, and for some, a few minutes a day goes a long way to forming a connection with their partners.

Survival Tip # 35

Use a video camera to record a *Day in the Life* story for your partner. You can begin by placing the camera next to your bed the night before. When you wake up, the first thing you do is pick up the camera and say "Good morning!" Take the camera with you throughout the day. Ask your coworkers to help tape a few shots of you during the day. Add in some mundane chatter with your partner as if they were present. Tape yourself making dinner, or working out in the evening. Record your nightly routine and then say, "goodnight," to your partner. You'd be very surprised how much people love these little tapes.

Heidi and Gary gave me permission to share their story with another couple, Michelle and George, whom I've already introduced. Michelle teaches school in

Indiana and George, like Gary, is stationed in Japan with the Navy. After discussing the videotape technique, which Michelle and Gary agreed to try, they mentioned their own way of keeping up on day-to-day events. Both have purchased relatively inexpensive handheld dictation recorders. Throughout the day they each "talk to" one another when various things come up.

"Not only does George get to find out about my day, but it helps me to vent as well," Michelle said. "If I'm upset or depressed or excited and I feel like I want to share something with George, I just talk into my recorder like he was here. I think it helps keep me sane."

George does the same, although he usually talks only at night before he goes to bed. Michelle listens to the tapes in the car while commuting to and from work. Again, their system is relatively inexpensive and, as Michelle mentioned, it has the added benefit of providing an outlet to express excitement or frustration when a telephone isn't available.

Survival Tip # 36

Carry a handheld tape recorder and talk to your partner throughout the day as if they're present. Each tape allows a little more bonding to develop between the two of you. You share the world together, despite the distance and the time delay.

Whether you use the telephone, email, letters, videotapes, audiotapes, or all of these, the key is to focus on sharing the details of your day-to-day activities that essentially constitute the bulk of all of our lives. "I love yous" are important and heartwarming to hear or read. But ultimately intimacy requires the interrelatedness that comes from being a part of the seemingly mundane details of your partner's life.

Chapter 13

How Often to Visit, Call, and Write

Catherine and John

"When Catherine first moved back East, I ran out and tried to find books on long-distance relationships. One of them said that to keep from breaking up we had to talk to each other every day. Well, calling daily from California to Illinois isn't cheap. Catherine suggested three times a week, which I agreed to, but I couldn't help but think we were endangering the relationship by not talking daily like this particular book had said we should."

Sarah and David

"When Sarah began her MBA work, we had to decide how often we would see one another. She lived four hours away, which meant that we could theoretically see each other every weekend or more. My first thought was 'of course, we'll see each other as often as we can.' It seemed right that if you loved someone you'd want to be with him or her all the time. Sarah wanted time to work on her studies, and so she proposed seeing each other every two weeks. I'll admit that I was hurt by the thought that she didn't want to see me every weekend. It took a while to de-program myself from presuming that, because she needed time away, she didn't care anymore. Eventually I began to enjoy that weekend I had entirely to myself."

These couples embody two of the issues that every LDR must face. John, a chemical engineer, was searching for data to help him decide what would be best for the relationship. He was looking for the right frequency of telephone calls and face-to-face visits. When their budget couldn't support what he had been told was the right amount of telephone calls, they cut back, but at the expense of John's anxiety that the relationship would fall apart.

Almost invariably while talking with someone newly involved in an LDR, the question of "how often should we . . ." comes up. While John searched for data in a book, David and Sarah searched for a mutually acceptable plan with each having their own idea of what was right. All LDRs face these questions: First, what is the right frequency of telephone calls and face-to-face visits for us? Second, what process will we use to decide what that right amount will be? This chapter will discuss both of these questions, and provide some actual data from our study, showing how often the average couple in an LDR visit, talk on the telephone, and write letters.

What Is the Right Amount of Visits and Telephone Calls?

Many researchers have tried to answer this question, as it could prove very important for separated couples. Suppose that research were to show that you had to visit once a week to make an LDR work. This would be critical information for those of us who counsel couples in separated relationships. In my own studies and review of the literature, I've focused heavily on trying to discover the answer to this question.[11] Ultimately, the answer is both complicated and straightforward. It's complicated because the studies have somewhat conflicting results. Some say that a certain amount of face-to-face visits is important, while others suggest that this variable plays little importance. I'm going to give you a brief primer of these studies and discuss how I view their results. (If this gets too technical, feel free to jump ahead a few paragraphs and just read the conclusions.)

Historically, relationship researchers and therapists have been of the opinion that separated relationships need fairly frequent face-to-face visits.[80] Several articles, based on either professional opinion or interviewing techniques, have suggested that separated couples need to see one another about once a month to maintain intimacy.[14, 29, 32, 61] I have great respect for these researchers and take their conclusions seriously. Generally, the next step after developing an idea through interview and professional opinion is to test the idea through rigorous research. This requires studies of large numbers of people in LDRs using some objective measures of relationship quality, frequency of face-to-face visits, and relationship success.

One of the first studies to address this issue looked at 50 people currently in an LDR (considered the *successful* group) and 50 people who had been in an LDR, but had later ended their relationship (the *failed* group).[17] The latter group answered the researchers' questions by attempting to recall details about their failed LDRs. The authors found that the reported frequency of face-to-face visits was greater in the group of successful LDRs than in those of failed LDRs. However, they found that this was true only when they compared men in the successful LDR group to men in the failed LDR group. When they looked at women in the two groups there was no difference in the reported frequency of visits. The apparent conclusion is that for men in LDRs (but not for women) more frequent visits lead to a greater chance of staying together.

There are two difficulties with this study. The first revolves around the idea that a group of people who have been involved in an LDR, that eventually broke up, should be considered a "failed" LDR, while those currently involved in an LDR at an arbitrary point in time are "successful." Certainly, many people in the "successful" LDR group will eventually break up. These people, who should eventually be correctly classified as being in the "failed" group, were considered "successful" simply because the researchers surveyed them at a point prior to their relationship ending. The second difficulty lies in the assumption that people in failed LDRs accurately recall the frequency of face-to-face visits. I've already mentioned that men in failed LDRs like to blame the distance for the breakup, rather than other factors.[7-9, 81] Quite conceivably, the men in the failed LDR group recalled fewer visits than actually occurred during their separation, in order to keep their theory of why the relationship ended consistent. They didn't see their partners very often and, in their minds, this was what caused their relationships to fail.

A second study examined 134 people in LDRs and found that people who visited less than once a month were less satisfied with the relationship compared to those who visited more than once a month.[18] Unfortunately, the researchers considered people to be in an LDR if they were separated by more than two miles. I'm concerned that this short distance might mean that large numbers of people in this study would not be in what most of us would call a long-distance relationship.

A third study looked at 37 married couples in LDRs.[43] This study found that those who visited more frequently were "more happy with the commuter-marriage relationship." Hopefully, all of you in an LDR would be happier with your relationship if you were able to visit one another more frequently. Unfortunately, this study did not address whether more frequent visits would lead to more successful relationships or more relationship intimacy, trust, or commitment.

In contrast to these earlier studies, research involving 89 people in LDRs, followed over a three-month period, found that the frequency of visits did not predict which couples stayed together and which did not.[82]

The largest study, which Dr. Clifford Swensen and I undertook, examined 202 people in LDRs.[3] In this study, we found no connection between the frequency of face-to-face visits and any measure of relationship quality. We did additional studies to determine if this was accurate, as it seemed to run against common sense. First, we attempted to copy one of the earlier studies[17] but redefined what it meant to be a "successful" LDR. We looked at 90 couples who had been in an LDR and then closed the distance after achieving their career or educational goals and continued to date (the "successful" LDR group). These were compared to those LDRs that had broken up while separated. In this comparison, we found that those who broke up visited just as often as those who stayed together.[3]

This still didn't particularly satisfy me, as it seems obvious that separated couples should visit one another frequently. Therefore, we did another study.[3] We followed couples in LDRs over six months and looked at those who had broken up, as compared to those who stayed together. Once again, there was no difference in the frequency of face-to-face visits.

What does all this mean? My interpretation of these studies is that the research is inconclusive. Any time that several studies show conflicting results, it usually means that there is no large effect. If, for example, it were vitally important to visit one another at least once a month, than most, if not all, studies should show this.

While ultimately there may be an advantage to those who see one another more often, this advantage is small, if it exists at all.

My own opinion is that no right amount of visits exists. The same concept applies to telephone calls. In fact, there's even a trend for less satisfied couples to talk *more* often on the telephone, as they may be trying to work out problems in the relationship.[3] This is good news for LDRs. It means that rather than having to try to maintain a certain minimum amount of contact, you and your partner can work out the amount that best fits you both. If talking on the telephone once every two weeks works for you, keep it up. If you decide to visit every three months, that's fine. It doesn't matter when it comes to keeping a good LDR going strong. One caveat, however: Because so few participants visited their partner less than once every six months, we simply don't know what happens to these special LDRs. But if you plan on visiting more than twice a year, you can be confident that whatever frequency you and your partner pick will probably be the right one.

Survival Tip # 37

Remember that research has shown little connection between how frequently you visit your partner and how successful your LDR will be. Decide for yourselves how often you can get together. Whatever your decision, be comforted that it is the right amount for *your* relationship.

How Often Do Most People Visit and Call?

Geographically close relationships constitute the norm in our society and, as a result, those of us in long-distance relationships have relatively little exposure to role models of LDRs. How often do most people in LDRs visit one another? How often do they call one another? How long do most people expect to be separated before moving closer to one another? Is our LDR a normal LDR or are we a special case? Answers to these questions help us develop realistic expectations and provide us a background with which to compare our own experiences.

We all have numerous occasions to observe geographically close relationships: our parents, friends, and television characters (far from normal I realize, but they reflect *society's* norms.) Once we have a framework of society's expectations, we can then accept or reject them as we please. A complete lack of norms to guide expectations can lead to trouble.[83, 84] Therapists routinely see couples whose difficulties stem from one or both partners failing to meet the expectations of the other. This is hard enough when in a relationship with relatively clear expectations, let alone in an LDR.

To help provide some idea of what others in LDRs are doing, I've constructed a table with the results of our study of more than 200 LDRs.[3] A separate study looking at 124 people in LDRs has numbers very similar to these, so I believe the numbers are a reasonably accurate representation.[85]

These statistics come primarily from couples in premarital relationships, so married couples likely differ to some extent. By providing these numbers I am in no way suggesting that your own LDR should struggle to conform to the group norms. As I've said in earlier chapters, the success or failure of your LDR depends very little on these demographic issues. These numbers should simply help you understand the social context in which your own relationship takes place.

The following table shows both the average (median) response and the range of 95% of the LDRs.

Some Interesting Statistics About LDRs

How far apart?
Average: 125 miles
95% range: 30 miles to 950 miles

How often do you visit one another?
Average: 1.5 times a month
95% range: once a week to once every four months

How often do you call one another?
Average: once every 2.7 days
95% range: at least once a day to once a month

How long are your telephone calls typically?
Average: 30 minutes
95% range: 2 minutes to 1 hour 20 minutes

How often do you write one another (not including email)?
Average: three letters a month
95% range: never to every other day

How long do you expect to be separated before you can move closer to one another?
Average: 14 months
95% Range: one month to four years

Survival Tip # 38

Take a minute to compare your LDR to those of others shown in the table. Feel free to break these norms and do whatever you like in your own relationship. But realize that simply knowing what others are doing helps support your relationship at a distance by giving you a framework in which to place your own unique situation.

Chapter 14

Making the Most of Your Telephone Time

Steven and Jessica

"Early in our time apart, we knew that we couldn't afford to talk for an hour every day. Our first telephone bill was over $300, and that put an end to long conversations. We didn't know how often we should call, so we used trial and error. First we tried twice a week. I'd call him on Tuesday and he'd call me on Friday. Unfortunately, the call on Friday night always made us miss each other more, and pretty soon were also calling on Saturday. Our telephone bill improved but was still much too high. We tended to spend about an hour and a half on the telephone each time. Then we had to make a decision between two or three very brief calls a week or one longer call.

"We tried both plans. I enjoyed the one longer call because it takes me a while to warm up on the telephone, and brief calls don't give me a feeling of closeness. Steven preferred having three short calls a week because he liked to keep track of things going on in my life. We ultimately decided to alternate: One week we'd talk once for about 90 minutes, and the next we'd talk three times for a half-hour each time. We weren't always great about sticking to the schedule, but we did finally reach a point where we were both relatively happy and the bill was tolerable."

John and Catherine

"We've found that living in different time zones makes it difficult to schedule our telephone calls. I don't usually get home until about 8:00 P.M., which makes it 10:00 P.M. where Catherine is. Because she has to be up fairly early we can only chat briefly. Thursday nights we don't talk at all. This sounds kind of stupid but we each like to watch the same TV shows that night, and because of the time difference, the entire evening is out. For a while she'd call me during one of the programs and I'd always answer, but I'd be a little annoyed at having to interrupt what I was doing. We eventually agreed not to call Thursday nights. One of

99

Catherine's friends thinks we're strange. 'You'd rather watch TV than talk to Catherine?' she'd ask. As much as I'd like to say that I'd always drop everything to talk with her, it doesn't work that way. Sometimes I'm simply not in the mood to chat, and I've found that trying to force myself doesn't work. She always picks up on my ambivalence and asks what's wrong. There's really nothing wrong. I didn't feel like chatting at that moment. Try telling that to someone on the telephone without starting a serious argument."

All but a few of us in LDRs spend a good deal of time on the telephone with our partners. In fact, many couples spend more time on the telephone than face-to-face. This means that much of the relationship satisfaction, intimacy, and trust must develop and flourish within the unique constraints of telephone conversations. For some people such a task seems essentially impossible, while others have virtually no difficulty achieving wonderfully satisfying connections over the telephone. We all differ in our level of comfort with the telephone. These differences mean little within the context of a geographically close relationship, because poor telephone skills don't typically interfere with such relationships. Obviously the same is not true for LDRs. This chapter examines some of the research on the unique aspects of telephone conversations, and then provides some hints on how to improve your own telephone skills.

Is the Telephone the Next Best Thing to Being There?

Virtually all of the people I speak with in LDRs would agree that, next to seeing their partners face-to-face, they prefer communicating via the telephone. Telephone conversations allow immediate interaction and feedback with your partner, unlike letters and most email. But telephones have their drawbacks. Steven and Jessica in the opening vignette mention the most frequent complaint–the cost. For all but the wealthiest of you, the expense of using the telephone demands some structure as to how often and for how long you'll speak with your partner.

A second drawback to using the telephone is what sociologists have called its *insistency.* [55] We've all felt this when the telephone rings when we're in the shower. The urge to begin the hassle of drying off and scrambling toward the telephone is strong. The telephone seems to require us to participate in the conversation immediately, whereas other forms of interacting don't have this demand. Email and regular mail can be set aside until we choose to read it.

This insistency often leads to trouble when one person doesn't feel like talking, yet senses that he or she *must* or *should* answer the telephone. This is the situation John and Catherine described also. Both wanted to enjoy watching a TV show, yet one felt obligated to answer the telephone and miss the program. The caller often detects subtle anger and ambivalence. The person answering frequently feels guilty for wanting to do something else at that moment. The comment made by John and Catherine's friend embodies the social norm that says we should always drop everything to answer the telephone (especially if it's our partner). As I'll discuss later, giving into this insistency and dropping everything whenever the telephone rings, may work for the occasional important call, but this isn't the best approach for your LDR.

Another aspect of telephone calls that I've seen lead to anger and ambivalence, involves the actual physical discomfort of holding a telephone to your ear or scrunching it between your ear and shoulder. Hour-long calls are common in LDRs, and holding any position for that long will cause a lot of discomfort. I personally can't hold a telephone to my ear for more than about 15 minutes before my ear hurts. The irritation can usually be picked up by my partner, and she can mistakenly attribute this to something she may have done or said. My solution was to purchase a hands-free headset for the telephone that has a soft cushion earpiece, an inexpensive item that makes me much more comfortable while on the telephone.

Survival Tip # 39

Early in your separation, invest in equipment that makes talking on the telephone more physically comfortable. Headsets with soft cushion earpieces are quite inexpensive. Other options include speakerphones for those couples who have privacy or don't mind others listening in. These can give the impression that your partner is in the room with you. Finally, I suggest purchasing the shoulder holders for all other standard telephones you use. These are the plastic, banana-looking devices that connect to the back of telephone handsets and allow you to hold the telephone between your ear and your shoulder, freeing up your hands.

Another problem with telephone talk revolves around what sociologists call *parallel* versus *serial* communication.[55] *Serial* communication requires that both parties be focused on the same task and that information generally run back and forth between them. Telephone conversations virtually demand serial communication. *Parallel* interactions occur when both parties do different activities while together, with only occasional interaction. For example, if you and your partner were studying together for an exam by quizzing each other, that would be serial communication and could be done easily by telephone. If you and your partner, together, were each studying for two different exams, with occasional brief breaks to chat, you would be involved in parallel interaction.

The limitations of the telephone make parallel interaction exceptionally difficult, though not impossible. Unfortunately, healthy relationships may well require a good deal of parallel activities.[20, 21] There is something unique and important about interacting with your partner while you're each working on separate activities. Perhaps it's a special blend of independence and intimacy that helps promote a feeling of being a couple.

Finally, the most obvious difficulty with using the telephone is the lack of visual cues. Psychologists and sociologists have shown that a tremendous amount of spoken information relies heavily on nonverbal cues for its specific meaning. Many studies have been done examining how the lack of these visual cues affects our ability to communicate.[55] To help all of us who spend a great deal of time on the telephone talking with our partners, I've put together the following pointers.

The Six Pitfalls of Telephone Talk
and How to Avoid Them

1. Conflicts are less likely to be resolved when discussing them over the telephone compared to face-to-face.[86]

This should come as no big surprise. Sociologists have explored the details of why this happens, and the reasons are quite varied and complicated. The removal of all nonverbal signals that we normally use during face-to-face discussions certainly doesn't help to move negotiations along. Additionally, we tend to view our partners in a less favorable light when talking with them over the telephone. This effect taints the entire experience of conflict management and makes it much less likely to end in resolution.

What this means for those in LDRs is that you need to choose carefully those conflicts you're willing to attempt to resolve over the telephone, and which should be dealt with face-to-face. Obviously, if you are dealing with very important issues, such as the fundamental rules of your relationship, these should probably be dealt with in person if possible. Second, you should become astutely aware that sometimes the fights that occur over the telephone may have more to do with the medium through which you're communicating, than with the topic you're discussing. Often, these discussions become moot when you get to discuss them in person.

2. We're much less able to guess another person's opinions, desires, or preferences when talking over the telephone versus face-to-face.[86]

Trying to interpret your partner's preferences via a telephone call may be difficult. The loss of nonverbal cues prevents us from seeing gestures or emotions that put a verbal comment in perspective. For example, when your partner says, "No, I don't mind if you can't make it this weekend," they may in fact feel exactly the opposite. But the information you need to correctly notice this, and address the issue, is lost when you're unable to see the disappointment in their facial expression. Geographically close relationships often develop ground rules and manage difficult issues without ever explicitly discussing them. Their access to nonverbal cues allows them to place in context the statements their partner makes, and therefore they can come to more accurate estimations of their partner's true preferences. Without nonverbal communication, you must be explicit in your opinions and preferences. Discuss issues clearly rather than assuming that everything is understood.

3. When we talk to someone face-to-face, we tend to have much more confidence in our estimates of the other person's personality traits.[87]

For example, we're more confident that someone is trustworthy when we talk to him or her in person compared to talking with him or her over the telephone. However, additional research shows that although face-to-face discussions make us more *confident* in our judgments they do not increase our *accuracy;* that is, we'll be wrong about our judgments just as often over the telephone as in person, but we'll think we're more accurate in person. What this research means for those in LDRs is that you're likely to feel less sure about how your partner is feeling than you would if you were face-to-face. You'll still be wrong as often, but the lack of confidence means more time spent wondering "Was he (or she) really angry (sad, upset, etc.)?" Work on expressing your own emotions as directly as possible and ask your partner to do the same. Conversely, don't expect your partner to read your mind when you're talking on the telephone. Thinking to yourself that she or he "should have realized I was upset" isn't going to work over the telephone (and, in most cases, probably not face-to-face either).

4. We tend to perceive others as more dominant when we talk to them over the telephone versus face-to-face.[88]

In day-to-day talks with your partner, perceiving them as slightly more dominant on the telephone than in person may not be a big deal. But during the inevitable telephone argument, this factor can cause problems. Some people react poorly to perceived dominance, either by responding with immediate submission or by brisk confrontation. The best solution would be to avoid arguing over the telephone, but this isn't practical. Instead, try paying careful attention to your own posturing during a fight. Realize that the telephone can exaggerate hostility and dominance, so think hard before insulting or verbally bullying your partner (not that you'd do that anyway, right?) A small insult that would normally be ignored in person can have a much bigger impact than you had anticipated when it is relayed by telephone.

5. Telephone conversations, compared to face-to-face conversations, are more likely to leave us feeling misunderstood.[89, 90]

Talking in person allows us to estimate whether the listener is paying attention. Quizzical looks from our partner allow us to reiterate or reformulate our message, while nodding the head in comprehension relays the message, "I hear you and understand." These cues are absent in telephone conversations, leaving us with a good deal of uncertainty. To avoid this, try to provide more verbal cues that communicate to your partner that you hear and understand them. Repeat the message in summarized form more frequently: "I can't believe he wanted you to work on the weekend!" This explicitly shows you heard and understood the message. Also try to switch from nodding your head in agreement to a quiet "um-hmm" over the telephone when you're listening. I've seen many people on the telephone nodding excitedly over some idea, forgetting that this emotion is totally lost on the caller. The key to overcoming the loss of visual cues is learning to replace them with spoken ones.

6. *We tend to perceive others as less intelligent, less sincere, and generally less favorable when we talk over the telephone compared to face-to-face.*[90–93]

Perceiving our partners as less sincere is obviously not a good thing. Trust represents one of the foundations of a good LDR, and this unfortunate side effect of the telephone must be counteracted whenever possible. As I've said in earlier chapters, honesty is paramount in your relationship, so don't lie to your partner over the telephone. The temptation is great to try and alter your story slightly, to make things easier or to keep your partner from worrying. Unfortunately, each time your partner discovers that you lied, you erode his or her confidence in what you say over the telephone. The inherent loss of trust built into telephone conversations, combined with a history of little white lies, can lead to a tremendous amount of anxiety, guilt, and disruption.

The Anatomy of a Telephone Disaster: An Example of the Good, the Bad, and the Ugly

Telephone conversations are so fundamental and yet so potentially explosive that I'd like to dwell on them a little longer. I've put together a telephone script to illustrate how these pitfalls come into play and what you can do to avoid them. Below, you'll find a telephone conversation between Jon and Sydney. In the first version, I've shown what they said to one another. In the second, I've added what they're thinking and chimed in with my own commentary on where they went wrong. Hopefully, you can use these examples to catch yourself when you may be stumbling into your own telephone pitfalls.

Jon and Sydney

Jon: So, what do you want to do this weekend?
Sydney: I don't really care. I thought we'd go to the wine festival on Saturday and catch a movie Saturday night. I want to go to church with you Sunday.
Jon: Do we have to go to church?
Sydney: Jon, we've talked about this over and over. You know that my religion is very important to me. Why can't you understand this?
Jon: Come on, how am I supposed to answer that? I do understand. Now how come you don't understand that I don't want to go to church? It may be an important part of your life, but it isn't in mine.

Sydney: Forget it. I don't want to argue with you right now.
Jon: Fine. I'll talk to you tomorrow.

Now, I've added what each is thinking as well as my own commentary.

Jon: So, what do you want to do this weekend? (*Thinking: I want to play it by ear. I hope she hasn't planned every hour down to the minute.*)

An innocent appearing question, but within it hides a deeper issue. Jon is probing to find out if Sydney has planned the weekend in more depth than he likes. Hopefully, he and Sydney can sit down and discuss the true issue in greater depth: How much planning should there be? This would potentially defuse this whole matter and turn the question into a legitimate request for information, as opposed to a reconnaissance attempt. The telephone is not a good way to discuss these important ground rule-type issues.

Sydney: I don't really care. (*Thinking: I don't want to sound too pushy.*) I thought we'd go to the wine festival on Saturday and catch a movie Saturday night. I want to go to church with you Sunday.

Sydney's concern about sounding pushy might come from a realization that during telephone calls she is perceived as more dominant than she means to be. Unfortunately, she is essentially misleading Jon by claiming that she doesn't really care, when in fact she does care. This opinion, that she "doesn't care," confuses Jon. This may be, in part, due to the lack of face-to-face cues. Perhaps if they were seeing one another, he would see the nonverbal cues that place this comment in perspective. Sydney may be saying this only to mean that she hasn't thought it through yet.

Jon: Do we have to go to church? (*Thinking: For someone who doesn't really care, she sure seems to have an itinerary. She knows I don't like going to church. Why is she putting me in this situation?*)

Jon is falling into a couple of the pitfalls discussed earlier. First, he is beginning to perceive Sydney as assaulting him (". . . putting me in this situation"). Again, this shows that there is a tendency to perceive others as being both more dominant and less sincere over the telephone. This results in people mistakenly assuming that others are out to take advantage of them. Second, he has given too much meaning to Sydney's comment about not caring what they do. Both Sydney and Jon contributed to this confusion: Sydney by not being explicit, and Jon by forgetting that the telephone makes such a statement very hard to interpret accurately.

Sydney: Jon, we've talked about this over and over. You know that my religion is very important to me. Why can't you understand this? (*Thinking: Here we* *go again. Every time we get together on the weekend this issue comes up. He knows how important this is to me. Why is he trying to push my buttons?)*

Sydney and Jon have collectively stumbled together into a serious pitfall. They already know that this issue is a hot one in their relationship, yet they seem to want to pursue it over the telephone. Clearly, it needs to be thoughtfully explored, but this should be done when they are together. At this point, one of them could mention to the other that the telephone is probably not going to lend itself to a better understanding of this issue. They could collectively agree to postpone discussing this point until they can be face-to-face. Yet, they move on because the egos involved find it difficult to resist forging ahead. Sydney begins to mirror Jon in assuming that her partner has some malicious intent when there may be none. Again, the telephone may be contributing significantly to this perception. Also, Sydney has forgotten that the telephone will make you believe your partner doesn't understand the message you're trying to get across. With an issue this emotional, the temptation to simply assume that your partner doesn't understand is hard to resist.

Jon: Come on, how am I supposed to answer that? I do understand. Now how come you don't understand that I don't want to go to church? It may be an important part of your life, but it isn't in mine. *(Thinking: Why is she attacking me? She's the one who says she doesn't care what we do. I don't want to get into this. She knows that I understand how important her religion is to her, so why does she pretend that I don't know?)*

Again, this is a missed opportunity to bail out of this disaster. Both Jon and Sydney are developing anger over what they perceive as mean-spiritedness. Jon is sensing Sydney as being overly dominant, partly due to the nature of telecommunications. He is also feeling misunderstood.

Sydney: Forget it. I don't want to argue with you right now. *(Thinking: Now we're fighting. I want him to understand my concern, and now he's just trying to win the argument.)*

Sydney is sensing that things are going poorly and has decided to exit the conversation. Unfortunately, she again does not say quite what she means. Obviously, she doesn't actually want Jon to "forget it." She really means, "Let's defer this to a different time." She is also sensing that Jon is just out to win. Again, the telephone conspires to add to this misperception. Ideally, Sydney could stop the topic at hand and process with Jon what seems to be happening. For example, saying something like, "I'm sensing that we're both feeling defensive about this. I wonder if this is too sensitive an issue to work on over the telephone. Are you feeling this way also? What do you think?"

Jon: Fine. I'll talk to you tomorrow. *(Thinking: Just like her to bring up the topic then drop it without addressing my concerns.)*

Jon still senses that Sydney is being dominant by taking control of the direction of the conversation. He also senses that things went poorly, but is still too angry and defensive to stop and process the discussion with Sydney. Perhaps they both need a little time to process the events in their own heads before they process it with one another. Hopefully, they can call one another a little later and discuss what happened–not the content (whether they should or should not go to church together) but rather what happened during this conversation.

Telephone Hygiene 101: Tricks for Getting the Most from Your Telephone Time

Once the inherent pitfalls of telephone conversations are overcome, the telephone becomes a pivotal instrument for your LDR. The vast majority of most people's time spent interacting with their partner while separated occurs through the telephone lines. Therefore, we all should put a great deal of effort into cleaning up our experience with the telephone to get the most out of our time. Here, I'll discuss some ways of maximizing the impact of telephone conversations on your relationship.

1. Ask your partner out on a telephone date.

Telephone dates are one of the best suggestions I've heard from the hundreds of people in LDRs with whom I've spoken. Telephone dates aren't the same thing as telephone sex (although for some people telephone dates may end up that way). A telephone date simply involves having a specific time set aside to spend with your partner on the telephone. As mentioned before, one of the drawbacks to telephones is the caught-by-surprise nature of the telephone ring. Sometimes you or your partner may not be in the best mood to chat. Telephone dates allow a degree of preparedness for the call. Telephone dates also provide two other important ingredients: predictability and romantic ritual. Predictability is important in LDRs because often people feel that they have little control within their relationship.[14] If you and your partner call only at random times, then some of the potential for feeling more control is lost. Explicitly planning a telephone date on Wednesday nights at 9:00 P.M., for example, allows you to predict when your next interaction will take place. As noted in earlier chapters, predictability and control are important components to maintaining your sanity during your LDR.

Survival Tip # 40

Set a specific time for some of your telephone calls. Consider these as telephone dates and guard this time preciously. The predictability of these dates gives you a sense of control in the relationship–control that often is lacking in other aspects.

The second advantage of telephone dates is to help establish romantic rituals. These are activities that usually take on a stereotyped pattern (like any ritual) that symbolize your coupleness. Geographically close relationships have multitudes of these every day: holding hands while walking, going to the movies and sitting side-by-side, telling the hostess at a restaurant that they need a table for two, or even casually mentioning to friends that they're going out with their partner. Each of these actions subtly reinforces the feeling of being together, and simultaneously projects the message to others that you're "taken." Those of you in LDRs have far fewer opportunities for these romantic rituals, and loss of these can sometimes lead to difficulty feeling close to your partners.[61] Telephone dates help provide a much needed romantic ritual. Some couples go to great lengths to ritualize these telephone calls. I'll let one couple, Sasha and Andy, describe how detailed some of these dates can become.

Andy and Sasha

Andy

"Sasha and I have schedules that change relatively frequently, so we can't have a set time to call each other each week. Toward the end of each call we decide on the time for the next one. We both write that time down in our calendars as if it was a real date. I let my roommate know that I'll be on the telephone for an hour or so. That way we don't get interrupted and I don't feel rushed. I take out a picture of Sasha right before I call her. I usually pick out some cool music to have on softly in the background."

Sasha

"The day of our telephone date I think a lot about Andy. After I'm done for the day I usually like to tidy up my room in preparation for our date. I know he doesn't see it, but I think it's a carryover from the days when he'd come over in person. I always like to light a few candles in the room. The dim lighting and the perfume of the candles are really sensuous. Neither one of us would forget about a telephone date. This makes me feel special. It's usually very easy to say I'll call you Tuesday and then get too busy. Our telephone dates are different. We both view them as our special time together. I even tell my friends that I have a date on Friday night or whenever. Most of them know what I mean."

2. Purchase a hands-free cordless telephone.

Remember I said telephone dates are one of the best ideas for telephone time? Well, a hands-free cordless telephone is *the best* idea. I strongly recommend that anyone who spends significant time on the telephone with their partner look into these technological wonders. These are your typical cordless telephones with hands-free headsets (like telephone operators use) that plug into the telephone. My own model has a belt clip that allows me to attach the telephone to my waist and roam virtually anywhere in or around my house, with no cord and both hands free. Why is this so great? Remember what I said earlier about the importance of parallel activities (you and your partner doing two separate things together)? Geographically close relationships do this constantly: watching TV, studying, doing chores around the house. There is very good reason to believe that these parallel activities form the backbone of any intimate relationship.[20, 21]

Telephones don't usually facilitate these parallel activities; either you're talking with your partner (and focused entirely on this) or you're not. Hands-free cordless telephones allow you to work on chores while talking with your partner. After I purchased my hands-free telephone, I realized that telephone calls to my partner were either of two very different types. One involved a telephone date in which I was very focused on simply talking with her on the telephone. Typically, I didn't try to do anything but talk with her during this time, just as you wouldn't try to do your laundry during a face-to-face date. The second type of telephone call occurred when I rang her up while I cooked dinner and did chores. With the hands-free cordless, I could walk all around the place chatting with her *as if she was in the same room*. In some ways I felt even closer to her during these second type of calls, because I could more easily forget that I was on the telephone. I wasn't holding a telephone to my head and I wasn't limited to a certain vicinity by the telephone cord. These are perfect times to chat about the day-to-day events and really feel interconnected.

Of all the strategies I've come across in talking with people in LDRs, the hands-free cordless telephone made the most difference in my own LDR, and I think it can do the same for yours. The technology is fairly inexpensive, so strongly consider purchasing one. A caveat: Cordless telephones can be intercepted by certain radio receivers so if you plan on being amorous over the telephone, try to purchase a model that has scramble security to prevent radios from picking up your frequency. You never know when your roommate, boss, children, or grandparents may be listening.

Survival Tip # 41

Purchase a hands-free cordless telephone as soon as possible. Then, make sure that you and your partner allow yourselves plenty of both casual telephone calls, during which you're doing other chores, and deeply focused and intimate telephone dates.

---

3. Talk with your partner about telephone ground rules.

If you're in the middle of watching a riveting murder mystery and the telephone rings, do you miss the climax of the show to answer the telephone or do you let it ring? Do you prefer to end a conversation with your partner relatively quickly, or would you like to know in advance how much time is left to talk? Do you think it's okay to hang up on your partner if you're really angry, or would that make things much worse?

It's 2:00 A.M. and you wake up from a nightmare. Is it okay to call your partner at that hour? If you and your partner are going to try telephone sex, is it okay to try it with your roommate home or is that too risky? Are you going to each take care of your own telephone bills, or will you pool the two telephone bills and split the cost? Are there certain topics you'd prefer to talk about face-to-face instead of over the telephone? Is it okay to call her or him at work? Are there specific times that you would prefer not to be called?

Telephone ground rules constitute an important focus of discussion for you and your partner. Often people in LDRs feel awkward about discussing many things explicitly. For some, the issues all work out implicitly without any direct discussion, but these relationships are few. Many people struggle through a process of passive-aggressive conflict until a system that works finally develops. Either approach may ultimately succeed, but the more comfortable you and your partner become with discussing relationship issues directly, the more easily many of the aspects of LDRs will come to you both.

4. It's okay not to answer the telephone.

It's been mentioned before but it's worth repeating. Sometimes if you're not in the mood to talk, it's better to let your machine take a message than to answer the telephone. You can always call back when your mood changes. Conversely, remember that you should grant the same freedom to your partner because both of you will have fluctuating needs for intimacy and autonomy.

In geographically close relationships this is expected, and the way couples interact in their relationships varies depending on their moods. Unfortunately, telephones don't provide much variety in terms of the process of interaction. While geographically close relationships can often satisfy each other's needs by simply being together without actually focusing on one another (once again, the idea of parallel activities), telephones ask for more focused involvement. Allow yourself the additional option of letting the telephone ring and returning the call at a time more convenient for you (or at a prearranged telephone date).

5. Use pictures to help establish intimacy over the telephone.

Earlier you learned that people vary in their ability to process information in verbal, visual, and tactile modes. If you forget which mode fits you best, close your eyes and imagine seeing, hearing, and then touching your partner. The one you perceive most clearly is your primary modality. As you might expect, telephones typically gratify verbal individuals more than visual and tactile persons. Fortunately, I'm a verbal person. I have no difficulty imagining my partner's voice. Her touch is slightly more difficult to imagine, and her appearance takes a great deal of focus for me to picture clearly.

To compensate for this, I always had a collection of pictures to peruse during our telephone dates. This allowed me to create more of a whole person from the voice I heard. Similarly, people who are visually focused can benefit from using pictures simply as a method of satisfying their primary modality while on the telephone. Eventually video telephones will solve these issues. Until then, keep a well-stocked photo album by the telephone. If you are a computer-savvy person, you can use the real-time video feature available through many Internet providers. This allows you to interact with your partner via the Internet, while both of you have a "Web cam" filming you. Talk to someone at a computer store for more information on this option.

6. Keep track of the time (and money).

It is easy to lose track of the time while chatting with your partner. I've had my own share of three-hour telephone calls. There are a variety of techniques to help keep tabs on the time. The easiest is a wristwatch with a timer. Also, some telephones have a built-in digital timer that shows the elapsed duration of the call.

One of the most interesting techniques I learned was from an engineering doctoral student, Griffin, whose partner lived across the country. They had agreed that they could afford only three hours apiece each week on the telephone. Griffin purchased a countdown kitchen timer. Each Sunday night he'd reset the time to three hours and he would keep track of his ration of time throughout the week. Ultimately, he even used a marker to replace the minute markings with dollar amounts. When he had two hours remaining in his allotment, the timer showed $9.00 (the amount he'd be charged), and when he had only five minutes left it read $26.25. Griffin felt that seeing the dollar amounts motivated him to stick to his budget.

Telephones constitute an integral part of LDRs, and they can either help or hurt the relationship. Telephones have many drawbacks, and several couples I've talked with have had significant difficulties associated with these issues. Yet careful planning and a little effort can make the telephone a real ally in your LDR rather than a source of conflict. Understandably, few people would give up their telephone time. But the couples who thrive in LDRs have learned to use many of the techniques outlined in this chapter to their full advantage.

Unlike the telephone, few couples reported conflicts around letter writing–aside from complaining that their partner didn't write often enough. The next chapter will discuss why letter writing may be essential to your LDR.

Chapter 15

Your Secret Weapon: Sending Letters

Michelle and George

"George and I rely heavily on letters, because we rarely have access to telephone calls." (Recall that George is in the Navy.) "I try to write about twice a week. He sends a letter every other week, but his letters are much longer than mine. Usually he sort of keeps a diary for me with an entry for each day over the past two weeks.

"Every day when I check my mail I get excited wondering if I'll have another letter from him. When there is one, I begin a sort of ritual. First, I never read the letter right away. I always read all of the other mail first. Then I have dinner and take care of some other chores with his letter sitting on the dining room table. After a while I settle into my favorite chair, turn on some soft music, cuddle up under my comforter, and finally open his letter. Usually I spend at least an hour reading and rereading it.

"Throughout the week I'll come back to my favorite parts and read them over and over. Some nights when I'm particularly lonely, I'll get out an old letter and read it first, kind of like watching last week's TV show again before seeing the new episode."

Michelle and George have little choice but to use the post office to keep in touch. While telephones and email can be wonderful ways to keep in touch, especially to keep up on day-to-day issues, the good old-fashioned letter packs a lot of power. Amazingly, a large number of those in LDRs have never sent their partner anything by mail. Letter writing takes substantially more energy than simply picking up the telephone and hitting speed dial. But before you decide that letters aren't for you, let me share some interesting research on writing and sending them.

Letter Writing Beats Out
Phone Calls and Face-to-Face Visits

Toward the end of World War II, a sociologist reviewed a very large study examining the effect of wartime separation on the families back home.[45] The results

113

showed that the more often the soldier wrote home, the better the relationship and the lower the likelihood that the marriage would break up after the war. Telephones simply weren't available for the intercontinental calls that are now possible, so soldiers had little choice but to write.

Half a century and great technological leaps later, research has surprised some of us by showing exactly the same thing now as in the 1940s study.[3] When we looked at the frequency of face-to-face visits, telephone calls, and letter writing, and compared them to measures of the quality of the long-distance relationship, we found two interesting things. First, as already mentioned, the frequency of visits and telephone calls was not related to how satisfied people were in the relationship, the relationship intimacy, the commitment to the relationship, or the amount of trust in their partner. Second, the number of letters written *did* correlate with relationship quality. The more letters written the more satisfied, the more intimate, the more committed, and the more trusting the couples were.

I was initially skeptical about these findings so I looked at a second study of ours that followed LDRs over time, and looked for differences between those couples who broke up and those that stayed together.[3] Once again the frequency of visits and telephone calls was the same between the two groups. The only factor that made a difference was the frequency of letters: *Those couples who were still together wrote one another nearly twice as often as those who broke up.* While it's easy to believe that couples who wrote more often also were more satisfied with the relationship to begin with, at the beginning of this particular study the two groups reported being equally committed, intimate, and satisfied. Admittedly, we don't know for sure that writing letters *causes* long-distance relationships to stay together. However, there are some strong reasons to think that it may.

Survival Tip # 42

Research suggests that perhaps the most important thing you can do to help your relationship survive the distance is to write letters. This is fantastic news for those in LDRs–a powerful factor that you can control. Don't let this opportunity slip away.

The Peculiarities of the Letter

Near the turn of the century, scholars began examining how letters impacted our relationships. Since that time, with the advent of cellular telephones and email, few researchers seem to care about old-fashioned mail. Letters have several obvious disadvantages when compared to telephones and email. Letters take much more energy. Personally, writing a letter seems like a tremendous hassle (finding the paper and envelope, handwriting a message, addressing the envelope, writing in the return address, finding a stamp, finding a postal box) compared to hitting speed dial or logging onto email. Letters also have a significant time delay compared to the instant transmission of email. Finally, letters are *unidirectional,* meaning that one person sends the message and the other receives, as compared to telephones where there is a combination of sending and receiving simultaneously.

So if letters are such a hassle what gives them this apparent power to influence the outcome of LDRs? Several things, but partly the fact that they *are* such a hassle. In discussing our research results with couples in LDRs, I asked for people's opinions about why letters have such an impact. The most common answer was that, because letters took so much effort, they meant more than a telephone call or email message. You feel special when someone takes the time and effort to write to you.

Another significant advantage of letter writing involves the tangible nature of the letter. It's hard to hold a telephone call in your hand. Some psychologists would call this a transitional object, similar to the fuzzy pole you learned about in Chapter 11. The physical presence of the letter allows us to draw an unconscious connection with the sender of the letter. It acts as a tangible transition between the reader and the sender.

Some people find this hard to believe, so I have a little experiment I ask them to try. Imagine if suddenly everything you own connected to your partner vanished. No pictures, no gifts, no cards or letters, no ticket stubs from movies, nothing. But you could still see him or her occasionally and talk on the telephone. Most of us would still feel very cut off from our partner with this scenario, even though it allows for communication by visits or telephone. Physical objects related to our partners make us feel emotionally closer to them.

Several couples shared with me that having the letter in their presence was comforting. One woman even carried the letter in her purse until the next letter arrived. Besides this effect, the tangible nature of the letter allows it to be reread as often as desired. Few people I spoke with ever read a letter from their partner just once. Most couples keep their letters in a library of sorts, whether they reread them or not.

Some of you more technologically minded readers will remind me that email can be printed out as a hard copy. While this is true, and I myself printed copies of certain emails from my partner, there simply isn't the same connection that occurs with handwritten letters.[29] When I've discussed this with others in LDRs, the letter wins out on three counts. First, the particular handwriting seems to draw a connection to the writer compared with a computer printout. Second, the fact that at one point your partner sat down and created *this particular letter,* which then traveled several hundred miles to land in your hands, seems to enhance its connection. And finally, letters can be scented, an idea shared by Michelle, whose vignette opened this chapter. Michelle had read in psychology books about the power of scent, and so she has taken to scenting her letters with George's favorite perfume. As noted before, your sense of smell is the only sense that goes directly to the emotion centers of your brain without first being processed in the switchboard of the thalamus. Scenting letters has been done for centuries, well before the neurology of smelling was discovered, and I think there is a reason: it works.

Survival Tip # 43

Try applying a small amount of cologne or perfume to your letters. Consider adding some other personal touches to your letters as well. For example, Leslie Karsner, in her book, *The Long Distance Romance Guide,* suggests writing on personalized stationery or tracing your hand on the envelope.[94]

One final advantage to letter writing over telephone calls: Research suggests that because of the relative ease and speed of telephone calls, we tend to use it for relaying both good news and bad.[3] When we're upset with our partner, we reach for the telephone. This explains why, in our study, we found that the more conflict a couple had, the more often they called one another. The effort involved and the time delay inherent with letters usually relegates them to carrying mostly positive messages. People who do write about issues that need to be discussed usually end up getting a telephone call as soon as the letter arrives. This isn't to say that the letter should never be used to speak your mind. In fact, it does provide ample time to plan out what you'd like to say and to proofread your message. But generally for most people in LDRs, letters contain primarily positive messages, and this gives the letter a constructive association for the reader that helps explain part of its power in keeping the relationship alive.

Getting the Most Out of Mail

The biggest obstacle to overcome with letters is the effort required to write and mail them. If not for the research, I'll admit that I would rarely have written and I certainly wouldn't push others to take up a pen. But the research is convincing, so the next step involves making the process easier.

The best suggestion I've heard for this came from a professor in California whose wife lives in North Carolina. He has over 50 envelopes, preaddressed with computer-printed labels, and he has prestamped all of them. This way he simply composes a letter in between his administrative meetings and drops it in the mail at his office. Once the initial investment of time required to label and stamp the envelopes is complete, the effort involved drops off sharply.

This strikes me as one of the most productive and beneficial tricks of the trade for LDRs. A similar trick is to keep a number of greeting cards around. I had a drawer in my filing cabinet containing various cards (with the envelopes preaddressed and stamped, of course).

Survival Tip # 44

Take a half-hour to gather a bundle of envelopes, address them to your partner, and stamp them. Once this is done, the likelihood that you will write a little note and drop it in the mail increases substantially.

One last note: Keep in mind that an occasional small package can mean a great deal. Some creative souls keep a stack of items that they cut out of the newspaper or magazines for their partner. Once a month or so, they send a small package with these clips. Packages can also be used to send an audio- or videotape. And for those interested in a little long-distance loving, packages can help keep your sex life interesting as well.

The next chapter discusses ways of keeping the sexual spark in your relationship alive, even when you have to be apart.

Chapter 16

Long-Distance Loving:
Sex While Separated

Kevin and Stephanie

"I think our sex life was one of the better areas of our relationship during our separation, but it took some work," Stephanie explained. *"The sex was always fantastic the first night of a reunion. There were even times when we didn't make it home from the airport without a brief detour. Being apart heightens the honeymoon effect when it comes to sex. What I needed to work on more was the stuff we tried when we were apart. Kevin had no problem with telephone sex. One night he started off a call saying, 'You know what I'd really like to do to you tonight?' He went on to get me so excited, I thought I'd ignite. I knew he wanted me to talk back to him using the same words he did, but when I first tried I struggled with saying those things.*

"Finally a girlfriend loaned me a book of sexual fantasies, which I read cover to cover. Kevin asked me which one I liked most and then asked me to read it to him. When I did, I found it much easier. We tried that for a while and then I decided that none of the fantasies fit mine perfectly so I wrote my own. I planned on sending it to Kevin but one evening I decided to read it to him instead of reading from my book. I think because it was so personal it really turned him on."

Separation affects sexuality tremendously. The distance and deprivation lead to very intense couplings upon reunion and an exploration of new ways of being sexual while apart. In this chapter, I'll explore some issues surrounding what I've called *honeymoon sex* (those first few hours or days after reuniting), and then I'll share with you various ways that couples have found to keep their sex life active while separated.

Honeymoon Sex: Sexuality Upon Reuniting

Most couples in LDRs, like Stephanie and Kevin, report very lively and intense sex the first day back from a separation. This is one of those advantages LDRs have over geographically close relationships. (Try your best to emphasize this

119

whenever your friends in normal relationships complain about their sex life.) But if your relationship doesn't seem to have the same honeymoon effect as Kevin and Stephanie, you're not alone.

Some couples found that they needed time to reconnect with their partner in an emotional way before connecting in a sexual one. Usually, once this emotional reconnection is reestablished, the sex can proceed in a manner as steamy as those who need nothing but some privacy after reuniting. The difficulty arises when one partner needs time to reconnect and the other can't get to the bedroom fast enough. Sometimes one partner feels that they need sex to become more emotionally connected, while the other partner feels that they need to be more emotionally connected to become more sexual.

Although this sounds like a difficult Catch-22, it's an issue that sex therapists deal with routinely. If you find that your relationship fits in this category, there are a couple of suggestions that will help you and your partner negotiate a solution.

The wrong answer is for the sexually "slower" partner to give in. Typically, this simply leads to difficulties later down the road. It also surrenders the bonding experience that sexuality can have for the relationship when both partners truly crave it. The solution lies in negotiation.

First, realize that sexuality has a tremendous range of expression, from holding hands to sexual intercourse. Very often people think about sex as meaning only intercourse. Within the field of sex therapy, being sexual is often defined as *any activity that causes someone to feel erotically charged.* This can mean anything from feeling sexy as you get ready for a reunion to actually making love. There is plenty of ground for both partners to give and take. If immediate sexual intercourse is uncomfortable for one partner, perhaps something less sexually intense would suffice until the emotional connection is more established.

If having an orgasm is important, and intercourse is too intimate for one partner, then other options should be explored. One woman I talked with found that a shower taken with her partner allowed her to feel more intimate, and she often would stimulate her partner with her hand. Although he usually preferred much more on the first night, this was a good compromise because he achieved some sexual release and she had time to become more emotionally connected.

Survival Tip # 45

At some point, discuss explicitly with your partner the different ways that the two of you react sexually to a reunion. Who seems to need more time together prior to sex? Are there things other than intercourse that you would like to do early in the reunion to give you time to warm up? Talk about these issues before they develop into something more difficult.

A second helpful approach involves a little psychological preparation. A day or two prior to reuniting, the partner who prefers to go slower can begin fantasizing about past sexual experiences with their partner that he or she really enjoyed–experiences that may have helped them feel emotionally as well as sexually closer. Realizing that sexuality can lead to feeling more emotionally connected can help accelerate the process once a reunion takes place.

Virtual Sex: Sexuality While Apart

We all have a sexual appetite, and the fact that our partners may be hundreds of miles away doesn't change that reality. This situation creates the opportunity to try some sexual practices that most people in geographically close relationships don't typically explore. One thing that most of these techniques has in common is the practice of self-pleasuring.

Given our current, more liberal perspectives on human sexuality, the term "masturbation" tends to have a lot of old baggage attached to it. In the past it was often viewed as sinful, immoral, adolescent behavior, or a regression in sexual development. Therefore, many adults have grown up with ambivalent attitudes regarding this common activity. So let's update the word. Most sexual health experts refer to masturbation as *self-pleasuring* or *self-stimulation.* Today, sexual health educators believe that self-stimulation is an important step in personal sexual development. It is the primary way that an individual learns about his or her body and what pleases them sexually. Once we learn about our own body, we can better inform our partner as to what pleases us. Learning to be comfortable with self-pleasuring can take a lot of pressure off of the relationship over time.

If self-pleasuring makes you feel uncomfortable, you're not alone. Many women in particular were taught that their genitals are dirty and that self-stimulation is wrong or evil. If you believe on religious grounds that self-pleasuring is intolerable, I respect your belief, though you may have a more difficult time with sexuality in an LDR. If your religious beliefs don't constrain you, but you find self-stimulation difficult anyway, you might consult a couple of books for women on the topic such as Lonnie Barbach's *For Yourself* [95] or Heiman and LoPiccolo's *Becoming Orgasmic: A Sexual and Personal Growth Program for Women.* [96] If you find that touching yourself is simply too difficult, you may consider purchasing a vibrating massager. Most people find them very arousing, and because they can be used over your clothes, they provide a solution for those who feel uncomfortable directly touching themselves.

Survival Tip # 46

Self-pleasuring can be an important component of any separated relationship. If you feel uncomfortable with the idea, consider starting a program to help ease your anxieties. A good place to start is your local bookstore or Internet-based book marketer.

Telephone Sex

In this section I'm not referring to the 1–900 telephone sex lines that charge by the minute. Rather, I'm referring to the most common means of sexual play that couples in LDRs use while apart. Roughly three-quarters of all couples in LDRs admit to having telephone sex at least once, and a healthy proportion use it on a regular basis. For those of you who haven't tried it, let me explain what exactly it is people do on the telephone. Basically, one or both people talk about sexy things they would like to do, while one partner, or both together, pleasure themselves. Some couples take turns, with one partner talking and the other self-pleasuring, and then they switch roles. Others like to switch rapidly back and forth, carrying on an erotic conversation with both partners stimulating themselves simultaneously.

What exactly do they talk about? Usually, they simply tell their partner what things they would like to do if they were actually there. Alternatively, reading fantasies like Stephanie and Kevin did is fairly common, and a good way to ease into sexy telephone talk. More advanced telephone lovers enhance the connection by directing the activity of their partner while they talk to them.

"Spread out on the bed."
"Now I want you to take off your shirt."
"Take your right hand and . . ."

By taking charge of the action, you increase the relationship between you and your partner and help overcome the distance implied by the telephone. I've known one couple who were too shy to talk dirty over the telephone, but both would self-pleasure with each focusing on the sounds of breathing and moaning made by their partner. The eroticism of being focused entirely on what your partner *sounds like* during sex is something many couples in geographically close relationships don't experience, because the visual aspect of sexuality often dominates. One of the great gifts of an LDR is to allow us to explore the auditory aspect of our sexuality, and hopefully retain this discovery when we return to a geographically close relationship.

Five Steps to Great Telephone Sex

1. Learn to say it like you mean it.

The most common obstacle to great telephone sex is discomfort with saying sexual words. Many people are turned on by hearing them, but can't bring themselves to say them naturally. Like everything else this simply takes practice. Most bookstores carry books with sexual fantasies such as *Letters to Penthouse,*[97] Nancy Friday's *My Secret Garden*[98] or *Women on Top,*[99] or Lonnie Barbach's *Shared Intimacies: Women's Sexual Experiences.*[100] Another helpful book is Andrew Stanway's *The Joy of Sexual Fantasy,*[101] which focuses on developing one's sexual fantasy life. The Internet also has a tremendous variety of sexual fantasies online.

Try reading these to yourself first, then outloud in private. Get used to saying the words to yourself. Once you get comfortable reading them to yourself, try reading them to your partner. If there are certain words that you simply don't find sexy, then substitute others for them. One woman who considered herself an expert at telephone sex purchased a book that detailed how to write erotic novels, which she then used to enhance her vocabulary and her stories while on the telephone. Most of us have a fairly limited erotic vocabulary that can be remedied by the sexy synonyms, adjectives, and adverbs contained in books like Bonnie Gabriel's *The Fine Art of Erotic Talk: How to Entice, Excite, and Enchant Your Lover with Words.*[102]

2. Get a hands-free headset for your telephone.

As discussed previously, there are numerous advantages for a hands-free telephone, but if you're still not convinced, try undressing with one hand and you'll be sold.

3. Pictures! Get out the instant cameras.

Instant cameras have been out for decades now and we all know the erotic subject matter of many of the pictures. These cameras develop one picture at a time within seconds of taking it. Instant cameras are often used for sexy pictures–ones you wouldn't want (or couldn't get) developed at your local store. One increasingly popular alternative to the instant camera is the digital camera. These can also take a single image at a time that you can then print on a color printer.

Digital camera technology has become inexpensive enough that many people substitute this technology for instant cameras. Some couples find that while talking on the telephone they enjoy having something to look at as well. This ranges from the typical picture you'd put on your desk at work to those that are actually illegal in some states. (Remember that there are still laws in several states against certain common sexual activities, even between consenting adults.) Instant cameras are relatively inexpensive. The film, however, ranges around a dollar a picture.

4. Pay for separate telephone lines if you have children or roommates.

Second lines usually aren't terribly expensive, and they're worth the price for the knowledge that you and your partner won't be interrupted during a moment of passion. What sounds terribly sexy to you will not sound that way to your roommate or child.

5. If you use a cellular or cordless telephone, pay for the scramble technology.

As mentioned briefly earlier, certain radio receivers can often intercept cellular and cordless telephone conversations. If you don't want your neighbors listening in on your latest fantasy, pay the extra money for this technology.

Erotic Letters

The next most common form of long-distance loving is the good old love letter, updated to today's erotic standards. Sexy letters give a different feel than telephone sex. Usually they're enjoyed in private, rather than with your partner, and the more interesting parts can be read over and over. Erotic letters are a good alternative for people who just don't enjoy telephone sex. But they're also a great supplement for those who regularly use the telephone as well. In addition to helping out your sex life, you'll also get all of the advantages of the letter discussed in Chapter 15. One caveat: If you don't trust your partner with a sexy story in your handwriting, don't write one. It could turn up in unwanted hands if the relationship goes sour.

The Instant Camera Revisited

I've already discussed how instant and digital cameras can help enhance telephone sex, but they have many uses apart from this. An earlier chapter mentioned how they can be used to take nonsexual pictures once a week to help maintain a sense of connection. Of course, if you could get pictures developed one at a time, you could use ordinary film rather than the more expensive instant film.

Couples have used instant cameras to enhance their sex life in three different ways. First, as a prop during telephone sex. The second involves taking pictures during reunions. These are action shots showing both partners involved in various activities together. Finally, some couples take occasional pictures of themselves to send to their partners as a little reminder of what they're missing. Unfortunately, the standard instant cameras do not have a timer that allows for easy self-portraits. Most people either simply hold the camera at arms length or they use mirrors. For less explicit pictures, friends can sometimes be enlisted.

One caveat to erotic pictures: Many states have laws that regulate what can be photographed and developed at standard film shops. People have been arrested for turning in rolls of film with photographs that are considered legally obscene in their particular state. Before taking or sending any explicit photographs, you will want to check the laws in your state.

Once again, while photos can lend a spark to your love life, you need to trust your partner to keep them secure and to return or destroy them if the relationship should end. Instant cameras have the additional advantage of having no negatives that could be used to make copies.

Videotapes

A few of the more adventurous couples have turned to videotapes to help spice up their long-distance love life. If you don't own a video camera you can rent one for those special occasions. Couples either tape their activities and then watch them again while separated, or they use them to create videotape care packages. Most video cameras can be rented with a tripod that allows for solo performances to be easily recorded (unlike instant cameras, which require a little more dexterity).

At the risk of being repetitive, trust your partner before you create any X-rated videotapes that could come back to haunt you.

Audiotapes

A less expensive alternative to both videotaping and instant cameras, audiotapes allow an experience similar to telephone sex, but permit you to listen to the best parts over and over. Most couples who use audiotapes record themselves reading fantasies. More adventurous lovers also include their own sounds of arousal as they self-pleasure during the fantasy. Audiotapes work well in situations where telephone sex is either too expensive, or the telephone line is not secured.

Audiotapes are less likely to be discovered by outsiders than videotapes or instant camera photos, but they have their own risks. One young man in an LDR shared with me his embarrassment when his roommate, who had been knocking on his door repeatedly, opened it to find him with his headphones on in a rather awkward position. Suggestion: Lock your bedroom door before putting on the headphones. An adventurous woman with a very curious fifth grader at home avoided a similar encounter by listening to her tapes in her car. She and her partner had a standing telephone date on Friday night, and for two or three days prior to that date she would listen to a different fantasy on her way home from work.

Survival Tip # 47

Keep your sexuality creative. One of the many advantages of a long-distance relationship is the novelty that comes with each new reunion. Take advantage of this and work on exploring new ways to express yourself. If you're comfortable with it, use sexy pictures, videotapes, and even audiotapes. Find out what your partner enjoys. Send him or her one picture a day that slowly builds on a favorite fantasy.

Email: Sex on the Internet

With so many couples using email to stay in touch, it's no surprise that email also provides an opportunity for sex. Almost everyone with access to the Internet knows that online sex is big business. Both pictures and text detailing almost every conceivable facet of sexuality can be downloaded in an instant.

Couples in LDRs have used the Internet to enhance their sex life in a variety of ways. First, some couples use the Internet to find interesting stories and fantasies to share with their lovers. Some download these fantasies to their own computer and then forward them to their partner after doing any necessary editing. Second, couples can use email to send their own fantasies much faster than with traditional mail. Finally, a few couples use email to talk directly with their partners in real-time, split-screen fashion. This option allows one person to type on half the screen where the message is instantaneously relayed to their partner, who is also logged onto the Internet. The partner can respond immediately so that a virtual conversation occurs.

Because many couples have free access to the Internet through their business or educational institution, virtual conversations can be much less expensive than conversations on the telephone. Email has one major drawback: very little security. Don't ever assume that a third party (including bosses, family, and housemates) can't intercept what you send via email. I have heard several stories of intimate messages falling into the wrong hands. Remember that most businesses with email have the legal right to review all emails sent or received through their office. However, as of this writing it is generally illegal for an employer to *knowingly* eavesdrop on an employee's personal conversations. The court has yet to decide about many aspects of privacy and email, so for now use a great deal of caution.

Timing Is Everything

Some couples spoke to me about trying to schedule reunions around the woman's menstrual cycle. During menstruation, couples vary with regard to how disrupted their usual sexual routine becomes, from absolutely no sex to no change whatsoever. For those couples who severely restrict their sexual repertoire during a woman's period, scheduling their one weekend a month at the wrong time can become very frustrating. While simply working out a better schedule is one answer, some couples have very little flexibility with their calendar.

Couples have dealt with this issue in different ways. Many simply learned to accept sexuality during menstruation as perfectly acceptable (although theoretically there is a slightly higher risk of transmitting certain sexually transmitted diseases if either partner is previously infected). Other couples discovered that the timing of a woman's period could be manipulated, to some extent, if she is taking birth control pills. Athletes have been doing this for years when their period falls on the day of a big event. Check with your doctor for details on how to do this.

Sexuality will often play a central role in intimate relationships. While distance can sometimes frustrate our desires, ultimately most couples in LDRs find that their sex lives are as good, if not better, than their friends in geographically closer relationships.

Chapter 17

Hello/Goodbye:
Parting and Reuniting

Michelle and George

"The worst part of this relationship for me happens after we've spent a week to-gether, and George has to leave again for another few months. For two or three days before he has to leave, I notice that I begin to change. I know he's going to leave and I'll be alone again, and I find that I start to pull back a bit. Sometimes I get angry with George because he's leaving, and that also puts some distance between us. Once he's gone, I start hating myself for ruining the last couple of days we had together. We see each other so rarely that I don't need to go ruining it by being so irritable. The night before he has to leave, we usually have a nice dinner, and then we always go for a walk in the same park where we went for a picnic early in our relationship. I can't en-joy the last night together because all I think about is him leaving in the morning.

"When I drive him to the airport, I probably wouldn't say a word if he didn't talk. I have to fight to keep from crying the entire drive. For a while we tried hav-ing me come in with him and wait until his plane would begin boarding. That was absolute torture for me. I loved being able to spend the extra few minutes with him, but it prolonged the inevitable. I would sob in front of everyone at the gate, and I felt pretty uncomfortable with that.

"One time I had to drop him off at the curb and hurry back to work, so I couldn't go into the terminal with him. I still cried, but I found that it seemed much easier for me than our usual plan. After that we decided I'd drop him off at the curb rou-tinely and it worked much better for me than going into the airport with him."

Michelle and George have a particularly difficult relationship because of George's commitment to the Navy. They tend to see one another for about a week every three to four months, and in between they rarely can talk on the telephone. Thus, when they have to part again after getting together, they both find the expe-rience quite difficult.

Everyone in an LDR faces a similar experience with varying levels of diffi-culty, depending on personality, coping skills, and some demographic factors such as the length of time between visits. Previous chapters have already addressed some of the issues that come with being apart. This chapter examines the actual process of leaving one's partner: the "saying goodbye" part of the long-distance relationship. Later sections will discuss the process of temporary reunions–those times when you do get together again.

For many of us, saying goodbye tops the list of our least favorite things to do. While we often hope that the unpleasant emotions that this process brings will fade with each subsequent parting, the research suggests otherwise. Puppies separated from their mother show the same grief (or even a little more) with each separation–they don't seem to adapt to the process with time.[58] While we all have far more adaptability than puppies, studies of human separations have shown the same thing–people in LDRs report the same difficulty saying goodbye the hundredth time as they did the first time.[3] What this means for those in LDRs is that they must develop strategies to ease the inevitable sorrow that comes with saying goodbye, rather than simply waiting for it to get better with time.

Survival Tip # 48

Research has shown that the pain of having to say goodbye when your get-together has ended does not seem to improve with time. Later separations will invoke similar reactions as earlier ones. You must develop a strategy to help cope with these emotions, rather than hoping the goodbyes will get easier and easier.

Saying Goodbye

The way couples say goodbye varies tremendously. Michelle and George succumbed to the belief that they should try to be together up until the instant that George actually had to board the plane. Unfortunately, this led to more grief for Michelle until she stumbled upon a better process for her, which was dropping George off at the curb rather than going to the gate. Other couples would strongly prefer to stay together until the last bittersweet moment. Usually, deciding on the actual process of saying goodbye takes some trial and error and a lot of communication. After talking with many couples and reviewing the few studies that examine this process, I've established some guidelines for helping to make this uncomfortable event a little easier.

Six Tips to Making Goodbyes a Little Easier

1. Recognize the tremendous variety of healthy ways that people say goodbye and find the one that's right for you.

Several couples I spoke with seemed to believe that they were crazy for not wanting to spend every last second together. Somehow many people believe that if you love someone you should be together as much as possible. Obviously, this isn't true. In fact, the more a couple loves and trusts one another, the more comfortable they are spending time apart. Feel free to explore different styles of saying goodbye. Some couples even say their formal goodbyes before they get in the car on the way to the airport. There is no right way to say goodbye. If what you're doing doesn't work for you, try something else without worrying about what you *should* be doing.

2. Consider developing some goodbye rituals to ease the transition.

Many couples found that having a certain routine helped make the goodbye a little easier. Psychologists have found that these rituals (a series of routines that mark a special occasion) help people through difficult times. Rituals mark the beginning or ending of an event, and in so doing allow us to begin to refocus on what lies ahead. They also provide an automatic routine that allows our energy to be focused on the emotional aspects of the event rather than on the minute-to-minute tasks that must occur.

I've heard many examples of goodbye rituals. In my own relationship, as I discussed earlier, I made a ritual out of examining our schedules on the last day of a reunion, picking the next time to visit, and then buying the ticket. I never felt like it was time to leave until we would sit down and open our calendars at the airport. Once that was over, I would begin to focus on the upcoming flight, and what I needed to get done for work. Every two weeks we would do the same thing. It made the experience seem more familiar and more comfortable. Regardless of what exactly the routine may be, developing a plan that you follow each time you part will help ease the transition.

3. Avoid "leaving" your partner before you actually leave.

Pulling away from your partner before the parting occurs is referred to as *anticipatory distancing*. Essentially it's a natural defense against the pain of separation. Rather than continuing to become closer and cling tighter and tighter, some people react to the impending separation by pulling away to help prevent the sudden shock of loss. Occasionally, some couples find that one or both of them become angry or irritable with one another. Unfortunately, this is also a normal reaction to separation.

Evolutionary sociologists suggest that anger may have once served to prevent an impending separation all together. It may even be hardwired into our brains. The best way of dealing with anticipatory distancing and separation-related anger is to understand its source; that is, the separation itself, *not* each other. Typically, as the LDR progresses and couples experience more separations without any catastrophic consequences, the anticipatory distancing becomes less necessary.

4. Realize that not all get-togethers will be fantastic.

Because couples in LDRs have such little time together, the desire to have an absolutely wonderful reunion each and every time is understandable. We often place a great deal of pressure on our partners and ourselves to do whatever is necessary to make each reunion special. Unfortunately, no relationship can sustain an unending number of wonderful reunions without at least a few disappointing ones.

When these inevitable crummy reunions materialize people often feel quite upset and disillusioned. Some people in LDRs cannot resist the temptation to use each reunion as a benchmark for the relationship as a whole. If the reunion went well then the relationship is on track, while if the reunion went poorly the relationship is in trouble. Unfortunately, relationships simply don't progress in a linear fashion, always getting better and better. LDRs, like any other relationship, have their ups and downs. In order to grow and become closer to one another, couples must have periods of conflict and turmoil–times that allow them to learn more about one another, to develop problem-solving skills, and to emerge from the conflict more intimate than before. It is natural, healthy, and indeed inevitable, that your relationship will have its share of crummy reunions.

5. Early in your LDR, try to call one another soon after you leave.

Like many other aspects of LDRs, communication plays a major role in developing a satisfactory process of saying goodbye. This is especially true early in LDRs, before a process develops on its own. Spend a few minutes on the telephone talking about the actual separation, discussing the process and discovering what worked and what didn't, what things you liked and what things you didn't.

For example, one couple had a great deal of difficulty with saying goodbye. He tended to distance himself and was quite stoic, while she cried and hugged to the very end. Afterward, she felt hurt that he hadn't cried. In her mind, this meant he didn't care. Until they talked about this process, she never realized that for him, his stoicism was necessary precisely *because* he did care so much. After they talked, she began to see his distancing as his way of dealing with the same pain she felt when they had to separate.

6. It's okay to feel some excitement about leaving your partner.

Most people experience some mixed emotions when they say goodbye. Hopefully, there is some grief over having to separate from one's partner. But often separation also means refocusing on the world we live in when apart. A great many of those in LDRs have a tremendous career drive (often this is precisely what led to the choice of a long-distance relationship). The knowledge that they soon will be returning to their usual work can be exhilarating. After a brief reunion with my own partner, I often felt that my yearning for intimacy was satisfied, and so I was ready to get back to my career with renewed zest. So while I was sorry to have to leave her, I was also excited about returning home.

These mixed emotions are completely normal. With any luck, each partner can understand how both emotions can exist together without detracting from the sorrow of having to part.

Survival Tip # 49

Use the six strategies for easing the pain of saying goodbye: 1) explore different ways of saying goodbye; there is no "right" way for everybody, 2) develop some goodbye rituals to ease the transition, 3) recognize that you may feel angry or distant from your partner in order to emotionally prepare for the separation, 4) allow your relationship to have an occasional disappointing reunion, 5) call your partner soon after you leave one another to discuss how you both felt about the process of saying goodbye, and 6) allow yourself to be excited about leaving your partner and getting back to work if you feel that way.

Saying Hello

John and Catherine

"One of the more difficult issues that Catherine and I had to deal with was the amount of time we spent together when I would come back home to see her. I loved seeing her again, of course, and I spent the vast majority of my time with her. But I also wanted to see my friends as well . . . I found that spending so much time apart from her developed my independent side. After a few days of spending every second with her, I'd begin to feel a little smothered. She never seemed to have that problem. She could spend every second with me for two weeks and want more. I'm not like that.

"The first time I suggested that I was going to go check out this engineering fair by myself, she completely flipped. I was only home for a week, so apparently that meant I couldn't possibly be away from her. Well, I agreed to have her go with me, but I became irritable. I needed some space. It didn't mean that I didn't care for her. I can't switch back and forth from being completely on my own to being completely with her without a bit of a break."

John and Catherine discovered one of the defining issues of long-distance relationships–dealing with the sudden, and extreme, shifts between intimacy and autonomy. For most of us, the majority of our time is spent away from our partners, and we are forced to live a very independent lifestyle. Upon reuniting, we suddenly switch worlds and become exceptionally intimate and intertwined. No wonder many couples describe long-distance relationships as an emotional teeter-totter.

While most people in LDRs ask about how to cope with their time apart, few ask how to cope with their time together. They should, because many difficulties originate at reunion rather than while apart.[105, 106]

This section provides a few helpful hints for getting the most from your reunions.

Six Tips for Making Reunions Even Better

1. It's okay to schedule some time to yourself during your reunions.

Despite what many couples seem to think, there is no need to spend every second with your partner when you get together. In fact, many couples like John and Catherine find the transition from living alone to intense intimacy a bit confining. Some people recognize this feeling quickly, while others simply become irritable or angry with their partners for no obvious reason. We all need some space to ourselves, and when we can't obtain that distance physically we obtain it emotionally.

While separated we have plenty of space, but not so during reunions. I've known couples who, when reunited, are never more than 20 feet away from one another for an entire week. Some couples can deal with this intimacy easily but most can't. If you find yourself irritated or smothered, try scheduling some time away from your partner; for example, a jog, a journey to the bookstore, some solo shopping. Often couples find that an hour a day away from their partners makes the intimacy inherent in the reunion even more exciting.

2. Try to schedule some time with mutual friends.

A few couples I talked with had a tendency to spend all of their time together, alone as a couple. Because they saw one another so infrequently, they would withdraw from their usual social network, and spend all their time alone on the weekends they could get together. A reunion spent entirely with yourselves can be fun and quite rewarding. However, don't underestimate the importance of spending time as a couple with your friends.

Some very interesting studies have shown that the amount of time a couple spends with their social network (friends and family) *as a couple* is one of the best predictors of whether the relationship will eventually survive.[107–110] When friends and family see us interacting as a couple, it makes the relationship appear more real to them (especially given the rarity with which most people in LDRs see their partners). This, in turn, reinforces their role in supporting the relationship, support that has repeatedly been shown to help couples in the long run. So try and schedule at least some time with your friends or family or both.

3. Schedule some time out in public as a couple.

Even if you don't find time to get together with friends, try to find time to go out in public as a couple. Most couples have no difficulty with this, but a few become so isolated during reunions that they spend very little time in public. Spending time together around other people has an effect similar to spending time as a couple with your friends. The more society recognizes you and your partner as a couple, the more real the relationship will feel to both of you. Even the common question asked by hostesses at restaurants, "Table for *two?*" helps to reinforce the fact that you and your partner exist as a couple.

While this sounds somewhat trite, it isn't. Couples in LDRs often begin to feel like they aren't *really* in a relationship because they spend so little time together.

Society has propagated the myth that if you are in an intimate relationship, then you must spend a significant amount of time together. LDRs violate this standard, so some people struggle to accept that their relationship is as real as any other. And though we'd like to escape it, we're all subject to the influence of society. When we go out as a couple, others treat us as a couple. It is our recognition of this societal acceptance that helps bond the relationship together.

4. Expect to be disappointed periodically.

Another of the major themes that runs through long-distance relationships involves idealization and disillusionment. Researchers have shown that the majority of those in LDRs tend to focus on the positive aspects of their partners while downplaying the negative ones.[48, 65, 111–115] This probably represents one of the factors that helps protect their relationship from breaking up while they're apart. However, it also develops unrealistic expectations that rarely are met during reunion.

This idealization becomes more pronounced the less often they visit one another. Couples who spend several months away idealize their partners more so than couples who see one another every week. The major difficulty inherent in this fantasy occurs when disappointment sets in during a reunion. Disillusionment can lead to anger and frustration and ultimately emotional distance that leads to a feeling of a spoiled weekend.

The best way of avoiding this trap is to prepare just prior to reunion. While the excitement of seeing your partner is growing, remind yourself that your partner is only human. Try to make sure your expectations are realistic.

5. Don't schedule every minute of your time together.

Now that I've said you should schedule time alone, time with friends, and time together in public, I need to caution you not to "overschedule" during your reunion. As I've already discussed in earlier chapters, LDRs have difficulty because they lack the opportunity to engage in parallel activities. Recall that parallel activities occur when you and your partner are physically together but each doing different tasks. Reading different books while in the same room is a good example of a parallel activity. Research has shown that parallel activities help cement the relationship together, maybe even more so than joint activities. Joint activities are the kind of couple things we all do, like going to dinner together, where we are both focused on each other. Many couples in LDRs schedule their reunions with a great deal of joint activities, but they have little time left over for the more mundane parallel activities. Leave time for spontaneity and just lying around together.

6. Try to keep the timing of your reunions as predictable as possible.

Unfortunately, many of us don't have flexible schedules or schedules that are planned out well in advance. However, the more you can keep to a routine the better.[14] Routines help to ease the transition between life alone and life with our partner. Also, routines help provide the predictability, and therefore the control, that plays such an important role in LDRs.

Survival Tip # 50

Enhance your reunions with these six strategies: 1) if you like, schedule some time to yourself during a reunion, 2) during some reunions, try to schedule activities with friends as a couple, 3) find time to do things out in public, 4) expect to have disappointing reunions periodically, 5) keep some days unscheduled to allow for "downtime" as a couple, and 6) keep the timing of your reunions as predictable as possible.

Dealing with the goodbyes and hellos of separation can be one of the most frustrating components of long-distance relationships. They represent the ups and downs of the so-called emotional rollercoaster that comes with LDRs. Precisely because they are unavoidable, those in LDRs must learn early on how best to adapt to these joyful and painful times. With some effort, and a great deal of communication, most couples can learn to use these events to strengthen rather than threaten their relationships.

Chapter 18

Dealing with Conflict at a Distance

Ryan and Susan

Susan, a lawyer living in Phoenix, has been dating Ryan for four years. Ryan is a loan officer for a large bank and lives in southern California. While they know one another quite well, they still find themselves struggling with issues involving conflict resolution. When they were geographically close, they had a pattern that worked for them. Now, that same pattern leads to serious problems, as Susan explains.

"*I'm a fairly emotional person. When I get angry, I don't stew about it. I let him know in no uncertain terms. Before the separation I would sometimes hang up on him when I got really angry. I needed time to cool off and think things through. Then I'd hop in my car, drive over to his apartment, and we'd have a long talk until we'd worked things through.*

"*The first time this happened during the separation, we almost broke up. I'd said some unfortunate things and hung up on him. When I tried to call him back, he wasn't home. Then I felt bad about hanging up on him and so I avoided the issue for a day or two. He never called back. Finally, I called when I didn't think he'd be home to leave a message and he picked up. We finally worked things through, but it took us a four-hour telephone call. Not only did we work out the issue that had me so angry, but we also talked about what went wrong in our communication.*

"*I know that I sometimes need that cool-down time, and sometimes I need it abruptly; I simply can't go on talking. We agreed that I could take a 'time out' on the telephone call. The rule was that I had to say specifically when I would call back to talk again. This way I got my distance without annoying Ryan too much.*"

Ed and Donna

"*Before I left Donna, I had a whole bunch of friends who I could chat with when we had a problem. I'd get upset about something Donna did or said, but I'd be confused that I might be making too much out of it. Sometimes I'm a little too sensitive about things. I used to be able to chat with a buddy of mine who could set me straight. He'd tell me if I was being a jerk or if I had a legitimate gripe. I'd also be able to vent a bit and think things through. Now I don't really have anyone to do that with. I tried chatting with him once over the telephone, but it wasn't very comfortable. It seemed okay to talk about this stuff in a bar over a beer or two, or while shooting pool. But it's a little too 'girly' to call him up to talk about my relationship. I think I've been a lot more difficult for Donna to deal with lately."*

Many couples have significant difficulty dealing with conflict under the best of circumstances. When the unique issues of separation are added to the mix, some couples simply disintegrate, and then attribute the breakup to the distance rather than their own difficulties with communicating.

Long-distance relationships bring with them five fundamental issues that lead to problems with managing conflict:

- Unique issues related to distance and travel.
- Problems inherent in the use of the telephone for conflict resolution.
- Difficulties with conflict avoidance (no one wants to argue during one of their precious times together).
- Anger that comes solely from the separation reflex, but is mistakenly attributed to each other.
- An insistence that, but for the distance, everything would be okay.

Unique Issues Related to Distance and Travel

Long-distance couples argue about the same things that all couples do–the amount of time to spend together, who does the chores around the house when they are together, how much money to spend or save, and issues around sex, religion, and friends. The separation also brings with it other conflicts that most geographically close couples don't have to address. In my interviews with hundreds of couples in LDRs, I've uncovered the following common topics of conflict:

- When we're together, how much time do we spend with friends versus just the two of us?
- When we're together, how structured should our time be? Should we have everything planned out hour-by-hour or play it by ear?
- During reunions, is it okay to spend some time alone, away from one another?
- How much activity with members of the opposite sex (or same sex for homosexual couples) is allowed? Is it okay to have lunch, or dinner, or see a movie with them?
- How often should we visit one another?
- When one of us has to work all weekend should the other come and visit or not?
- Who pays for the travel?
- Who should travel to see the other?
- How long will we stay separated?

- After we get together, how long do we wait before having sex?
- How often do we talk to one another on the telephone?
- How long should we talk? If we have limited funds, do we try to have one longer call or many shorter calls?
- How do we split the telephone bill?
- How often do we write one another?
- When we're together, who does the chores?
- When one of us flies to see the other, should we be met at the terminal, picked up on the airport curb, or take a taxi?

The list could go on and on. These are simply the most common issues that cause aggravation. Unfortunately, along with some unique problems come some unique factors that hamper your ability to deal with these issues.

Using the Telephone

Many couples use the telephone as their primary means of dealing with conflict. Our research found that the more conflict couples reported with their relationship, the more they called one another.[3] This correlation goes in both directions: Conflict results in people calling one another more often, and calling more often can result in more conflict.

Let's look first at the more obvious relationship: When someone is upset, they use the telephone. During a separation, people prefer to use the telephone whenever an issue comes up. The reasons for this are many. Most importantly, the telephone gives immediate access. When we're upset, emotional, or angry, we want to talk *right now*. Often, writing things out on email or sending a letter seems inferior to a telephone call because of the time delay involved.

Additionally, the telephone allows the easiest real-time interaction. Conflict resolution requires multiple cycles of expressing oneself, learning more information about the situation, integrating that information, then reformulating one's concerns. This back-and-forth occurs almost unnoticeably on the telephone or in face-to-face discussions, but is quite laborious when email or letters are involved.

This cycle represents a critical process if conflict is going to lead to improvement rather than simply more conflict. If the point of conflict were simply to let someone know that you're upset, email might do this as well as the telephone. Yet, the purpose of telling your partner that you're upset is typically to facilitate improvement within the relationship, not just to send a message.

While it's relatively obvious that conflict will increase the number of telephone calls, the opposite proposition–that more telephone calls may cause more conflict–is less clear. Remember that, compared to face-to-face discussions, telephone conversations are:

- Less likely to result in resolution of conflicts.[86]
- Less likely to provide an accurate guess at our partner's opinions.[86]

- Less likely to make us feel confident in our understanding of our partner's personality traits.[87]
- More likely to make us think of our partner as trying to dominate the relationship.[88]
- More likely to leave us feeling misunderstood.[89]
- More likely to leave us thinking that our partner is insincere.[92]

Each of these can erode any couple's communication to a point that a routine argument becomes a serious conflict. Over the telephone, a point of contention that may have been resolved easily face-to-face could result in feeling misunderstood, attacked, and swindled. Consequently, each conflict that is processed over the telephone has the potential for worsening the situation. Here we can see how the connection between increasing conflict and an increasing number of telephone calls runs in both directions.

One solution to this dilemma that I've seen recommended by a few authors is simply to avoid arguing over the telephone. Unfortunately, this solution has several serious problems. First, it does not address the emotional imperatives that come with conflict. When we're upset, we want to deal with it now. Trying to somehow box up that anger and fear for a more convenient time simply does not work. Second, if you agree not to argue over the telephone, and you indeed do have a gripe to deal with, you have exactly three options: 1) don't call your partner at all (thereby cutting off communication), 2) call your partner and pretend that you're not upset (possibly worsening everything by hiding your emotions, something few people can accomplish), or 3) call your partner, tell them you're upset, but that you're not going to talk about it until you get together again (torturing your partner mercilessly).

The telephone, for better or worse, is an integral part of how those in LDRs process conflict. How then do you attempt to overcome the inherent problems with telephone arguments?

Fighting on the Telephone:
Tips for Productive Telephone Discussions

1. Decide if a face-to-face discussion is needed, rather than a telephone call.

Some issues are so critical or emotional that a telephone call will almost certainly worsen the situation. Determining which problems should be dealt with face-to-face can be difficult and varies from couple to couple. When the two of you live a thousand miles apart, the issues that necessitate an immediate visit may be very few indeed, while a couple living an hour apart may visit frequently to discuss problems. As the cost of a trip increases, couples tolerate more emotional upset. Before making a telephone call that has the potential to threaten the relationship itself, consider a face-to-face visit. The issues that usually fall in this category include:

- The revelation of an affair.
- An allegation that your partner had an affair.

- A significant change in the ground rules, such as a desire to start dating others.
- An unexpected pregnancy.
- The need to discuss the possibility of ending the relationship.
- A change in the expected duration of the separation (for example, taking a job that will add two years to the separation).

These types of issues should be addressed in a setting that provides the best possible chance of constructive discussion.

2. Decide if the issue needs urgent attention.

Many minor problems that don't need rapid correction seem to come up during telephone calls. These small annoyances should probably be dealt with face-to-face, rather than risk the conflict escalation that comes from using the telephone. To determine if a problem should be dealt with over the telephone, answer these two questions: First, do I have a lot of emotion over the issue? Second, will the situation get worse if I wait until we're together again? Strong emotions–be they anger, guilt, or fear–usually can't wait for reunion.

3. Try to forewarn your partner of the incoming "conflict call."

One of the problems with telephone arguments is the feeling of being ambushed. Often, there is virtually no warning that our partner is upset until we pick up the telephone and dive right into an unexpected quagmire. Couples who live close to one another often unconsciously preface their fights with body language that clearly says, "I'm upset." This allows a moment for us to psychologically prepare for constructive conflict. This preparation can help prevent a defensiveness that often comes when we feel unexpectedly challenged.

Consider sending an email, page, or voice message noting that you have an issue that you need to talk about. Make sure both of you understand that this does not mean a critical problem with the relationship, but rather an issue that needs attention to help the relationship grow.

Survival Tip # 51

When you feel the need to work out a disagreement over the telephone, email your partner or leave a brief message that you need to schedule a *conflict call* to discuss something. Allowing some mental preparation prior to dealing with difficult issues will help prevent the excessive defensiveness that often accompanies telephone fights.

4. Create the best possible environment to address difficult issues.

This refers to your physical comfort while on the telephone. While it seems a trivial issue, it can play a more significant role than many realize. Telephone calls that deal with conflict often can go on for hours. If you are holding a telephone to your ear and standing in the kitchen for two hours, trying to work out who should pay for the last airfare, you're not helping the process. The cartilage of the ear can only take so many minutes of being deformed against the skull before it throbs. The arms and shoulders get tired. You feel rushed to prematurely end the call simply to alleviate these little aches and pains. If possible, lie or sit down, turn off or escape background noise, and use a hands-free telephone with a soft foam earpiece.

5. Focus on the telephone call.

You've already learned the critically important role of what are called parallel activities–simple, everyday things that each of you do separately, but in one another's presence. Recall that I suggested getting a hands-free telephone so that you could partake in these parallel activities without having to be as focused on the telephone call itself. However, the one time that doing parallel activities creates a problem is during the high-intensity telephone argument, because the telephone has a tendency to make people feel misunderstood and taken for granted. Therefore, you must do everything possible to make your partner feel listened to and understood.

When you sense that the discussion is becoming heated, stop whatever else you're doing, turn off the television or radio, and focus all of your attention on your partner. Some people find this difficult, as they may be focused on a particularly important or interesting television program. If this happens to you, routinely have a videotape ready so that you can simply record your program while you work things out on the telephone. Few arguments will go well if you try to split your attention between your partner and other activities. Even if you are one of the few who can focus your attention on the telephone call, even while the television is playing in the background, your partner can't tell that you're paying attention. They're unable to watch your body language, and the noise in the background suggests that your attentions are divided.

6. Let your partner know that you're listening and trying to understand their point of view.

As noted before, one of the biggest disadvantages of using the telephone is its tendency to make us feel misunderstood.[89] Perhaps the most common way we determine if someone is listening to us involves the almost unconscious recognition of the listener's body language. Think about someone you believe is a good listener. What do they do to make you feel that way? Almost certainly, they lean slightly toward you, they make and maintain good eye contact, and they nod their head in agreement as you speak. These behaviors give the speaker the sense that the other person is interested, listening, and respects what they have to say. Telephone conversations obviously lack this important feedback. Therefore, you have to make up for this deficit. You must signal to your partner verbally, rather than non-verbally, that you are listening, attentive, and respectful.

There are three ways that you can accomplish this. *First, let your partner speak.* Don't interrupt them every few sentences to defend yourself or correct them. Frequent interruptions not only worsen your partner's feelings of being misunderstood, they magnify their perception of being dominated.[88] By focusing on understanding your partner's position, before you begin to explain your own, you transmit a feeling of sincerity and understanding.

This takes a great deal of practice and patience. If you find that you and your partner are simply not able to do this, consider structuring your calls with slightly more formality. Once it's clear that you are trying to work out an issue that is somewhat heated, either of you can call a time-out, declare the call a *conflict call,* and then each of you has five uninterrupted minutes to discuss your feelings and perceptions. During these five minutes the person not talking simply listens to the other. After each person is done, the other must paraphrase back what his or her partner just said. If necessary, the first speaker than corrects any inaccuracies in the paraphrasing. Then the other takes their five minutes.

This ritual helps set ground rules that allow each person to feel that they've had an opportunity to speak and be understood. Paraphrasing your partner's position is important. Because it can only be done if you indeed were sincerely listening, it provides feedback to your partner that is unobtainable in any other way. Subsequently, the second way to make your partner feel understood is to *paraphrase what your partner has said and allow for corrections until you truly understand their position.*

When we talk with someone who seems intently focused on what we have to say, they almost always are nodding their head in agreement or making facial expressions that tell us to continue or to rephrase our point. They don't have to say anything at all to let us know that they are truly listening; we can see it in their actions. Unfortunately, you can't project these over the telephone. The third way to project your attention to your partner is by *conveying frequent verbal messages that you're focused and listening.* Work on saying "okay," "uh huh," "right," "I see," "oh," "got it," or any other phrase or word that conveys the impression that you're attentive. Resist the temptation to follow these words with your own discussion. You don't want to interrupt, only to convey attention.

Conflict Avoidance: "Let's Not Fight, Okay?"

When we studied hundreds of couples in LDRs, we found that they argued with their partners less frequently than couples in more traditional geographically close relationships.[2] "Fantastic!" you say? Before you get too excited, consider this: The same couples who fought less also progressed more slowly in their relationships.[3] One other study found almost exactly the same thing: Although separated couples fought with one another half as often as geographically close couples, they also reported less relationship progress.[16]

Survival Tip # 52

Arguments are important to the development of the relationship and you will definitely have fights over the telephone. You have to become proactive with these conflicts and create the best possible outcome. Consider using a checklist with the six tips previously discussed: 1) decide if the issue is too important to be addressed over the telephone, 2) decide if the issue is so trivial that it should wait until you are visiting one another (so you can avoid the dangers inherent in using the telephone), 3) let your partner know ahead of time that a *conflict call* is needed, 4) create a comfortable physical environment, 5) direct all of your attention to the telephone call, and 6) let your partner know you are truly listening. Keep this list nearby so that it can be quickly referenced should a call begin to become confrontational.

While conflict may be unpleasant, it is fundamental to the development and growth of any intimate couple. As a therapist, if I would hear a couple discuss how they never fight, it would make me quite worried. Typically, this means that one or the other is simply giving in, rather than expressing their own needs and desires. While this works for a while, it usually fails in the long run. Conflict provides an opportunity to learn more about your partner, to develop and fine-tune communication skills, to learn how to gracefully apologize and humbly accept responsibility, and to gently and lovingly express your frustrations and disappointments.

Often when couples feel that their relationship is already tenuous, they avoid rocking the boat at all costs. Many couples in LDRs describe a fear of conflict. They believe that even trivial matters could result in the end of the relationship. This comes from the mistaken notion that the distance itself places the relationship in great jeopardy. Consequently, they seek to avoid arguments by giving in, not expressing themselves, hiding their frustrations, and ignoring problems, with the assumption that they'll all vanish after the separation ends.

Many couples report that if they argue during a reunion they feel like they have spoiled their time together.[14, 149] Part of this results from the almost universal tendency to idealize their partner while separated.[5] They strive to have a perfect get-together and dealing with difficult issues doesn't seem to be on the agenda.

A second problem involves the easy ability to simply exit the conflict. Sociologists who study interpersonal conflict describe many strategies for fighting. One of them, *exiting,* simply means avoiding the issue all together and minimizing physical contact. Couples in geographically close relationships don't have this option, as they come in contact with one another almost daily. For them, an issue such as who does the dishes after dinner is quite hard to avoid. Their level of contact usually compels them to work these issues out if they genuinely want to work on the relationship. Those in LDRs simply think, "I don't want to mess up the weekend and I'll be leaving shortly anyway, so I'll let this go." The fact that we spend brief periods of time together and then leave provides us a built-in excuse not to fight.

Unfortunately, this conflict avoidance may well represent a fatal flaw in the long run. One portion of our study looked at couples who had been in an LDR, closed the distance, and then eventually broke up. We compared them with couples who had never been long-distance who also broke up. We found that the LDR couples had dated one another for a much longer period of time prior to ending their relationship.[3] Their relationships had met with the same end, but at a much slower pace. Hence, geographic separation can slow the natural progress of a relationship, whether it is progressing toward greater intimacy or toward a breakup. This effect probably results from the avoidance of conflict. Couples who broke up after they reunited would probably have done so earlier, had they been geographically close. They would have had more opportunities to deal with conflict, and either grow from the process or realize that they were not a good match for one another. No one wants to avoid conflict while separated only to become embroiled in heated turmoil after reunion.

Survival Tip # 53

Separated couples seem to avoid conflict more often than those in geographically close relationships. While it may seem easy to put off an important issue if it will result in a confrontation, it will ultimately hurt the relationship to do so. Conflict helps focus us on issues that must ultimately be resolved to move forward. When you find that you're talking yourself out of pursuing an argument simply because you don't want to "rock the boat," remember that you're conspiring to slow down the relationship, and then think again.

The difficulty thus becomes–how do we effectively discuss important controversial issues without spoiling our time together? One of the best techniques I've learned was from a journalist in southern California, highlighted below.

Tammy and Kevin

"Kevin and I have struggled with several problems during our separation. When you talked about the idea of spoiled time, I thought, 'that's us exactly.' I was always ignoring things that bothered me, because I didn't want to ruin the weekend.

"Kevin has a tendency to sulk over things, and a discussion on Friday night could change the tone of the whole weekend. We had a serious problem with the amount of time he would spend working when we got together. He would usually bring his laptop computer and spend one of the two weekend nights working. This frustrated me, but each time I'd bring it up, we'd fight and it would ruin the whole

time. Finally, I just ignored it. But I found that I got more and more angry. We absolutely had to deal with this. I raised the issue prior to Kevin coming and told him we would need to talk about it. The first time was rough. It had a lasting negative effect on the whole weekend. The next time, it was a little less difficult. We forced ourselves to deal with these issues every single time we got together, and amazingly, it got easier each time.

    "We found that, for us, talking through our issues routinely at each get-together helps. We have what we call a 'problem debriefing' (Kevin's term) each time we get together. This is a time that we schedule into our reunions that is explicitly for airing our problems and working on solutions. We tried various times during our reunion. For us, doing this at the beginning or end of the get-together didn't work. At the beginning, it offset the honeymoon excitement and caused too much grief. At the end, it didn't leave us time to get past any hurt feelings. We decided to do it pretty much in the middle of our trip. We don't look forward to it, exactly, but we know it's important for the health of our relationship."

Any time we're forced to do something unpleasant, such as hashing out our differences with our partner, it helps to ritualize the situation. Once you make the time more formal (by naming it, setting ground rules, scheduling it clearly, and making it a routine), it will become easier. Tammy and Kevin's idea of a *problem debriefing* has worked well for many couples in an LDR. The ground rules for the problem debriefing are fairly straightforward and are outlined below. Not all of them work for every couple, but the concept represents an important one to prevent serious stagnation in your relationship.

The Problem Debriefing Ground Rules

1. Both partners must commit to scheduling a problem debriefing once a month (or more if needed).

For any relationship to grow, you must face conflict head on and work on the process of managing disagreements. Because the natural tendency of those in LDRs is to avoid conflict, we must actively schedule time to address these issues. Even if you believe everything is going well, you still need to hold a debriefing, even if only a short one.

2. Either partner can call for a problem debriefing for any reason.

The process of beginning a discussion on difficult issues stymies many attempts to deal with conflict. Simply speaking the words that you know might lead to a fight can be overwhelming. Once again, you must make it easier to discuss problems in the relationship. Many couples find it easier to simply say, "It's time for our problem debriefing," than, "We need to talk."

3. Have some ritual that marks the beginning and end of the debriefing.

Often discussing issues that provoke some unpleasant emotions can lead to a prolonged period of ill will. If raising an issue results in a weekend-long tirade, you'll be very hesitant to raise that issue (or any other) at your next reunion. Sometimes hurt feelings are inevitable, and no matter how hard you both try to smooth things over, your time together simply isn't the same. One way to help contain the discussion and prevent it from spilling over into the rest of the time together involves ritualizing a beginning and an end to the debriefing. Perhaps you both go for a "debriefing" walk, or have a special park bench you sit on to talk. Other couples have a set time for the debriefing and mark the start and stop by setting a timer. Perhaps you keep track of the things on a notepad during the debriefing. Then, getting out the debriefing record and putting it away ritualizes the beginning and end. Whatever you pick, if you formalize the time by some ritual, you'll find it much easier to both work on critical issues and avoid "spoiling" the limited time you have together.

4. Plan the debriefing somewhere in the middle of your get-together.

Most couples find that scheduling their problem debriefing sometime in the middle of their time together works best for them. If you begin a reunion by discussing problems on the very first night, it seems to ruin the excitement of the get-together. More couples wait until the last night to raise important issues. Unfortunately, this often leaves people feeling angry or guilty after their partner has already left. This then requires discussion over the telephone, which has its own disadvantages. If you find time in the middle of your get-together, you will have the fun of the honeymoon, along with enough time to deal with any lingering anxiety that the debriefing may have caused. As with every suggestion in this book, you should see what works best for you. No one rule for LDRs applies to everyone.

5. Establish who will talk first.

Similar to the way you handle conflict by telephone, set up your problem debriefings so that each partner has a turn. Decide who will go first. That person then talks for five minutes while the other partner listens. Then you switch roles. These debriefings require tremendous attention and patience. All relationships require good communication, and the true test of how well any couple interacts is determined during the heat of argument. The critical element is not how well you make your point, nor how often you prove your partner was wrong. The most important thing you can do during these debriefings is to *listen*. See how often you interrupt or how often you're thinking about what you're going to say next, rather than paying attention.

After your partner finishes talking, try to repeat back to them what they just said. Try to put yourself in your partner's position and see things from their point of view. Once you can understand what your partner has to say, how they feel, and what their concerns are, then you have listened. Oftentimes, you'll find that simply understanding your partner's concerns results in an end to the issue.

6. Schedule something fun right after the debriefing to help get back into a loving mood.

Many couples feel disconnected after a debriefing and need a little boost to get back into the excitement of the reunion. As part of the tradition of your problem debriefing, find something that you both enjoy and schedule it to follow your discussion. Tammy and Kevin found that going to a movie seemed to clear the air for them and allowed them to move on. Other couples would go shopping, have frozen yogurt, go on a hike, or make love–whatever works to help bring your focus back on the fun aspects of your reunion.

Each couple can develop their own process of discussing difficult issues, and many variations of the problem debriefing work wonderfully. The worst possible approach you can have is to fool yourself into thinking that you don't need to discuss anything. Don't allow the fear that your relationship is at risk to hold you and your partner back. If you wish to develop and grow as a couple, you must develop and grow in your communication during conflict.

Survival Tip # 54

Although difficult to do, you and your partner must set aside time to address perceived problems in the relationship. These routine debriefings should address difficulties head-on rather than waiting for them to grow out of control. As difficult as these debriefings can be early on, they will prevent a substantial amount of grief and pain as the relationship matures and progresses.

Separation-Related Anger: "If He Loved Me, He'd Stay"

Back in Chapter 10, I discussed the emotional stages of separation. Most people find that they go through these stages to varying degrees whenever they separate from their partners. In many ways, these stages are somewhat similar to those elucidated by Elizabeth Kubler-Ross when she studied the process of grief.[161] Dr. Kubler-Ross found that we go through five stages when faced with the thought of our own or a loved one's death: denial and isolation, anger, bargaining, depression, and finally acceptance. While these studies focused on death, which is one of the most profound causes of grief, their results nevertheless apply to much less traumatic events.

Many processes of grief follow the same pattern, but with less intensity. Couples often describe how, prior to departing one another, they begin to pull away and isolate.[61] They talk of becoming upset easily and even seeming to pick a fight.

Most of us are familiar with the bargaining stage, whereby we ask our partners to rearrange their schedule and stay one more day. The next stage, depression (which has been covered in previous sections) accompanies most separations, though it is often mild.

In a very different style of research, which I discussed earlier, Scott elucidated a pattern of grief seen in animals.[58] Scott's stages progress from protest, to depression, and finally to emotional detachment. The protest phase most closely mimics the anger phase of Kubler-Ross' research.

Two characteristics of this anger-protest reaction complicate attempts to manage conflict at a distance: 1) its cause is unclear at the time we experience it, and 2) it persists despite repeated experience with separation.

In his animal studies, Scott found that the protest phase seems to react very much like an *emotional reflex* coming from the act of separation itself.[58] Researchers and therapists working with separated couples have reported the same reaction: Whenever we leave our loved ones, we encounter this reflex that generates some degree of anger.[37, 50, 51, 65]

Typically, anger signals to us that something is wrong and demands our attention in an effort to right the situation. Unfortunately, short of ending the separation or ending the relationship, little can be done to stop the pain. Often we recognize that we're angry, but cannot identify exactly why. Many times I've had couples talk to me about their difficulties with the last few hours prior to separation. One person senses the anger in the other, and they become embroiled in a fight over the question of what is wrong. The angry partner undertakes an internal search for the cause of the anger, only to find none, or at least none that can be addressed. This can leave them feeling guilty,[50] and then they withdraw from their partners even further.

The anger that develops from this emotional reflex demands expression and, unfortunately, just about anything or anyone will do. In explaining the anger stage of coping with death and dying, Dr. Kubler-Ross writes, ". . . this anger is displaced in all directions and projected onto the environment at times almost at random."[161] Very often, this can be said also of those in LDRs.

The second problem with this emotional reflex is its persistence. Rather than getting easier with each separation, it seems to maintain its intensity despite our efforts to cope with it. This holds true for both puppies separated from their mothers[58] and for those of us in LDRs.[2, 35, 36] This means that you can't ignore the anger related to separation in hopes it will simply vanish with time. Learning to deal constructively with this anger is essential to negating its destructive effects.

There are four steps to overcoming separation-related anger.

Step 1: Direct Your Anger Where It Belongs

Anger is very much like steam. Kept pent up it will blow in any direction if given the opportunity. Because you don't want to aim it at your partner undeservedly, it has to go somewhere. The best way to release pressure requires getting angry at the separation itself. After all, this is its origin. Releasing anger toward an idea, rather than a person, takes ingenuity. First, you must have some physical object that represents the separation. A few suggestions from other couples:

- The used airplane ticket stubs from the most recent visit.
- A candy necklace, cut in the middle to make a long string, each candy represents time apart from one another.
- A strip of air pocket packaging bubbles (the ones that are fun to pop after opening a package containing them).
- A piece of paper with the word "Distance" scribbled on it.
- A soccer ball, baseball, golf ball, or tennis ball that represents the distance.

Now, once you have something tangible at which to direct your anger, you can develop a ritual that helps blow off some of the steam. Right after you separate (or right before if you find your anger peaks just prior to leaving), focus on the distance and the pain involved in separating, and then take it out on your special object. Tear up or burn the used tickets, take off a candy and smash it under foot, twist and pop the bubble-wrap, tear up the paper, or smash the tennis ball. This ritual helps to dissipate some of the energy that the reflex anger creates, so that it does not spill over onto your partner.

Step 2: Accept Responsibility for the Separation

Although anger seems to come invariably from separation, its magnitude varies greatly. Fortunately, you have some control over this magnitude. When something frustrates us, the degree of anger depends to a great extent on how much we believe we can manipulate the situation. When people feel the most anger, they usually feel the least power. Often, people in LDRs seem to believe they are at the whim of destiny. They assume they have no choice in the matter and, thus, no control. The frustration and anger that develops at the thought of each separation thrust upon them seems great.

Except for a few couples, most people make the ongoing choice to continue their relationship at a distance. As discussed earlier, those in an LDR make the decision, day-in and day-out, to stay in their relationship. At any point, they could decide to end the frustration and simply breakup with their partner. They choose not to. At any point, they could decide to give up personal goals, move closer, and thereby end the separation. They choose not to.

While it's sometimes hard to believe, you do have some element of control. If nothing else, you have veto power. While it takes two to create a relationship, it only takes one to end it.

When you feel frustrated and angry, stop for a moment. Ask yourself these questions:

1. At this very moment, what am I going to choose to do? Am I going to end the relationship, or am I going to choose to continue it?
2. At this very moment, what am I going to choose to do? Am I going to give up my life here and move closer to my partner, or am I going to choose to continue this relationship at a distance?

Once you stop and realize that you do have a choice, and that you choose to stay in an LDR, the anger from the separation diminishes somewhat. Ultimately, the role that this reflex anger plays in complicating your relationship rapidly decreases as you realize your own control of the situation.

Step 3: Learn to Recognize the True Source of Your Anger

One of the most profound effects of reflex anger arises when you direct your anger toward those who have no part in its origin. Often, as the separation approaches, we project our anger at the nearest target: our partner. They feel attacked, we feel guilty, and everyone feels confused.

The natural tendency to assume that our anger stems from the closest person results in serious and predictable problems. As your separation looms near, be on the lookout for anger. When you note its arrival, monitor your thoughts and actions.

When you notice your own frustration or anger, get in the habit of telling yourself:

"Stop! Why are you frustrated or angry? Is it really something my partner said or did? Or am I experiencing the usual reflex anger that separation brings?"

Being aware of the issue brings you the power to deal with it in an effective manner.

Step 4: Focus on the Positive Aspects of the Separation

Earlier we discussed the many different advantages that come with the choice you've made to continue a relationship at a distance. While you cannot easily alleviate the frustration and anger that come with separation, you can balance them by filling your thoughts with all of the benefits you enjoy. Consider creating a list of the good things that come from the separation and reviewing it whenever the anger seems to be dominating your feelings about the LDR.

Survival Tip # 55

Research shows us that the mere act of being separated from someone we love causes us to be angry. This reaction acts like a reflex and is quite difficult to control completely. When you notice yourself getting angry, try this four step approach: 1) direct your anger where it belongs, 2) accept responsibility, 3) learn to recognize the true source of your anger, and 4) focus on the positive aspects of your separation.

Blaming the Distance: "Everything Would Be Fine if Only . . ."

Every relationship has its moments of conflict. LDRs are no different. Yet, when we fight, there is an almost overwhelming desire to place the blame squarely on the distance. Indeed, as mentioned previously, separation does invoke certain emotions within us in an almost reflex manner. But these reactions do not seem to affect the quality of the relationship nor its ultimate outcome.[3] Despite a huge volume of research showing that LDRs are very similar to more traditional geographically close relationships, few of us are willing to give up the tempting scapegoat of blaming any difficulties on the separation. While the distance does contribute to a few interesting moments, the vast majority of any difficulties within the relationship stem from the same issues every intimate couple navigates.

Although displacing the blame away from ourselves feels good, it frames the relationship in an inappropriately negative manner. Blaming the distance contributes to the idea that everything would be okay but for the separation. The result is an avoidance of dealing with the issues. After all, if the only real problem is the distance, why should you bother trying to work out any conflict?

Try to catch yourself when you begin to think that all of your problems stem from the separation. Be realistic. Focus on the issues, rather than the distance.

Overall, remember that conflict, despite its emotional difficulty, is a *good* thing for your relationship. Strive to accept it as part of growth, rather than avoid it as too risky. When sociologists studied conflict within developing relationships, they found that couples only began to verbally fight with one another when they start to feel emotionally committed.[118] When couples don't ever fight, it usually means they are either too insecure with their relationship to risk the conflict, or they simply don't care enough about one another to put the energy into an argument. As uncomfortable as it is to fight, it represents a necessary process of growth.

Chapter 19

Sexual Affairs: While the Cat's Away the Mice Will Play?

Donna and Ed

"When Ed and I first decided to live apart, I had several friends warn me that long-distance relationships never work because someone always cheats on the other. I've never worried about Ed cheating on me, but with so many people telling me the same thing I wondered if it could happen.

"Early in our separation I had a coworker, who knew I was seeing Ed, ask me out. He said later that he assumed that Ed and I were having trouble because we were living so far apart. Although I was never seriously considering having an affair, I realized how easy it could be. I began not only wondering about Ed but also about myself."

Kevin and Stephanie

"From the beginning Stephanie and I weren't as serious as a lot of them (other couples in our study). We tried to see just each other, but we usually couldn't see one another more than once every other month or so. Stephanie decided that she missed the companionship and she wanted to start dating some people nearer to her as well. There were a couple of people I was interested in also, so I agreed.

"We tried very strict ground rules at first–no sex, only kissing, and if we started getting serious we were to tell each other about it. I think Stephanie tried to stick to those rules, but I found out later that she had gone farther with one guy she was dating. I began obsessing about her. Every time that I would call her and she wouldn't be home, I'd assume she was on a date. One Saturday night I tried to reach her from 7:00 until about 4:00 in the morning. She eventually admitted that she was out with this guy, which was technically okay because we had agreed to that, but it frustrated me. I decided that I couldn't deal with the whole idea of dating others."

Many couples in long-distance relationships must face at least one of two serious issues:

1. What is the risk that one of us will have an affair?
2. Should we consider trying to date other people while we're apart?

More established couples, and those who are married, tend to focus on the first issue, because they already have an understanding that they will see only each other. Less established couples often give thought to both issues. Ultimately, all couples in LDRs need to decide on ground rules for seeing others, whether these rules include romantic dates or simply platonic encounters. Some couples agree to virtually no one-on-one interactions with eligible others; even a dinner with a friend is out, unless it's done in a group. Other couples allow any sort of encounter, up to and including sexual contact. Several couples allowed limited dating including kissing, and a few even accepted sexual intercourse. Finally, in our study we found that while almost half of all couples had explicitly discussed this issue, the majority had not.[3]

Affairs: Are LDRs at Risk?

Common sense suggests that because partners can't keep an eye on one another they might be more prone to wander. Researchers have examined whether couples in long-distance relationships have more affairs than geographically close couples.[3, 103, 104] These studies produced both good news and bad. The good news is that all three studies showed that couples in LDRs had no greater risk of having an affair than geographically close couples. It seems that the risk of having an affair is related more to the quality of the relationship between the couple, and the personalities involved, than on mere opportunity.

Now for the bad news: Despite what the statistics say, those in LDRs *worry much more* about affairs than those in geographically close relationships.[34, 61] Even after telling couples about these studies and reassuring them with regard to their risk, many still show a great deal of anxiety. This seems to relate not so much to the risk of having an affair, but rather to the risk of one's partner having an affair and *the other not being aware of it.* Although the studies tell us there is no greater risk of having an affair, they don't tell us how likely it is that one partner would know if the other were having an affair. Geographically close couples believe that their daily contact provides them enough information that they would know if their partner were cheating on them (although this often is not the case). Those in an LDR lack this kind of daily information, and, therefore, they may feel that even if the risk is the same, they have less knowledge, and, subsequently, less control.

This situation highlights the added importance of trust and communication within an LDR. In general, those couples who are equally concerned (or unconcerned) have the easiest time dealing with their fears. When neither partner is concerned, the issue rarely comes up. When both partners are very concerned, they both tend to elicit and reveal a great deal of information to help reduce their anxiety. "Who exactly is this guy?" "Is this person married?" "Who all is going to this movie with you?" These types of questions are natural for those who have more anxiety about this issue. Information helps us all feel more secure.

The difficulty usually arises when one partner has more concern about affairs than the other. In this situation, the more concerned partner will tend to ask many questions, while the less concerned partner will often begin to feel resentment at being cross-examined. This leads to a vicious cycle in which the less concerned partner begins withholding information out of resentment for their partner's prying or lack of trust. This leads to greater anxiety on the part of the more concerned partner, leading to more questioning.

The best way of avoiding this situation lies in open lines of communication. Talk about the risk of affairs directly and decide which partner has more concern. The partner with *less* concern about affairs now needs to understand that information is important to their partner. They must begin to *offer* extra information rather than waiting for their partner to *ask* for that information. This way the concerned partner receives the information they need to reduce their anxiety without having to ask, and the less concerned partner avoids feeling cross-examined.

I know many couples who routinely add little statements to their telephone conversations that help explain vague situations without having to be asked by their partners. Even the most trusting partners can occasionally feel uncomfortable without such information. Simply be aware that most people in an LDR are slightly more neurotic about the possibility of affairs than their counterparts in geographically close relationships.

Survival Tip # 56

Don't let anyone tell you that separated couples have more affairs. When they do, ask them how they know this, because research shows this isn't true. Don't get consumed with thoughts of your partner cheating on you. It's no more likely while you're living apart than if you were living near each other.

As to your own tendencies, almost everyone thinks briefly about having an affair. For most, these thoughts are mere fantasies with absolutely no intention to act on them. Others know early on that they will have a difficult time not acting on their impulses. Dealing with one's tendency to stray goes well beyond the scope of this book. Obviously, having an affair after agreeing on a monogamous relationship is ethically suspect. Perhaps more importantly, in today's climate of potentially lethal sexually transmitted diseases, it can lead to life-threatening consequences for those involved. Some couples do, however, explicitly agree to allow a certain amount of romantic or even sexual contact with others.

Dating Others: Should We or Shouldn't We?

For many couples the issue of dating other people never comes up, as it is clearly assumed that they will not date outside of their relationship. Virtually all long-distance marriages work under this assumption, as do most of the premarital couples in LDRs. Yet our own research found that about one-quarter of couples in premarital LDRs had agreed to date others during their separation.[3] Their reasons usually involved a lack of companionship, a need for sexual release, or a need to explore other relationships before committing to one person.

I'm often asked how dating other people affects an LDR. Usually people assume that it's not a very good idea. Unfortunately, the few studies that have examined this question have shown complicated results.

One of our studies looked at this question by following a group of couples in LDRs over a period of six months.[3] At the beginning of the six months, about 25% had agreed to date other people, while another 40% had agreed not to date others. The remaining 35% had never explicitly discussed the ground rules about dating others. At the end of the six months, we found that 30% of the couples who dated others had broken up, while 27% of the couples who dated only one another ended their relationship. Statistically, there was no difference between the two groups. From this study, it seems that for short periods of about six months, it doesn't matter whether couples choose to date others or not.

We tried to examine this question from another direction by looking at a number of relationships that at one point had been long-distance. We compared relationships that had broken up while they were long-distance to relationships that had survived the separation and then reunited as planned. Only 15% of LDRs that had dated others survived the separation, while 48% of LDRs who dated only one another ultimately stayed together.[3] While the first study looked at a period of six months, this study examined the entire duration of the relationship. However, far from being the superior study, this second study is *retrospective,* meaning that couples were asked to simply recall information about their LDR. Such retrospective studies allow people to change their memories about the events to better fit their understanding of what happened. This creates an element of bias in the research that the first study, known as a *longitudinal study,* doesn't have.

These studies together suggest that for brief periods of time, perhaps six months, dating others has little effect on your chances of staying together in the short run. However, in the long run, dating others may cut your chances of staying together by two-thirds.

Discussing Ground Rules: If You Don't, You'll Be Sorry!

Returning to the study in which we followed LDRs for six months, we found a very interesting result. I already mentioned that of those couples who agreed to date others, 30% broke up. Also, roughly 30% of those couples who agreed not to date others broke up. But what of those couples who never explicitly discussed any ground rules about dating others? Nearly *70%* ended their relationship within six months. These couples had more than twice the risk of ending the relationship compared to those who discussed ground rules, *regardless of what those ground rules were.*[3] This represents another stark example of the importance of explicit communication in your LDR.

Many couples understandably feel uncomfortable bringing up the issue of dating others. Hopefully, this study will underline the importance of discussing this topic with your partner.

Survival Tip # 57

Discuss with your partner your expectations with regards to spending time with eligible others. Explicitly discuss the ground rules about this issue. Couples who don't will more than double their chance of breaking up.

Chapter 20

Gender Differences in Separation

Jim and Jessica

Jim

"When Jessica and I first separated, we had dated for about six months. Neither of us looked forward to being apart, but I disliked the idea more than she did. I wasn't sure what I would do to fill my time on weekends. I'd always spent them with her, and maybe with her friends. For the first few weekends I rented a movie and entertained myself. Her friends didn't seem that interested in spending time with me if Jessica wasn't around. I found myself getting more and more lonely. Jessica seemed to have an endless supply of companions, and I'll admit I got jealous. Not that I didn't trust her. I was jealous that she handled the distance so well. It didn't seem that she was having a very hard time with this separation. I love her more than anything in the world, and this is killing me. She's taking this so easily that it makes me wonder if I mean that much to her."

Jessica

"I feel bad for Jim. He hasn't been able to adjust well to the separation. He doesn't really do much with anyone anymore. I'm the only one that he talks to about the distance. He's not comfortable talking to many people about his relationship or about his loneliness.

"Unfortunately, he seems to have the most problems on the weekends we're apart. This leaves me in a dilemma. I can stay home to talk with him on a weekend night and avoid my friends. Or, I can go out, but that leaves him on his own. Either way I lose. Part of me worries about whether we'll survive this separation. I look at this as a test. If we're meant to be together, and our relationship has what it takes to make it in the long run, then we should be able to manage a few months of being apart. But Jim seems to have so much difficulty. I can't tell if he doesn't trust me, if he's worried I'll break up with him, or if he's wondering about his own

157

choice to try to do this. It may seem strange, but I see his difficulties with the separation as a sign that the relationship may not be right for us."

When I heard Jim and Jessica discuss the difficulties they were having with their LDR, it appeared that part of the problem stemmed from the different meanings that men and women attach to long-distance relationships. Both of them could agree on the facts: Jim reported more emotional difficulty with the separation, and Jessica had more companions to keep her busy. Yet they interpreted these differently. Jim saw Jessica's apparent comfort in the LDR as a sign that she didn't care that they were apart. Jessica saw Jim's troubles as signaling that they were failing a test, suggesting that they weren't meant to be together.

The way in which we view the separation varies depending, to some degree, on gender. Men and women have different needs, different stresses during separation, and different ways of coping with the distance. In this chapter, I'll discuss what we know about men, women, and long-distance relationships. Obviously, not every woman or man acts or thinks the same way as all others. While research gives us an idea how *most* men or women respond to separation, it cannot tell us how any *particular* man or woman will react.

To understand our partners and the different ways they react to and cope with separation, we must first understand two key differences in the way men and women view romantic relationships in general.

Sexuality

Perhaps the most documented aspect of gender differences involves the importance of sex. As many would anticipate, men, compared to women, seem to feel that sexual intimacy plays a more important role in long-distance relationships.[3, 79, 164] This characteristic extends to most relationships, not just those that are separated. Why men focus more on sexuality is not entirely clear, although theories abound. (You probably have your own.) The importance of this, however, lies in its potential to cause difficulties as the separation brings a new context to sexuality. Long-distance couples must deal with the timing of sex after reunion, the ground rules for sex outside of the relationship, and a greater potential for misunderstandings related to sexual expression.

One common problem lies in the tendency for men to use sexuality to feel intimate, while women prefer to feel intimate prior to becoming sexual. This isn't true in all relationships, or for all men or women, but it does represent a relatively common scenario. In geographically close relationships this Catch-22 becomes moot, as partners feel more and more intimate as they spend more time together. However, in LDRs, couples often report feeling a little detached after a long separation.[14] Following reunion, this can translate into a longing to reestablish emotional intimacy. If differences exist as to the importance of sex, this period can become troublesome. Often men, who place a greater emphasis on sexuality, prefer to quickly resume sexual intimacy, while women prefer to spend more time talking and getting to know each other again prior to sex.

What It Means to Love

When we talk about love, it often seems that we all understand exactly what that slippery word means. Yet, when researchers dig a little deeper, they discover that love means many different things to many different people. Researcher John Lee conducted extensive interviews with people on exactly this topic and concluded that we think of love in six different ways, which he labeled with Greek nouns: eros, ludus, storge, pragma, mania, and agape.[165]

Eros refers to the romantic love that has tremendous passion, physical longing, deep intensity, and intimacy. *Ludus,* also called "game-playing love,"[166] is likened to the love of a knight for a princess. There are well-scripted, playful interactions but little drive for intimacy or deep intensity. *Storge* characterizes friendship-based love where there is strong companionship and shared values but little physical intimacy. *Pragma* refers to practical love in which someone actively searches for a partner with certain, predefined characteristics. *Mania,* the troubled love, stems from a combination of eros and ludus. This love has jealousy and dependence (often called co-dependency), great intensity, some intimacy, and many psychological symptoms related to the relationship. Many people would consider *Agape,* a blend of two other types (eros and storge), to be the "purest" form of love. This is the love of altruism, of giving without asking anything in return, and of sacrificing oneself for one's partner.

While all couples share a little bit of each of these, some individuals focus more on certain types. Researchers discovered that men tend to view love more in terms of the romantic, intense eros love, or the game-playing courtly love of ludus. In contrast, women often have a firm footing in the practical pragma love.[166–168] Why women approach love in a much more practical manner than men is a controversial issue in sociology. Historically, when women chose a marriage partner, their social status as well as their financial stability stemmed primarily from their partner's status and ability to support a family. Should a woman marry someone who later ended up a failure in his career, the woman's life was tremendously affected. Women in the past have had a great deal to lose in picking the wrong partner. Men have historically depended less on their wives for financial or social-status support. Men often had the perception that they controlled their own destiny, while their wives looked to them for social advancement. Therefore, women developed more practical expectations when searching for a mate. This situation is rapidly changing in today's world, of course.

Thus, many men tend to look at love in more romantic, idealized terms, while many women view relationships in a more practical, measured way. The implications for separated couples are complicated, but revolve primarily around difficulties during reunions. One can easily see how, with different frameworks for defining love, couples can struggle deciding how to prioritize their valuable time together.

Men and Women Separated

The majority of studies examining the psychological effect of separation have focused on women. This stems from the multitude of research on military families where the father or husband is deployed overseas. However, more recent literature has revealed interesting differences in the way men and women experience separation. Many of these differences originate from the two issues just discussed: different emphasis on sexuality, and a different view of what it means to love. Others result from well-known differences in the way men and women react to stress. We'll discuss each of these differences, starting with the most basic issue: Men, in general, report more difficulty dealing with separation than do women.

While this seems surprising for some, especially with the prevailing myth that women focus more on relationships than men, the research seems clear on this point.[7-9, 14, 62, 69, 81, 178] When I've discussed this in focus groups, many people don't believe the data. They can cite several cases of women who seem very much affected by the distance, and men who seem unfazed. Certainly, this does not apply to *every* man and woman. However, many men are suffering silently, and only reveal the degree of their discomfort when pressed to do so.

Early on sociologists and psychologists who studied loneliness found that women tended to report more difficulties being lonely than did men. Later, more detailed analysis found that the earlier studies actually measured two things: the amount of loneliness, and the willingness to admit to being lonely. When the researchers were able to separate these components, they found that women seem to have more loneliness only because they are more willing to admit to it. In reality, the men were having more difficulties related to feeling lonely, but were very hesitant to discuss it.[169] Unfortunately, society has reacted much more negatively to men who feel lonely than to women.[169] Somehow it seems more normal for a woman to want to discuss how lonely she is than to see the same from a man.

The prevailing idea that men tolerate separation better than women results primarily from the façade that men project. In reality many of them are quite shaken by the separation. For example, when men and women end a relationship, 41% of men say that the distance had a significant contribution to their decision to break up, while only 28% of women say the same.[7] A similar study of couples who had ended their relationship asked men and women to review common problem areas and decide which ones were a problem for them in their now-ended relationship. The only one that men cited more frequently than women was "living too far apart."[81]

In a fascinating study of gender, Julia Wood, a researcher at the University of North Carolina, asked people to write about a crisis that affected their relationships. She found that men tended to focus more on external circumstances than did women. In discussing LDRs she found that, for men:

> *Distance is represented as an empirical, absolute obstacle that precludes continuation of a relationship. These accounts evidence no recognition of possibilities for managing distance; neither do they acknowledge any personal responsibility for its impact on relationships.*[8]

All three of these studies suggest that many men, compared to women, react more negatively to LDRs. Two studies, however, reported somewhat different results. When men and women in LDRs were asked about a number of psychological symptoms, women and men reported the same level of difficulty.[3, 57] This equality is odd in itself, as most studies find that men tend to underreport their symptoms, and, therefore, seem less distressed overall.[169] The fact that men in these studies report the same level of difficulties, despite a tendency to underestimate their problems, suggests that the reality may indeed be that they suffer more than women.

Our own study of nearly 200 men and women in LDRs looked closely at the differences between the genders when it came to psychological symptoms. We found that men, compared to women:

- Felt uncomfortable around groups of people.
- Felt that their achievements had been overlooked.
- Felt that they were not given proper credit for their contributions.[3]

Why men in LDRs (and not men in general) feel uneasy when they are around groups of people is unclear. One possibility revolves around the concept I discussed previously: that men think of love as more romantic, and tend to succumb more to the concepts of what a relationship *should be*. When they see couples together, they may contrast their own, nontraditional relationship to those "normal" couples around them. We know that some people in LDRs do report feeling very uneasy at the sight of other couples enjoying themselves.[65] At this point, this is merely speculation, but you may see it develop in your own LDR.

The other problems that men reported (such as not being given proper credit and having their contributions overlooked) were also unclear in their origin. Men in geographically close relationships did not complain of these things.[3] Somehow, the unique issues of the LDR were interacting with the different ways men and women support one another. While I'm unsure why men feel their contributions are being overlooked, it does suggest useful strategies for coping. Make sure that they're thanked for even little things, such as a card or letter. Something more substantial, like flowers, or a care package, should be met with a good deal of gratitude.

Survival Tip # 58

Research shows that men in LDRs often complain that they don't get the credit they deserve for their contributions to the relationship. Therefore, you should consider being extra careful to acknowledge their efforts.

Men, Women, and Sex

Why men, compared to women, seem to have more difficulties with separation relates back to the issues I discussed at the beginning of the chapter: Men focus more
on sexuality, and they tend to idealize and romanticize the concept of love. One of
the frustrations that separated couples face is the inability to easily satisfy sexual
urges. These frustrations seem less intense for many women, and this may contribute to the difficulty that men experience.

A second, related issue revolves around jealousy. While both men and women
can appear very jealous at times, they become jealous over different things. As
most of us would suspect, men tend to become more jealous when they believe
there is a risk to their partner's sexual fidelity.[170] In separated relationships this can
occasionally result in significant problems, with one partner constantly investi-
gating the other through probing questions and nagging suspicions. Although people
in LDRs do not have any greater risk of having a sexual affair, the emotional energy consumed with incessant monitoring of one's partner can drain psychological resources. Men, with a greater focus on sexuality, and possessing greater sexual
jealousy, almost certainly perceive this aspect of the separation more negatively
than most women.

Men, Women, and Love

The second factor that contributes to men's difficulties in LDRs relates back to the
concept that they romanticize the concept of love. They tend to succumb more to
the traditional myths about what love is:[166, 168] "Lovers should always be together."
"Love is intense and passionate." "Love should come naturally; you shouldn't
have to work at it." "True lovers rarely fight." Now, obviously not all men are the
same, and many men have much more realistic ideas about love. But as a group,
when it comes to their own choice of a love partner, women often have much more
realistic expectations.

This romanticized concept of love can lead to some troubling difficulties
when applied to long-distance relationships. The distance violates many of the
myths. Couples often don't feel the intensity or passion that they think they should
when they're separated.

As I discussed in Chapter 14, one of the gremlins of LDRs lies in the disillusionment that can come with reunion. Occasionally, we all tend to create
overblown fantasies about how fantastic the weekend will be, or how marvelous
our partners really are. This idealization may work to help keep us together during the separation. Unfortunately, it means that when we do get together, and our
weekend isn't quite as fantastic and our partner isn't quite as marvelous as we had
hoped, we have to deal realistically with the letdown. If men tend to hold onto the
romanticized myths more so than women, it's easy to understand why each episode
of disappointment may have a greater impact on them. Women may be more likely

to see the usual setbacks related to separation as simply a test of the relationship.[139] If they survive the distance, then their relationship shows the necessary qualities to thrive. Men tend to see the setbacks and frustrations as external to the relationship and often don't acknowledge their own ability to manage the distance.[8]

Survival Tip # 59

For men, ask yourself honestly how many of the old-fashioned myths about love you embrace. Realize that love and relationships take a great deal of work, and that separated relationships are, throughout history, classic and romantic tales. Pay particular attention to any tendency to become overly frustrated when a reunion doesn't go as well as planned. Remember that for some people, your struggles represent the degree to which you're willing to suffer to be with your partner. You–not the distance–control your destiny.

Men, Women, and Coping Strategies

With all of the differences between men and women, it should come as no surprise that we adapt to the stresses of separation in somewhat different ways. Researchers have found that for any particular stressful event, women tend to turn to their friends and family for assistance, while men often turn inward, relying on their own sense of self-control.[171]

Take, for example, Lori and David, a couple from Utah who had recently been separated when David moved to Colorado for graduate school. They talked to me about the different ways they dealt with loneliness. Lori would rally the troops, get together with her band of friends, and commiserate with her buddies. David would tell himself that he didn't have time to lament over his loneliness, and then he would spend the evening working on his master's thesis project.

Very often, men in LDRs attempt to handle the emotional stresses of separation by ignoring or avoiding them. They either deny that they're present, or acknowledge them, then brush them aside as unimportant. Ultimately, this coping strategy has several flaws. Redoubling one's career or work efforts in an attempt to avoid having to deal with loneliness leads to further isolation from people who could provide much needed support. Additionally, simply ignoring emotions often leads to an emotional *blow out*, which is a harmful way of releasing repressed emotions. Every time we suppress fear, hurt, pain, or loneliness, it takes emotional energy to keep it tied up in our minds. In order to focus on career-related work, our subconscious must spend energy to guard against these painful thoughts and feelings. Ultimately, each little event builds up and finally overwhelms our ability to ignore it. By this time, the result may be unexpectedly intense, occasionally resulting in an out-of-the-blue decision to end the relationship because it is just too emotionally difficult.

This process is analogous to taking a soda bottle and filling it with little bits of soda pop each time something emotionally uncomfortable occurs. For a while, the bottle is still empty enough that if it's shaken the pop still stays in the bottle. Eventually, the bottle fills. Everything is still okay, so long as nothing shakes up the bottle. But as soon as something rattles the container, it blows out the top. The event that triggers the explosion often seems trivial, and its impact would be trivial if the bottle was not already stuffed full of emotions.

In general, avoidance or denial of the stresses that come with separation leads to serious problems. The more productive approach is to use your social-support system to process and deal with emotions before they get stuffed into the emotional soda bottle. This approach has the additional advantage of creating companionship rather than isolation. While this is good advice for everyone, men in particular must guard against withdrawing into an "I-can-handle-this-myself" attitude.

Men, Women, and Time

All separated couples face the dilemma of deciding how to spend the limited time they have together. The less often you visit one another, the more critical each moment together seems to become. Often, couples determine the state of the relationship by looking back on the quality of the most recent reunion. A reunion fraught with conflict and disappointment leaves them feeling disconnected and emotionally distant from their partner. A reunion filled with excitement, romance, and genuine sharing reinforces the idea that the relationship is on solid and comfortable ground.

However, men and women sometimes differ on what constitutes a constructive use of their limited time. Each of them wants to contribute to the relationship and help it grow. But how we do this depends, to some extent, on gender. Research has shown that men tend to prefer to use time together to do things with their partner. They have the unspoken belief that relationships are maintained and escalated by sharing activities with one another.[130] The reality of the relationship rests on the catalog of activities shared, and the expectation of more to come. With this understanding of how relationships develop, it comes as no surprise that men often see their limited time together as an opportunity to focus on joint adventures.

In contrast, women often perceive that relationships are based on the sharing of emotions and ideas. Couples move forward by engaging in episodes of intimate face-to-face discussions. Thus, with limited amounts of time, the priority goes to talking.[172] Conflicts erupt when a couple cannot find activities that satisfy both approaches to relationship maintenance.

Chapter 21

Ending the Separation: When You Finally Move Together

Almost all couples in LDRs consider their separation temporary.[3] Eventually they expect to get together again and lead a more "normal" lifestyle. Unfortunately, many of them don't realize how difficult a transition they will face when they try to close the distance.

Gerardo and Rebecca

"Honestly, I thought the first month of living together again was more diffi-cult than the three years of separation," began Gerardo. He had completed three years of graduate school in engineering, and had finally been able to move closer to his fiancée Rebecca. During the LDR they had managed the separation rela-tively well, as both of them had very independent lifestyles and plenty of things to keep them both busy.

"The first week or so was fantastic. Not having to think about how much more time we had together before one of us had to leave was a completely free-ing experience.

"After the first week, we began having trouble. I had moved into Rebecca's apartment, which created a number of problems. She lived there throughout our separation, so I had spent a lot of time there. But during our LDR I had my own place as well, so things seemed equal. Now I feel like I'm invading her space. About 10 days after we moved in together, we had a huge argument. Rebecca had always tended to leave her clothes strewn about, which always had bothered me. Normally I ignored it because I didn't want to ruin our brief time together by starting a fight. But now I had no real reason to avoid confronting her. It was my place too."

Heather and Mark

Heather

"Mark and I had a rough time when the distance ended. I was used to spending a lot of quality time with him when he was around. We would do fun things together like kayaking, hiking, and wine tasting. When I moved closer, we seemed to have lost this creativity. Mark spent much more time working than I anticipated. He would be gone by 7:00 A.M. and wouldn't come back until late at night. I asked him to spend more time with me, but he said that he had always worked this hard. I just hadn't noticed before. I became much more jealous of his time."

Mark

"Heather apparently didn't realize what it took to be an associate in a law firm. I'm up for partner in two years and I need to work hard. When we were still apart, I could focus heavily on work. I can't suddenly cut back now. Admittedly, I've begun to feel much more guilty about not spending time with her. I'm also noticing much more anger than I've had in the past. Now that we're not a thousand miles away and a telephone call is local, she calls me several times a day. This knocks me off balance at the office, as it eats up a lot of time. I feel like she's invading my work time. I'll get frustrated when she calls just to chat. Doesn't she know I'm busy?"

Just like these couples, the majority of LDRs will have a great deal of turbulence to move through when they finally come together. Reunion creates as much of a stress on relationships as the separation itself.[105, 106, 154] One study of couples looked to see what events in the life of the relationship were considered turning points. These could be good or bad, but represented a period of intense change. Almost as many people reported the reunion to be a turning point (7.5%), as did those who reported separation (10%). Then, the researchers asked which turning points involved the most time talking about the relationship and where it's headed. They found that only 37% of couples reported that the physical separation prompted them to talk about the relationship, while 50% of couples said reunion did.[75]

Personally, I would hope that 100% would talk about the relationship at both occasions, as this is by far the best strategy overall. Yet, this study suggests two things: first, that people are afraid to talk about the relationship, despite the clear need to do so; and second, that reunion is so significant that it prompts more discussion than the actual separation. It's possible that people simply avoid talking about the relationship while they're separated out of fear that this will prompt a breakup.[117] Then, during reunion, they see that this cannot be avoided. Clearly, if a relationship is so fragile that simply discussing issues related to separation may cause its demise, then the relationship probably has some fundamental difficulties that will need to be addressed.

Survival Tip # 60

Many couples look forward to the end of their time apart with understandable jubilation. However, studies suggest that the changes inherent with reunion can pose a more significant hurdle than the separation itself. Approach your own reunion with joy and excitement, and with a healthy dose of preparation. You and your partner will need to stay alert and focused to keep from having all of the successes of your LDR crumble amid the chaos of change that comes with reunion.

While people often understand the difficulties of separation, they fail to see the problems that can accompany reunion. Gerardo's thoughts exemplify a couple of difficulties that arise with reunion. We've already discussed the issue of idealization in earlier chapters. Remember that this refers to a natural tendency to focus on the positive things, while ignoring the undesirable aspects of our partners. This may well represent an important way of coping with the separation.

You'll recall that earlier I discussed research that showed that couples who view the relationship as optimistically as possible and accentuated the positive aspects seem to cope better overall.[27, 61, 118] Unfortunately, some of these people may have a difficult time during reunion, if they become too idealistic with regard to their partner and find themselves disillusioned after reunion. All of us have habits that annoy our partners. Typically, if these are not too frequent or too significant, we ignore them during separation. Either we don't want to provoke an argument and spoil our time together, or we realize that we can deal with the annoyance exactly *because* we can exit the situation when we leave. Both of these excuses vanish with reunion, and a new means of coping with these day-to-day annoyances must be worked out.

A second difficulty with reunion, that Gerardo also raises, involves the surrendering of some of the advantages that come with an LDR. Separation provides a great deal of autonomy, free time, self-reliance, and the ability to focus intently on one's personal goals. During reunion, each of these diminishes to some extent. Often, people find that the autonomy they once enjoyed is sorely missed. Now, they find an implied obligation to let their partners know where they are, what they're doing, and when they'll be back. This degree of information-sharing was not expected when it required long-distance telephone calls. Couples often felt much more freedom to come and go as they pleased when they were separated. This sudden decrease in autonomy comes simultaneously with a peaking of the level of intimacy. For many, this imbalance is very difficult to manage and requires a period of intense adjustment.

The amount of free time also seems to diminish after reunion. Relationships demand time, and this competes with other obligations, particularly career or professional advancement. During the separation, most people have significantly more time than their geographically close counterparts.[3] This free time allows for an intense focus on work projects, usually one of the main reasons that the couple decided to separate. Often people find that this combination of free time and the autonomy inherent in the separation allows for tremendous work and career progress. Once the couple reunites, they either attempt to persist in the usual routine of intense work without interruptions or they surrender that approach. If they attempt to persist, they often feel guilty about not spending more time with their partner. This guilt is exacerbated by the implied imperative that living close to one another means spending large amounts of time together. Additionally, one or both partners can become angry with the other; one person is "ignoring the relationship," while the other is "too demanding."

The alternative is to surrender this intense approach to work altogether and return to the piecemeal approach, which means no longer being able to devote large chunks of uninterrupted time to career advancement. With this approach, someone usually feels some degree of anger, not so much toward the partner, but with the frustration of losing a small part of his or her industrious self.

Similarly, other areas outside of the relationship can suffer. With the loss of free time and autonomy, other relationships often diminish to some extent. Typically, one person has moved to reunite with their partner, leaving their own friends and support network behind. Then, the reunited couple often withdraws from the friends that are geographically close as they spend more time with one another. Jointly, they suffer by losing elements of their support network that could continue to play an important role in relationship stability. The partner who moved often suffers doubly, as they have given up one or more special friends or confidants that played a critical role in their own coping styles. Now, in this time of increased stress and adjustment, they find themselves without that much-needed support.

The couples quoted earlier also touch on issues of control and territoriality. While separated, most couples almost unconsciously develop a *yours and mine* mentality. When both individuals have their own apartments or houses, the other becomes the guest during times together. One person often cleans up, stocks up on groceries, and plans events for the reunion. The day-to-day chores during the brief get-together usually fall on the host. This routine no longer applies after reunion, and the well-defined roles of guest and host evaporate, leaving a miniature power struggle. Typically, the individual who did not have to move to reunite continues to play host for a few weeks. But this duty rapidly becomes burdensome, and the couple has to go through a period of readjustment. Occasionally, one person feels so strongly that they are invading the other's space that the couple must move together into a new home or apartment to feel equal again.

All of these changes often create a great deal of conflict. Unfortunately, one of the primary means of coping with conflict often learned during the separation–ignoring it–no longer seems tenable. As you learned before, *exiting* worked to some extent during the separation. Now, there is no rationality behind simply ignoring conflict and relying on the idealization that typically exists during separation to smooth over anger or resentment.

Reunion constitutes a period of change in your relationship that will demand as much attention and effort as the separation. Accordingly, I've put together a few tips on dealing with reunion.

Surviving Reunion: Tips on Reintegration

1. Talk! Talk! Talk!

You'll probably do this naturally, but many couples don't formalize their conversations to best address the new issues that reunion raises. Make a weekly ritual out of discussing how the reunion is going. Address the topics raised in this chapter explicitly and see if there are any issues festering behind unexpressed frustration. Communication was critical in pulling through the separation and, as the research shows, it's critical now. During these talks you can start working out new ground rules for your relationship. Additionally, you can begin to learn more about your partner. Researchers found that even couples who talked a great deal during separation still have much to learn about one another to feel intimate once again.[134] Don't let your guard down just because you survived the separation; now you have to survive the reunion.

2. Schedule a debriefing session every other day for the first two weeks.

Researchers studying reunion found that there is a honeymoon period within the first couple of weeks of reunion.[29, 34, 61] During this period, we tend to be more receptive to readjustment and conflict resolution. Some couples like to simply ride out the high of this period. They worry that talking about any touchy issues will signal the end of this blissful time. Unfortunately, sooner or later, those issues will have to be addressed. The tenderness and love typically associated with this honeymoon provide the perfect backdrop for discussion and negotiation.

3. Schedule time apart.

This seems a little odd. You've just been through a long separation and now you're back together. The last thing either of you wants is more time apart. But as noted above, this period of change typically creates a huge swing of the intimacy-autonomy pendulum. Both of you are accustomed to a great deal of autonomy, and now, thanks to the honeymoon period, you're both getting inundated with intimacy (as pleasant as this may be). Many people begin to feel a little overwhelmed by this change and desire a little more time for themselves. Unfortunately, this often seems selfish at this point in the relationship, and a combination of guilt and frustration develops. Short-circuit this typical reaction by recognizing that reunion is a very intense process that requires an occasional time-out. Wanting to take a short break from one another is both healthy and normal during this period of your relationship.

4. Keep things fresh and creative.

Research on separated couples found that they tended to do more fun, novel, and creative things with one another than did their geographically close counterparts.[3] During brief reunions, couples often would plan special activities to make the most of their time together. This seemed to create a feeling that the time they did share together was quality time and not spoiled. However, after reunion this tendency to plan exciting get-togethers no longer exists, and couples tend to fall back on the common routine of renting movies and watching television. For some, this loss of novel and exciting activities seems a great disappointment and further contributes to the problem of disillusionment. They begin to feel bored and disappointed that the relationship has lost some of its excitement.

Prior to the end of the separation, or soon after, plan out a list of all the exciting things the two of you can do in the area. Try to schedule several of these early on in the reunion. Ultimately, creative dates will help keep all relationships fun and exciting, and this should become a long-term goal for yours as well.

5. Make an effort to spend time with friends.

An earlier chapter discussed the central role of friends and social support during your separation. During reunion, their support remains critical. Couples often become self-sufficient after reunion, relying on one another for companionship, support, and friendship. The person who moved has already cut off their support system to some extent. The other person often must surrender some time that they had spent with friends to spend more time with their partner. Occasionally, reunited couples alienate their friends altogether. They become so focused on doing things together that they suddenly stop calling on friends, and start declining invitations to do things with their colleagues. Before long, their support network begins to feel abandoned and they stop attempting to connect with the new couple. This is often akin to the well-known phenomenon of withdrawing from friends during the first few weeks of a new relationship.

Along with planning a list of exciting things to do after your reunion, plan a list of all of the people you and your partner consider friends (or prospective friends). Once a week, look ahead and try to find a time when you can plan something with one or more of the people on this list. Ultimately, this helps develop support for you as an individual and for your relationship.

6. Schedule date nights.

Once again, this may seem odd. You've just closed the distance and you spend as much time as possible with one another. Why would you need to plan dates? Actually, this helps deal with several problems that arise after reunion. First, it addresses one of the biggest issues: dealing with changes in intimacy and autonomy.

As I discussed previously, the sudden loss of autonomy, coupled with this huge increase in intimacy, can be quite uncomfortable for some people. Spending time away from one another seems unnatural after such a long separation. Creating a ritual (such as a formal date night) helps fill the intimacy side of the equation, allowing us to feel more comfortable doing things alone. A night out on a date seems to give permission to spend time doing one's own projects–guilt-free time in which you can take a breather from the intensity of the relationship.

Second, date nights help to bring back a hint of the compartmentalizing that dominated the separation. During times apart, most people feel that they compartmentalize the relationship and their work. At very clear times, they were either focused heavily on the relationship or focused heavily on work. After reunion, the boundaries between the two blur; work intrudes on the relationship and vice versa. There will likely be no returning to the degree of compartmentalizing that came with being geographically separated. However, ritualizing each of these can help to some extent.

Creating a date night manufactures some degree of boundaries, artificially indicating that this is "us" time now. This often creates less need to then intrude into one another's work time to feel close again. This feeling of being interrupted, and the guilt that comes with it, plagues many reunions. Date nights can help focus this need for intimacy and help soothe these frustrations.

Survival Tip # 61

Approach your reunion with a plan–don't just hope everything works out in the end. Review the six strategies in this chapter above on a weekly basis for the first several months: 1) discuss the changes that come with reunion, 2) keep having *problem debriefings* like you did during the separation, 3) have some time apart from one another, 4) work on staying creative and playful with your time together, 5) spend plenty of time with friends, and 6) schedule one night a week as a *date night* and plan something fun.

And They Lived Happily Ever After?

Everyone wants their relationships to survive the separation, reunite, and then live happily ever after. Unfortunately, some couples will discover that this dream will never come to fruition. Many couples do break up or divorce during the separation (but no more frequently than couples living near one another). Additionally, many couples find that after spending more time with one another after reunion, they are not as compatible as they once thought. Research on military separations suggests that many more couples divorce or break up after they reunite than during the actual separations.[120] We don't know if the same is true of civilian couples, but certainly the stresses necessary to cause a relationship to fail exist during this period of reunion.

For some couples, reunion allows them to better get to know one another and determine if the relationship truly is one they both want to continue. Occasionally, couples find that the unique situation of separation allowed them to characterize their partner in an unrealistic way. They often fantasized about the reunion in a similarly unrealistic light.[38] The separation itself had become a coping mechanism for an already troubled relationship. The time apart allowed them to avoid conflict that needed to be addressed, rather than ignored. At the same time, it allowed them the safety of not being alone in the world, and not having to be out looking for a new relationship. Upon reuniting, the negative aspects of their relationship, coupled with the disillusionment of a less than perfect reunion, begin to weigh in favor of ending the relationship.

While no one enjoys the pain of realizing that they and their partner should go separate ways, sometimes this truly is the right thing to do. Many couples who end a long relationship lament over the fact that they "wasted" so much time before leaving. They realized relatively early on that the relationship would not work out, yet they persisted for a variety of reasons.

Subsequently, some people in LDRs will undoubtedly find that they no longer seem to be happy and fulfilled with their relationship once they reunite. I suggest allowing some time to work through this period of change prior to making any final decisions on ending the relationship. Occasionally, the discontent stems more from the difficulties inherent with reunion than anything fundamental to the couple.

Ultimately, most couples who have managed to maintain their relationship throughout the separation will find reunion exciting and fulfilling. I hope this is true for your relationship and I hope you and your partner do live happily ever after.

Chapter 22

Resources for Your LDR: An Annotated Bibliography

One of the most frustrating problems for people in LDRs seems to be the lack of information about these types of relationships. Admittedly, it takes a great deal of effort to find what little is out there. However, over the past decade that I've been researching separated couples, I've amassed a great deal of information.

Most of the sources are studies published in professional journals for therapists, relationship experts, psychologists, or sociologists. A few are books written for people actually in LDRs. Because I believe that knowledge is power, I've put together a bibliography of the most useful of the studies and books available. I've tried to keep the technical jargon to a minimum and focus on information that may be helpful to those of you in an LDR. Go to the bibliography under the referenced number to find the full citation of any book or article mentioned here. Many of the journals will be available at your local library. Some may require a trip to a university library or even a medical school or graduate school. Librarians can assist you in finding any particular journal, and many places will order copies of articles through a system called *interlibrary loan.*

Other than the books written for laypeople in LDRs, most of the research may seem fairly technical, as it addresses some particular theoretical concerns related to separated relationships.

Sources Written for Couples in LDRs

Books
At the Heart of Your Long Distance Relationship, by Catherine Day. Writers Club Press, 2002.[175]

A short paperback, this is one of the newest additions to the sparse literature on LDRs. The author, a corporate manager and a participant in an LDR herself, provides several lists of helpful tips and workbook-type projects for those in separated relationships. While there is no research cited for the suggestions made, they all seem to have utility for most LDRs.

The Long Distance Romance Guide, **by Leslie Karsner. Writers Club Press, 2001.**[94]
Written by a self-proclaimed "romance coach," this 140-page paperback has good tips to help you through your LDR. It's one of the most recent books and helps fill the void. The scientist in me would like to see some reference to research; however, her expert opinions are very helpful.

How to Stay Together When You Have to Be Apart, **by Karen Shanor. Warner Books, 1987.**[61]
A therapist who also is personally in an LDR wrote this 213–page book, one of the more complete paperbacks. Though this is a helpful book, it can be hard to find. She mentions a couple of studies, but the majority of the book seems to be based on expert advice. In a couple of spots I'm concerned about some advice that isn't well supported by research, but use Dr. Shanor's book in conjunction with this one and you'll find it a good resource.

Loving Your Long-Distance Relationship, **by Stephen Blake. Anton Publishing, 1996.**[121]
A self-proclaimed personal experience, this short 93–page paperback carries the reader along the journey of an LDR as experienced by the author. For those who would like to see that others share the same experiences, this is a helpful text. The author doesn't cite any research, as the book is more of a description of his relationship, with some personal suggestions, rather than a scientific work. A helpful edition to what little is available.

Still Loving Your Long-Distance Relationship, **by Stephen Blake and Kimberli Bryan. Anton Publishing, 1998.**[122]
In this sequel to the first book, Blake and Bryan provide the reader with a collection of letters written by those in LDRs in response to reading *Loving Your Long-Distance Relationship*. Again, this is a nice resource to see the range of experiences that people report during their separation.

Loving Your Long-Distance Relationship for Women, **by Kimberli Bryan. Anton Publishing, 1998.**[123]
Essentially the third in this series, this 93-page paperback describes the LDR from a woman's perspective. Although no research is cited, the author has some very good suggestions that generally seem to fit with more rigorous studies. The format follows the original book in the series with the author describing her own experiences and elaborating on coping strategies that seem to work for her. Personally, this is my favorite of this three-book series.

Long Distance Couples: An Activities Handbook for Strengthening Long Distance Relationships. **Developed by The National Institute for Building Long Distance Relationships, 2000.**[124]
This 28-page handbook provides several lists of activities to help strengthen and build your relationship while separated. Explanations are relatively limited,

but the handbook does not attempt to be an extensive work on LDRs. This is a nice edition to help churn up creative ways of coping with the distance.

***Commuter Marriage: Living Together, Apart,* by Farlie Winfield. Columbia University Press, 1985.**[29]

A slightly older book directed toward separated marriages but still useful for dating couples. Difficult to find but fairly helpful.

***Commuter Marriages,* by Naomi Gerstel and Harriet Gross. Sage, 1984.**[14]

Written by two experts in the field of separated couples, this was one of the first well-researched reviews. The work stems from several articles that these two authored and incorporates a great deal of information about commuter marriages. The flavor is slightly more academic than the other books listed. If you can find it, it is a good resource (though its focus is primarily toward dual-career marriages).

***Today's Military Wife (4th Edition),* by Lydia Sloan Cline. Stackpole Books, 1998.**[125]

Written for wives of servicemen in general, there is a chapter on dealing with deployments that contains both tips on emotional issues (dealing with anger, stress, etc.) and dealing with military paperwork and procedures. An excellent guide for all military couples and it also has some good tips and suggestions from those experienced in military deployments.

Articles and Stories

"Long-Distance Relationships and Emergency Medicine Residency," by Gregory Guldner, MD, MS. 2001.[126]

A brief article I wrote discussing the basics of LDRs. Although the focus is on couples separated due to training in emergency medicine, the bulk of the article simply reviews the data on LDRs in general. It's a brief summary ideal for handing out to skeptical friends and coworkers.

"Commuter Marriage," by Joan Wickersham.[127]

An entertaining story discussing one couple's attempt at an LDR.

Sources Written Primarily for Research and Academics

For those of you who truly want to read everything out there, refer to the complete bibliography at the end of the book, where you'll find almost every piece of written work that I used in researching this book. For the rest, I've put together a collection of articles that most directly address the issue of separated relationships. You may find some that sound interesting to you and your own situation. They are divided into groups based on the types of separations. In fairness, I've included some studies that make conclusions with which I don't personally agree. Generally, I've discussed the details of these elsewhere in this book.

Separated Marriages and Families (Nonmilitary)

"The Corporate Executive Wife's Coping Patterns in Response to Routine Husband-Father Absence," by **Pauline Grossenbacher-Boss, Hamilton McCubbin, and Gary Lester.**[128]

A pilot study examining the ways families and wives deal with work-related separations.

"Commuting Married Faculty Women and the Traditional Academic Community," by **Irving Allen and Jane Wilkie.**[129]

Reviews the difficulties associated with women in academics and the choice to maintain a long-distance marriage.

"Children's Reactions to Temporary Loss of the Father," by **Frank Crumley and Ronald Blumenthal.**[130]

An older article that may be helpful to those with children.

"Ending the Commute: Communication Strategies of Couples During Reintegration (Doctoral Thesis)," by **Pamela Dunkin.**[131]

A difficult to find source (write to the University of Oregon), but a good example of the difficulties that come with reunion after an LDR.

"So Near Yet So Far: The Non-Resident Father," by **Carol Michaels.**[132]

An interesting review, useful for those fathers involved in a separated marriage.

"Commuter Marriages: Personal, Family and Career Issues," by **Melissa Groves and Diane Horm-Wingerd.**[43]

A study of issues surrounding separated marriages including ways of coping with the distance.

". . . Until Careers Do Us Part: Vocational and Marital Satisfaction in the Dual-Career Commuter Marriage," by **Kathrijn Govaerts and David Dixon.**[13]

A nicely done study comparing dual-career couples who live together with those that have geographically separated. Factors that predict satisfaction with the relationship are also explored.

"Commuting," by **Agnes Farris.**[32]

A smaller study of intense interviews with couples in long-distance marriages. Easy reading that may generate good conversation with your partner.

"Dual-Career Couples Who Live Apart: Two Types," by **Harriet Gross.**[133]

Discusses the results of interviews with separated couples and compares younger couples who are still adjusting to those who are more established.

"Commuter Marriage: Couples Who Live Apart," by **Naomi Gerstel and Harriet Gross.**[134]

A review of separated marriages with an entertaining description of the commuting experience.

"Living Apart: A Comparison of Merchant Marine and Commuter Couples," **by Naomi Gerstel and Harriet Gross.**[135]

One of the very few articles looking at marriages separated for reasons other than academic or military reasons.

"Commuter Marriages: A Review," **by Naomi Gerstel and Harriet Gross.**[34]

Another good review from these two researchers.

"Two-Location Families: Married Singles," **by Betty Kirschner and Laurel Walum.**[52]

A discussion of separated marriages with a focus on how career development issues now affect women's decisions to undertake an LDR.

"Effects of Work-Related Separation on Children and Families," **by Chaya Piotrkowski and Lisa Gornick.**[41]

A review of the literature examining the effect of work-related separations on the family, along with a few hints on coping strategies.

"Marital Non-Cohabitation: Separation Does Not Make the Heart Grow Fonder," **by Ronald Rindfuss and Elizabeth Stephen.**[1]

A large intriguing study looking at census data to determine if couples living apart later divorce. Unfortunately, the study cannot differentiate between marriages that were physically separated because they were having relationship problems, and those that were simply long-distance. The study's conclusions, that LDRs are associated with divorce, is likely a result of including many couples whose relationships were already on the rocks.

"Attachment Theory as Applied to Wartime and Job-Related Marital Separation," **by Julia Vormbrock.**[136]

An outstanding, albeit technical, review of the process of attachment and separation for marriages.

"Dual-Career Couples and Geographic Transfers: Executives' Reactions to Commuter Marriage and Attitude Toward the Move," **by Ann Taylor and John Lounsbury.**[137]

An interesting study designed primarily for executives and human relations administrators, looking at how managers integrate issues of commuter marriage into geographical transfer decisions.

Miscellaneous Relationship Issues
The Psychology of Separation and Loss: Perspectives on Development, Life Transitions, and Clinical Practice, **by Jonathan Bloom-Feshbach, Sally Bloom-Feshbach, and Associates.**[138]

Although it does not focus on LDRs, this book provides a good framework for understanding all sorts of various stresses related to separation.

" 'Secret Tests' Social Strategies for Acquiring Information About the State of the Relationship," **by Leslie Baxter and William Wilmot.**[139]

A fascinating study of the ways people test their relationships. The article briefly discusses how physical separation is sometimes used as a test to determine the importance of the relationship.

"Separation as Support," **by Elizabeth Douvan and Joseph Pleck.**[31]

An uplifting article focusing on the advantages of LDRs.

"Prisoner's Families," **by Donald Schneller.**[140]

A somewhat older article examining the effect of prison separation on families.

"Flying Apart: Separation Distress in Female Flight Attendants," **by Jim Jupp and Paul Mayne.**[141]

A study of 36 flight attendants and how even short separations can cause problems, especially during reunion.

"Doesn't Anybody Stay in One Place Anymore? An Exploration of the Under-Studied Phenomenon of Long-Distance Relationships," **by Mary E. Rohlfing.**[174]

An excellent review of the literature on long-distance romantic relationships and long-distance friendships.

"Love at First Byte? Building Personal Relationships over Computer Networks," **by Martin Lea and Russell Spears.**[173]

This is a detailed but easily read review of relationships that take place predominantly via the Internet. Probably the best place to start if you're looking to untangle the mysteries of online LDRs.

Separated Students

"Relationship Maintenance of College Students Separated During Courtship," **by David Carpenter and David Knox.**[17]

A study that attempts to find out what factors help maintain college LDRs. I discuss a couple of the issues with the study design earlier in the book, as I disagree with some of their conclusions. They also report on some interesting gender differences that may prompt discussion with your partner.

"Does Distance Make the Heart Grow Fonder? A Comparison of Long-Distance and Geographically Close Dating Relationships," **by Mary Dellmann-Jenkins, Teresa Bernard-Paolucci, and Beth Rushing.**[16]

One of the larger studies of separated college students, and relatively well designed.

"Long-Distance Romantic Relationships: Prevalence and Separation-Related Symptoms in College Students," **by Gregory Guldner.**[2]

The largest study of college students, designed to estimate how common LDRs are in the college setting, and to quantify the types of stress and hassles related to separation.

"Time Spent Together and Relationship Quality: Long-Distance Relationships as a Test Case," **by Gregory Guldner.**[11]
Another large study comparing relationship qualities of those in LDRs with those in geographically close relationships.

"Long-Distance Romantic Relationships: Sex Differences in Adjustment and Break-up," **by Vicki Helgeson.**[57]
A study of 97 students in LDRs followed over three months focusing on gender differences related to the separation. A useful addition to the dearth of quantitative research on LDRs.

"The Effects of Self-Beliefs and Relationship Beliefs on Adjustment to a Relationship Stressor," **by Vicki Helgeson.**[142]
A study of college students in LDRs and how their beliefs about themselves, and their relationships, impact their ability to cope with the separation. A good study to show the utility of positive attitude.

"Needs, Coping Strategies, and Coping Outcomes Associated with Long-Distance Relationships," **by Paul Holt and Gerald Stone.**[18]
A study of college students in LDRs that tries to look at the differences between visualizers and verbalizers. There are a few problems with the study design (that I discussed in the text) but this is still one of earliest studies on students in LDRs.

"Coping with Moral Commitment to Long-Distance Dating Relationships," **by John Lydon, Tamarha Pierce, and Shannon O'Regan.**[143]
A somewhat technical article examining types of commitment in relationships that are undergoing the stress of geographical separation.

"The Medical-Student Spouse Syndrome: Grief Reactions to the Clinical Years," **by David Robinson.**[144]
A discussion of the emotional processes that occur when one partner becomes intensely committed to work at the expense of the relationship. Although not technically examining LDRs, this paper describes several of the common reactions to separation.

"Factors Associated with Relationship Stability in Geographically Separated Couples," **by Andrew Schwebel, Ryan Dunn, Barry Moss, and Maureena Renner.**[82]
A study of 89 college freshmen in LDRs examining how intimacy, satisfaction, self-esteem, frequency of contact, and other variables interact.

"Communication and Interdependence in Geographically Separated Relationships," **by Timothy Stephen.**[15]
An interesting study looking at university LDRs as a test of a theory of relationship dynamics. Much of the information is technical, but the author describes a great deal of information about separated couples that may prove helpful.

"Idealization and Communication in Long-Distance Premarital Relationships," **by Laura Stafford and James Reske.**[5]
A fascinating examination of the process of unrealistic expectations within LDRs.

"Physical Distance and Interpersonal Characteristics in College Students' Romantic Relationships," **by Roger Van Horn and Colleagues.**[4]
This study, comparing roughly 80 people in LDRs to 80 people in geographically close relationships, found that the two are more similar than different. A nice review and discussion.

"Coping with Long-Distance Relationships," **by John Westefeld and Debora Liddell.**[145]
A very brief discussion of the author's experience with a mini-workshop for college students in LDRs.

"Communicative Strategies Used to Terminate Romantic Relationships," **by William Wilmot, Donald Carbaugh, and Leslie Baxter.**[85]
These researchers wanted to study the process that occurs during relationships that end, so they chose LDRs, thinking they would break up more so than others. A somewhat technical paper, but still important given the dearth of research available.

Military Separations
"Depression in the Wives of Nuclear Submarine Personnel," **by Karen Beckman, Anthony Marsella, and Ruth Finney.**[146]
One of a handful of studies looking at the wives of Navy submariners, who are a somewhat unique type of LDR, given the long-stretches with very little contact.

"The Returning Veteran Syndrome," **by Douglas Bey.**[111]
A psychiatrist discusses the symptoms related to wartime reunion. A slightly less technical article than many, with a psychodynamic bent.

"Personal Transitions and Interpersonal Communication Among Submariners' Wives," **by Kathleen Boynton and W. Barnett Pearce.**[147]
An excellent, although somewhat outdated, review of separation in general, and the additional stress that comes with submarine deployment.

"Waiting Wives: Women Under Stress," **by Douglas Bey and Jean Lange.**[65]
This paper discusses the normal range of reactions that the wives of servicemen report during their separations. Most of these are applicable to nonmilitary LDRs as well.

"Family Readjustment of Veterans," **by John Cuber.**[112]
A post–World War II article discussing the problems of reunion.

"Coping with Sea Duty: Problems Encountered and Resources Utilized During Periods of Family Separation," by **Kathryn Decker.**[36]
A fairly extensive review of Navy families separated during non-wartime deployments.

"Navy Families in Distress," by **William Dickerson and Ransom Arthur.**[37]
An older article discussing Navy separations.

"Persian Gulf Sojourn: Stereotypes of Family Separation," by **Richard Dukes and Janice Naylor.**[148]
A study of how society perceives separation. Participants describe how they would react to several different vignettes. The only study of this kind to date. Very interesting with regards to the stereotypes that those in LDRs face.

"Loneliness and the Serviceman's Wife," by **Evelyn Duvall.**[35]
A World War II article that still is pertinent to many military separations.

"The Psychological Adjustments of Returned Servicemen and Their Families," by **Coleman Griffith.**[149]
Another post–World War II paper discussing the difficulties of reunion.

"Families of Prisoners of War Held in Vietnam: A Seven-Year Study," by **Edna Hunter.**[51]
This study focuses on families in crises examining the emotional processes and coping techniques over 7 years. Although it's based on a very specific type of LDR, many of the conclusions are applicable to all.

Families Under Stress, by **Rubin Hill.**[45]
An extremely detailed early study of families separated due to World War II.

"The Submariners' Wives Syndrome," by **Richard Isay.**[150]
One of the earlier studies that looked at the range of severe depression and anxiety connected with wives separated from their husbands on submarines.

"American Families and the Vietnam War," by **E. James Lieberman.**[151]
A detailed discussion of the impact of wartime separation on military families.

"The Returned Prisoner of War: Factors in Family Reintegration," by **Hamilton McCubbin, Barbara Dahl, Gary Lester, and Beverly Ross.**[152]
An in-depth study, by this prolific research group, of families trying to adjust after prolonged separation.

"Coping Repertoires of Families Adapting to Prolonged War-Induced Separations," by **Hamilton McCubbin, Barbara Dahl, Gary Lester, Dorothy Benson, and Marilyn Robertson.**[153]
Another well-done study by McCubbin's group looking at styles of coping with catastrophic war-related separation.

"Adaptation of the Family to the POW/MIA Experience: An Overview," by **Hamilton McCubbin, Edna Hunter, and Philip Meters, Jr.**[154]
A detailed study of over 200 families dealing with prolonged separation from military family members. There is a great deal of information about symptoms during separation, how people coped with the stress, and wives' perceptions of their marriages.

"Family Separation in the Army: A Study of the Problems Encountered and the Care Taking Resources Used by Career Army Families Undergoing Military Separations," by **Frank Montalvo.**[40]
Another good review of the issues facing military couples during separation.

"Prolonged Family Separation in the Military: A Longitudinal Study," by **Hamilton McCubbin and Barbara Dahl.**[155]
A review of military separations focusing on changes over time as the family and couple adapts to the distance and reunion.

"Separation Problems in Military Wives," by **Houston MacIntosh.**[24]
An early study of psychiatric symptoms in military wives separated from their husbands.

"The Families of U.S. Navy Prisoners of War from Vietnam Five Years after Reunion," by **D. Stephen Nice, Barbara McDonald, and Tom McMillian.**[156]
A fascinating study of couples as they attempt to adjust to reunion. This has one of the longest periods of observation, looking five years after the separation had ended.

"World War II and Divorce: A Life Course Perspective," by **Eliza Pavalko and Glen Elder, Jr.**[120]
A well-designed study examining the effect of World War II on marriages looking at several factors and following the relationships over time.

"Separation Reactions of Married Women," by **Chester Pearlman, Jr.**[28]
A psychiatrist discusses his experience with 485 women separated from their military partners.

"Social Support, Family Separation, and Well-Being Among Military Wives," by **Leora Rosen and Linda Moghadam.**[39]
A large study examining military couples and the role of social support during separations.

"Stressors, Stress Mediators, and Emotional Well-Being Among Spouses of Soldiers Deployed to the Persian Gulf During Operation Desert Shield/Storm," by **Leora Rosen, Joel Teitelbaum, and David Westhuis.**[44]
A study of 981 families of Gulf War veterans exploring issues related to military separation. A very important piece of research showing the critical importance of social support.

"Marital Adjustment of Army Spouses One Year After Operation Desert Storm," by Leora Rosen, Doris Durand, David Westhuis, and Joel Teitelbaum.[157]
A large study of families of Gulf War veterans and how they coped with reunion. Also includes a good discussion of the literature on military separation and reunion.

"The Dynamics of Grief of Wives and Families of Military Personnel Missing in Action," by Ludwig Spolyar.[158]
A psychologist discusses the emotional processes of wives dealing not only with separation, but also the uncertainty associated with a husband missing in action.

"The Homecomer," by Alfred Schuetz.[159]
Written in 1945, this discussion makes excellent reading, and provides great material to discuss with your partner prior to or just after reunion from deployment.

"Intensive Case Studies of Attachment Utilizing a Naturally-Occurring Separation in Marital Relationships (Doctoral Thesis)," by Stephen Stratton.[27]
A difficult to find thesis (write to Auburn University) that interviews five Army wives about their coping with separation. The material highlights several of the concepts I discussed in this book and reads very well.

"Children's Single-Session Briefings: Group Work with Military Families Experiencing Parents' Deployment," by Jane Waldron, Ronaele Whittington, and Steve Jensen.[106]
A rare look at methods of integrating children into coping strategies during deployments.

"Marital Satisfaction, Job Satisfaction, and Retention in the Army," by John Woelfel and Joel Savell.[12]
A somewhat technical article looking at how separation impacts career satisfaction in the military.

Internet Websites Dedicated to Long-Distance Relationships

Along with the advantages of email, the Internet provides a fantastic source of information for those in LDRs. The difficulty comes in locating the best sites without having to dredge through the volumes of irrelevant pages. A search for "long-distance relationships" tends to bring a barrage of sites for long-distance telephone service, Internet dating, and sexually explicit pages.

The next list provides a few of the sites that focus on long-distance relationships. Internet sites are constantly evolving with new pages born everyday and older sites routinely vanishing. Therefore, some of the sites listed may no longer be maintained or accessible.

Just as some of the books and articles give opinions regarding LDRs that are not supported by the research, websites can often have the same drawback. Be wary of taking too seriously some of the claims you may read about on their pages.

- *www.longdistancecouples.com*
- *www.theromantic.com/stories/longdistance/main.htm*
- *www.etoile.co.uk/Love/Long.html*
- *www.marriage.about.com/c/ht/01/04/How_Maintain_Long_ Distance0986863563.htm*
- *www.marriage.about.com/cs/militarymarriages/index.htm*
- *www.suite101.com/welcome.cfm/long_distance_romance*
- *www.sblake.com/*
- *www.wineberry.net/ltw/*
- *www.ldrexpert.com*
- *www.groups.yahoo.com/group/a-special-love/*
- *www.jfmilne.com* (publisher's website)

Epilogue

I hope this book helped provide you with some optimism, along with a few strategies to help improve your long-distance relationship. You are not alone. Many millions of us have gone through, and continue to go through, the same experiences
inherent in separated romantic relationships. Yours can survive and even grow during your time apart.

The suggestions in this book are based on a tremendous amount of research.
Every time I mention to someone the topic of my studies I'm asked, "What did
you find?" How does one succinctly summarize the findings of over 300,000
points of data, 400 couples who filled out questionnaires, and the hundreds of couples with whom I've personally spoken over the past decade or so (not to mention
my own years of experience in an LDR)? Eventually, I put together a brief top ten
list of the results that seemed to help couples the most. Each of these ten tips has
been discussed in more detail earlier in the book, but I think it helps to see them
all together.

Top 10 Strategies for a Strong and Healthy Long-Distance Relationship

1. Stay optimistic. Your LDR has as much chance as any other relationship.
2. Socialize. Get out and spend time with friends who can provide emotional support.
3. Find a confidant with whom you can talk about the relationship.
4. Discuss ground rules about what is okay and what is not in terms of interacting with others.
5. Prior to leaving one another, schedule your next reunion.
6. Plan the relationship in blocks of six months at a time.
7. Send letters.
8. Keep up on the daily trivia of each other's lives when you talk on the telephone.
9. Send photographs frequently.
10. Purchase a hands-free telephone so you can talk while you work on day-to-day activities.

Appendix

Separation Inventory–Part I
Answer Sheet

Instructions: Read the questions in the book and circle your answers below.

Question Number	Answer		
1	A	B	C
2	A	B	C
3	A	B	C
4	A	B	C
5	A	B	C
6	A	B	C
7	A	B	C
8	A	B	C
9	A	B	C
10	A	B	C
11	A	B	C
12	A	B	C
13	A	B	C
14	A	B	C
15	A	B	C
16	A	B	C
17	A	B	C
18	A	B	C
19	A	B	C
20	A	B	C
21	A	B	C
22	A	B	C
23	A	B	C
24	A	B	C
25	A	B	C

Separation Inventory–Part I
Answer Sheet

Instructions: Read the questions in the book and circle your answers below.

Question Number	Answer		
1	A	B	C
2	A	B	C
3	A	B	C
4	A	B	C
5	A	B	C
6	A	B	C
7	A	B	C
8	A	B	C
9	A	B	C
10	A	B	C
11	A	B	C
12	A	B	C
13	A	B	C
14	A	B	C
15	A	B	C
16	A	B	C
17	A	B	C
18	A	B	C
19	A	B	C
20	A	B	C
21	A	B	C
22	A	B	C
23	A	B	C
24	A	B	C
25	A	B	C

Separation Inventory–Part I
Scoring Sheet

Instructions: Each question on the Separation Inventory has a value of 0, 1, or 2. Locate each question along the left-hand side. Locate the column that corresponds to your answer to that question, either A, B, or C. Circle the number that corresponds to the answer for that question. For example, if you answered "B" on item 2, you would circle the number "1" located under the "B" across from the item number 2. Then add each of the items together to obtain the subscores, and then a total score.

Your Answer

Item Number	A	B	C	
1)	2	1	0	
2)	2	1	0	
3)	0	1	2	
4)	0	1	2	
5)	2	1	0	
6)	2	1	0	
7)	2	1	0	
	Total _____			**(Demographics** Subscore)
8)	2	1	0	
9)	0	1	2	
10)	2	1	0	
11)	0	1	2	
12)	0	1	2	
13)	2	1	0	
14)	2	1	0	
15)	2	1	0	
16)	0	1	2	
17)	0	1	2	
18)	0	1	2	
19)	0	1	2	
	Total _____			**(Personality** Subscore)
20)	2	1	0	
21)	2	1	0	
22)	2	1	0	
23)	2	1	0	
24)	2	1	0	
25)	0	1	2	
	Total _____			**(Support** Subscore)

(continued)

Demographics _____**(0–14)**
Personality _____**(0–24)**
Support _____**(0–12)**
Total (of all items) _____**(0–50)**

Separation Inventory–Part I
Scoring Sheet

Instructions: Each question on the Separation Inventory has a value of 0, 1, or 2. Locate each question along the left-hand side. Locate the column that corresponds to your answer to that question, either A, B, or C. Circle the number that corresponds to the answer for that question. For example, if you answered "B" on item 2, you would circle the number "1" located under the "B" across from the item number 2. Then add each of the items together to obtain the subscores, and then a total score.

Your Answer

Item Number	A	B	C	
1)	2	1	0	
2)	2	1	0	
3)	0	1	2	
4)	0	1	2	
5)	2	1	0	
6)	2	1	0	
7)	2	1	0	
	Total			(**Demographics** Subscore)
8)	2	1	0	
9)	0	1	2	
10)	2	1	0	
11)	0	1	2	
12)	0	1	2	
13)	2	1	0	
14)	2	1	0	
15)	2	1	0	
16)	0	1	2	
17)	0	1	2	
18)	0	1	2	
19)	0	1	2	
	Total			(**Personality** Subscore)
20)	2	1	0	
21)	2	1	0	
22)	2	1	0	
23)	2	1	0	
24)	2	1	0	
25)	0	1	2	
	Total			(**Support** Subscore)

(continued)

Demographics   _____(0–14)
Personality   _____(0–24)
Support   _____(0–12)
Total (of all items)   _____(0–50)

Separation Inventory–Part II
Answer Sheet

Instructions: Write down your answer next to the corresponding question below. Then write in your partner's answers under the corresponding column. Convert the letters to numbers with a = 1, b = 2, c = 3, d = 4, e = 5, and f = 6. For each item, subtract the larger number from the smaller and write this result under the column *Item Score*. Add all of the numbers in the *Item Score* column for a subtotal. Subtract this number from 50 for a total score. For details see pages 23 and 24.

Question Number	My Answer	My Partner's Answer	Item Score
1	_____	_____	_____
2	_____	_____	_____
3	_____	_____	_____
4	_____	_____	_____
5	_____	_____	_____
6	_____	_____	_____
7	_____	_____	_____
8	_____	_____	_____
9	_____	_____	_____
10	_____	_____	_____
11	_____	_____	_____
12	_____	_____	_____
13	_____	_____	_____
14	_____	_____	_____

Subtotal _____

Subtract Subtotal from 50
To Calculate Total Score

Total _____ **(0–50)**

Separation Inventory–Part II
Answer Sheet

Instructions: Write down your answer next to the corresponding question below. Then write in your partner's answers under the corresponding column. Convert the letters to numbers with a = 1, b = 2, c = 3, d = 4, e = 5, and f = 6. For each item, subtract the larger number from the smaller and write this result under the column *Item Score*. Add all of the numbers in the *Item Score* column for a subtotal. Subtract this number from 50 for a total score. For details see pages 23 and 24.

Question Number	My Answer	My Partner's Answer	Item Score
1	_____	_____	_____
2	_____	_____	_____
3	_____	_____	_____
4	_____	_____	_____
5	_____	_____	_____
6	_____	_____	_____
7	_____	_____	_____
8	_____	_____	_____
9	_____	_____	_____
10	_____	_____	_____
11	_____	_____	_____
12	_____	_____	_____
13	_____	_____	_____
14	_____	_____	_____

Subtotal _____

Subtract Subtotal from 50
To Calculate Total Score

Total _____ **(0–50)**

Separation Inventory

Scoring Circle

Instructions: Place a mark on the crosshairs that correspond to your Separation Inventory for each score–Demographics, Personality, and Support from Part I of the Separation Inventory, and the Relationship score from Part II. Then connect each of these marks to create a smaller circle within the larger one. Your total score is the sum of each of the four subscores (demographics, personality, support, and relationship). See Chapters 3 through 8 for how to use the circle to improve your LDR.

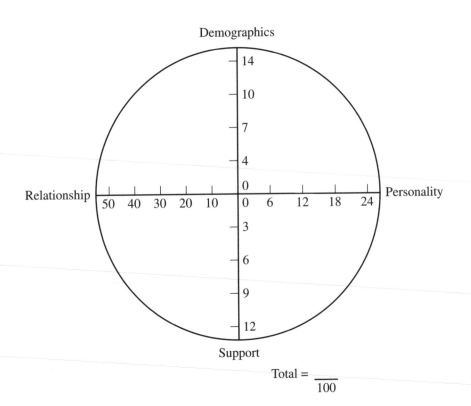

Total = ___
         100

Separation Inventory

Scoring Circle

Instructions: Place a mark on the crosshairs that correspond to your separation inventory for each score–Demographics, Personality, and Support from Part I of the Separation Inventory and the Relationship score from Part II. Then connect each of these marks to create a smaller circle within the larger one. Your total score is the sum of each of the four subscores (demographics, personality, support, and relationship). See Chapters 3 through 8 for how to use the circle to improve your LDR.

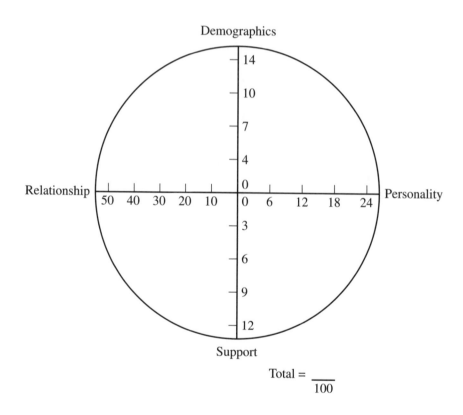

About the Author

Dr. Gregory Guldner, a graduate of Stanford medical school, is the leading authority on long-distance relationships. He has spent over a decade researching these relationships and is the author of the largest and most complete study of separated couples. During graduate training in clinical psychology, he completed several studies on long-distance relationships and gathered together volumes of research on separation. Over the ensuing years, he has continued to study the literature and to conduct interviews with hundreds of couples in LDRs. He has published several articles on issues of sexuality, romantic relationships in general, and long-distance relationships in particular. He has personal experience in separated relationships, having married his long-distance partner of four years. Currently, he is a professor at a university and teaching hospital in southern California.

Bibliography

1. Rindfuss, R.R. Stephen, E.H. "Marital Noncohabitation: Separation Does Not Make the Heart Grow Fonder." *Journal of Marriage and the Family,* 1990; 52:259–270.

2. Guldner, G.T. "Long-Distance Romantic Relationships: Prevalence and Separation-Related Symptoms in College Students." *Journal of College Student Development,* 1996; 37:289–295.

3. Guldner, G.T. "Propinquity and Dating Relationships: Toward a Theory of Long-Distance Romantic Relationships Including an Exploratory Study of College Students' Relationships-at-a-Distance." Department of Psychology. West Lafayette: Purdue University, 1992.

4. Van Horn, K.R. Arnone, A. Nesbitt, K. et al. "Physical Distance and Interpersonal Characteristics in College Students' Romantic Relationships." *Personal Relationships,* 1997; 4:25–34.

5. Stafford, L. Reske, J.R. "Idealization and Communication in Long-Distance Premarital Relationships." *Family Relations,* 1990; 39:274–279.

6. Stephen, T.D. "Symbolic Interdependence and Post-Break-Up Distress: A Reformulation of the Attachment Process." *Journal of Divorce,* 1984; 8:1–17.

7. Hill, C.T. Rubin, Z. Peplau. L. Anne. "Breakups Before Marriage: The End of 103 Affairs." *Journal of Social Issues,* 1976; 32:147–168.

8. Wood, J.T. "Different Voices in Relationship Crises: An Extension of Gilligan's Theory." *American Behavioral Scientist,* 1986; 29:273–301.

9. Hortacsu, N. Karanci, A.N. "Premarital Breakups in a Turkish Sample: Perceived Reasons, Attributional Dimensions, and Affective Reactions." *International Journal of Psychology,* 1987; 22:57–74.

10. Banks, S. P. Altendorf, D. Green, J. O. Cody, M. J. "An Examination of Relationship Disengagement: Perceptions, Breakup Strategies and Outcomes." *Western Journal of Speech Communication,* 1987; 51:19–41.

11. Guldner, G.T. Swensen, C.H. "Time Spent Together and Relationship Quality: Long-Distance Relationships as a Test Case." *Journal of Social and Personal Relationships,* 1995; 12:313–320.

12. Woelfel, J.C. Savell, J.M. "Marital Satisfaction, Job Satisfaction, and Retention in the Army." In: Hunter, E. Nice, D. Eds. *Military Families: Adaptation to Change.* New York: Praeger, 1978:17–31.

13. Govaerts, K. Dixon, D.N. ". . . Until Careers Do Us Part: Vocational and Marital Satisfaction in the Dual-Career Commuter Marriage." *International Journal for the Advancement of Counseling,* 1988; 11:265–281.

14. Gerstel, N. Gross, H. *Commuter Marriages.* New York: Sage, 1984.

15. Stephen, T. "Communication and Interdependence in Geographically Separated Relationships." *Human Communication Research,* 1986; 13:191–210.

16. Dellmann-Jenkins, M. Bernard-Paolucci, T.S. Rushing, B. "Does Distance Make the Heart Grow Fonder? A Comparison of Long-Distance and Geographically Close Dating Relationships." *College Student Journal,* 1994; 28:212–219.

17. Carpenter, D. Knox, D. "Relationship Maintenance of College Students Separated During Courtship." *College Student Journal,* 1986; 28:86–88.

18. Holt, P. A. Stone, G. L. "Needs, Coping Strategies, and Coping Outcomes Associated with Long-Distance Relationships." *Journal of College Student Development,* 1988; 29:136–141.

19. Weigert, A. *Sociology of Everyday Life.* New York: Longman, 1981.

20. Duck, S. *Human Relationships: An Introduction to Social Psychology.* Beverly Hills: Sage, 1986.

21. Stafford, L. Canary, D.J. "Maintenance Strategies and Romantic Relationship Type, Gender, and Relational Characteristics." *Journal of Social and Personal Relationships,* 1991; 8:217–242.

22. Kolb, D. *The Learning Styles Inventory: Technical Manual.* Boston, MA: McBer & Company, 1976.

23. Hunter, E. J. Nice, D. *Military Families: Adaptation to Change.* New York: Praeger, 1978.

24. MacIntosh, H. "Separation Problems in Military Wives." *American Journal of Psychiatry,* 1968; 125:156–161.

25. McCubbin, H. "Integrating Coping Behavior in Family Stress Theory." *Journal of Marriage and the Family,* 1979; 41:237–244.

26. Patterson, J.M. McCubbin, H.I. "Gender Roles and Coping." *Journal of Marriage and the Family,* 1984; 46:95–104.

27. Stratton, S.P. Intensive Case Studies of Attachment Utilizing a Naturally-Occurring Separation in Marital Relationships. Doctoral Thesis: Auburn University, Alabama, 1991.

28. Pearlman, C. "Separation Reactions of Married Women." *American Journal of Psychiatry,* 1970; 126:946–950.

29. Winfield, F.E. *Commuter Marriage: Living Together, Apart.* New York: Columbia University Press, 1985.

30. Rienerth, J. "Separation and Female Centeredness in the Military Family." In: Hunter, E.J. Nice, D.S. Eds. *Military Families: Adaptation to Change.* New York: Praeger, 1978.

31. Douvan, E. Pleck, J. "Separation as Support." In: Rapoport, R. Rapoport, R. Eds. *Working Couples.* New York: Harper & Row, 1978.

32. Farris, A. "Commuting." In: Rapoport, R. Rapoport, R. Eds. *Working Couples.* New York: Harper & Row, 1978.

33. Bloom-Feshbach, J. Bloom-Feshbach, S. "Introduction: Psychological Separateness and Experiences of Loss." In: Bloom-Feshbach, J. Bloom-Feshbach, S. Eds. *The Psychology of Separation and Loss.* San Francisco: Jossey-Bass, 1987.

34. Gerstel, N. Gross, H. "Commuter Marriages: A Review." *Marriage and Family Review,* 1982; 5:71–93.

35. Duvall, E. "Loneliness and the Serviceman's Wife." *Marriage and Family Living,* 1945; 77–81.

36. Decker, K. "Coping with Sea Duty: Problems Encountered and Resources Utilized during Periods of Family Separation." In: Hunter, E., Nice, D. Eds. *Military Families: Adaptation to Change.* New York: Praeger, 1978.

37. Dickerson, W. Arthur, R. "Navy Families in Distress." *Military Medicine,* 1965; 130:894–898.

38. Lagrone, D.M. "The Military Family Syndrome." *American Journal of Psychiatry,* 1978; 135:1040–1042.

39. Rosen, L. Moghadam, L. "Social Support, Family Separation, and Well-Being Among Military Wives." *Behavioral Medicine,* 1988; 14:64–70.

40. Montalvo, F. "Family Separation in the Army: A Study of the Problems Encountered and the Caretaking Resources Used by Career Army Families Undergoing Military Separation." In: McCubbin, H. Dahl, B.B. Hunter, E. Eds. *Families in the Military System.* Beverly Hills: Sage, 1976.

41. Piotrkowski, C.S. Gornick, L.K. "Effects of Work-Related Separations on Children and Families." In: Bloom-Feshbach, J. Bloom-Feshbach, S. Eds. *The Psychology of Separation and Loss.* San Francisco: Jossey-Bass, 1987.

42. Figley, C.R. McCubbin, H.I. *Stress and the Family, Volume 2: Coping with Catastrophe.* New York: Brunner/Mazel, 1986.

43. Groves, M.M. Horm-Wingerd, D.M. "Commuter Marriages: Personal, Family and Career Issues." *Sociology and Social Research,* 1991; 75:212–216.

44. Rosen, L. Teitelbaum, J.M. Westhuis, D.J. "Stressors, Stress Mediators, and Emotional Well-Being Among Spouses of Soldiers Deployed to the Persian Gulf During Operation Desert Shield/Storm." *Journal of Applied Social Psychology,* 1993; 23:1587–1593.

45. Hill, R. *Families Under Stress.* New York: Harper and Brothers, 1949.

46. House, J.S. *Work Stress and Social Support.* Reading, MA: Addison-Wesley, 1981.

47. Benson, D. McCubbin, H. Dahl, B.B. Hunter, E. "Waiting: The Dilemma of the MIA Wife." In: McCubbin, H. Dahl, B.B. Metres, P.J., Jr. Hunter, E. Plag, J.A. Eds. *Family Separation and Reunion: Families of Prisoners of War and Servicemen Missing in Action.* Washington, D.C: Government Printing Office, 1973.

48. Brown, D. Huycke, E. "Problems of Vietnam Prisoners of War and Their Families." In: Masserman, J. Schwab, J. Eds. *Social Psychiatry,* Vol. 1, 1974; 91–98.

49. Price-Bonham, S. "Missing in Action Men: A Study of Their Wives." *International Journal of Sociology of the Family,* 1972; 2:201–211.

50. Hall, R. Simmons, W. "The POW Wife." *Archives of General Psychiatry,* 1973; 29:690–694.

51. Hunter, E.J. "Families of Prisoners of War Held in Vietnam: A Seven-Year Study." *Evaluation and Program Planning,* 1986; 9:243–251.

52. Kirschner, B.F. Walum, L.R. "Two-Location Families: Married Singles." *Alternative Lifestyles,* 1978; 1:513–525.

53. Lewis, R.A. "Social Reaction and the Formation of Dyads: An Interactionist Approach to Mate Selection." *Sociometry,* 1973; 36:409–418.

54. Pueschel, J. Moglia, R. "The Effects of the Penal Environment on Familial Relationships." *The Family Coordinator,* 1977; 26:373–375.

55. Reid, A.A. "Comparing Telephone with Face-to-Face Contact." In: Pool, I.S. Ed. *The Social Impact of the Telephone.* Cambridge, MA: MIT Press, 1977.

56. Gottman, J.M. Krokoff, L.J. "Marital Interaction and Satisfaction: A Longitudinal View." *Journal of Consulting and Clinical Psychology,* 1989; 57:47–52.

57. Helgeson, V. S. "Long-Distance Romantic Relationships: Sex Differences in Adjustment and Breakup. Personality and Social." *Psychology Bulletin,* 1994; 20:254–265.

58. Scott, J.P. Stewart, J.M. DeGhett, V.J. "Separation in Infant Dogs: Emotional Response and Motivational Consequences." In: Scott, J.P. Senay, E.C. Eds. *Separation and Depression: Clinical and Research Aspects.* Washington, D.C: American Association for the Advancement of Science, 1973.

59. Derogatis, L. Melisaratos, N. "The Brief Symptom Inventory: An Introductory Report." *Psychological Medicine,* 1983; 13:595–605.

60. Schmale, A.H. "Adaptive Role of Depression in Health and Disease." In: Scott, J.P. Senay, E.C. Eds. *Separation and Depression: Clinical and Research Aspects.* Washington, D.C.: American Association for the Advancement of Science, 1973; 187–209.

61. Shanor, K. *How to Stay Together When You Have to Be Apart.* New York: Warner, 1987.

62. Hetherington, E.M. Cox, M. Cox, R. "Divorced Fathers." *The Family Coordinator,* 1976; 25:417–428.

63. Notarius, C.I. Pellegrini, D.S. "Marital Processes as Stressors and Stress Mediators: Implications for Marital Repair." In: Duck, S. Ed. *Personal Relationships 5: Repairing Personal Relationships.* New York: Academic Press, 1984.

64. Cohen, S. Hoberman, H.M. "Positive Events and Social Supports as Buffers of Life Change Stress." *Journal of Applied Social Psychology,* 1983; 13:99–125.

65. Bey, D.R. Lange, J. "Waiting Wives: Women Under Stress." *American Journal of Psychiatry,* 1974; 131:283–286.

66. Weiss, R.S. Loneliness: The Experience of Emotional and Social Isolation. Cambridge, MA: MIT Press, 1973.

67. Hartog, J. "Group Therapy with Psychotic and Borderline Military Wives." *American Journal of Psychiatry,* 1966; 122:1125–1131.

68. Rook, K.S. "Social Support Versus Companionship: Effects of Life Stress, Loneliness, and Evaluations by Others." *Journal of Personality and Social Psychology,* 1987; 52:1132–1147.

69. Cobb, S. "Social Support as a Moderator of Life Stress." *Psychosomatic Medicine,* 1976; 38:300–314.

70. Brown, G. W. Bhrolchain, M.N. Harris, T. "Social Class and Psychiatric Disturbance Among Women in an Urban Population." *Sociology,* 1975; 9:225–254.

71. Montague, A. *Touching.* New York: Perennial Library, 1972.

72. Lynch, J.J. *The Broken Heart.* New York: Basic Books, 1977.

73. Abramson, L.Y. Seligman, E.P. Teasdale, J.D. "Learned Helplessness In Humans: Critique and Reformulation." *Journal of Abnormal Psychology,* 1978; 87:49–74.

74. Overmier, J.B. Seligman, M.E. "Effects of Inescapable Shock upon Subsequent Escape and Avoidance Learning." *Journal of Comparative and Physiological Psychology,* 1967; 63:28–33.

75. Baxter, L.A. Bullis, C. "Turning Points in Developing Romantic Relationships." *Human Communication Research,* 1986; 12:469–493.

76. Skinner, D.A. "Dual-Career Family Stress and Coping: A Literature Review." *Family Relations,* 1980; 29:473–480.

77. Harlow, H. "The Nature of Love." *American Psychologist,* 1958; 13:673–685.

78. Bancroft, J. "Cardiovascular and Endocrine Changes During Sexual Arousal and Orgasm." *Psychosomatic Medicine,* 1999; 61:280–289.

79. Rettig, K.D. Bubolz, M.M. "Interpersonal Resource Exchanges as Indicators of Quality of Marriage." *Journal of Marriage and the Family,* 1983; 45:497–509.

80. Burgess, E.W. Wallin, P. *Engagement and Marriage.* New York: Lipppincott, 1953.

81. Rubin, Z. Peplau, L. Anne. Hill, C. T. "Loving and Leaving: Sex Differences in Romantic Attachments." *Sex Roles,* 1981; 7:821–835.

82. Schwebel, A.I. Dunn, R.L. Moss, B.F. Renner, M.A. "Factors Associated with Relationship Stability in Geographically Separated Couples." *Journal of College Student Development,* 1992; 33:222–230.

83. Sarbin, T.R. Allen, V.L. "Role Theory." In: Lindzey, G. Aronson, E. Eds. *The Handbook of Social Psychology. Vol. 1.* Reading, MA: Addison-Wesley, 1968.

84. Thibaut, J.W. Kelley, H.H. *The Social Psychology of Groups.* New York: Wiley, 1959.

85. Wilmot, W.W. Carbaugh, D.A. Baxter, L.A. "Communication Strategies Used to Terminate Romantic Relationships." *The Western Journal of Speech Communication,* 1985; 49:204–216.

86. Short, J.A. "Bargaining and Negotiation—An Exploratory Study." London: Communications Study Group, 1971.

87. Reid, A.A. Electronic Person-Person. *Communications.* London: Communications Study Group, 1970.

88. Young, I. *Telecommunicated Interviews: An Exploratory Study.* London: Communications Study Group, 1974.

89. Young, I. A Three-Party Mixed-Media Business Game: A Programme Report on Results to Date. London: Communications Study Group, 1975.

90. Weston, J.R. Kristen, C. Teleconferencing: A Comparison of Attitudes, Uncertainty and Interpersonal Atmospheres in Mediated and Face-to-Face Group Interaction. Department of Communications, Canada, 1973.

91. Williams, E. "Coalition Formation Over Telecommunications Media." *European Journal of Social Psychology*, 1975.

92. Williams, E. "Medium or Message: Communications Medium as a Determinant of Interpersonal Evaluation." *Sociometry*, 1975; 38:119–130.

93. Williams, E. Factors Influencing the Effect of Medium of Communications upon Preferences for Media, Conversations, and Person. London: Communications Study Group, 1972:E/72227/WL.

94. Karsner, L. *The Long Distance Romance Guide*. New York: Writers Club Press, 2001.

95. Barbach, L.G. *For Yourself: The Fulfillment of Female Sexuality*. New York: Signet, 1975.

96. Heiman, J.R. LoPiccolo, J. *Becoming Orgasmic: A Sexual and Personal Growth Program for Women*. New York: Prentice Hall Press, 1987.

97. Anonymous. *Letters to Penthouse*. New York: Warner, 1996.

98. Friday, N. *My Secret Garden*. New York: Pocket Books, 1973.

99. Friday, N. *Women on Top*. New York: Pocket Books, 1991.

100. Barbach, L.G. Levine, L. *Shared Intimacies: Women's Sexual Experiences*. New York: Bantam Books, 1981.

101. Stanway, A. *The Joy of Sexual Fantasy: Understanding and Enriching Your Fantasy Life*. London: Headline, 1991.

102. Gabriel, B. *The Fine Art of Erotic Talk: How to Entice, Excite, and Enchant Your Lover with Words*. New York: Bantum Doubleday, 1996.

103. Gerstel, N. "Marital Alternatives and the Regulation of Sex: Commuter Couples as a Test Case." *Alternative Lifestyles*, 1979; 2:145–176.

104. Ortner, J. Sullivan, J. Crossman, S.M. *Long Distance Marriage*. 1979.

105. Baker, S.L. Fischer, E.G. Cove, L.A. Master, F.D. Fagen, S.A. Janda, E.J. "Impact of Father Absence: Problems of Family Reintegration Following Prolonged Father Absence." *Journal of Orthopsychiatry*, 1968; 38:347.

106. Waldron, J. Whittington, R. Jensen, S. "Children's Single-Session Briefings: Group Work with Military Families Experiencing Parents' Deployment." *Social Work with Groups*, 1985; 8:101–109.

107. Parks, M.R. Adelman, M.B. "Communication Networks and the Development of Romantic Relationships: An Expansion of the Uncertainty Reduction Theory." *Human Communication Research*, 1983; 10:55–79.

108. Parks, M.R. Stan, C.M. Eggert, L.L. "Romantic Involvement and Social Network Involvement." *Social Psychology Quarterly*, 1983; 46:116–131.

109. Milardo, R.M. "Friendship Networks in Developing Relationships: Converging and Diverging Social Environments." *Social Psychology Quarterly*, 1982; 44:964–976.

110. Surra, C. "Courtship Types: Variations in Interdependence Between Partners and Social Networks." *Journal of Personality and Social Psychology,* 1985; 49:357–375.

111. Bey, D.R. "The Returning Veteran Syndrome." *Medical Insight,* 1972. July: 42–49.

112. Cuber, J. "Family Readjustment of Veterans." *Marriage and Family Living,* 1945. 7:28–30.

113. Frances, A. Gale, L. "Family Structure and Treatment in the Military." *Family Process,* 1973; 12.

114. Hill, R. "The Returning Father and His Family." *Marriage and Family Living,* 1945. 7:31–35.

115. Rogers, C. "Counseling with the Returned Serviceman and His Wife." *Marriage and Family Living,* 1945. 7:82–84.

116. McCubbin, H. Dahl, B.B. Meters, P.J. Hunter, E. Plag, J.A. *Family Separation and Reunion: Families of Prisoners of War and Servicemen Missing in Action.* Washington, D.C.: Government Printing Office, 1974.

117. Duck, S. *Understanding Relationships.* New York: Guilford, 1991.

118. Poloma, M.M. "Role Conflict and the Married Professional Woman." In: Safilios-Rothschild, C., Ed. *Toward a Sociology of Women.* Lexington, MA: Xerox, 1972.

119. Berger, P.L. Kellner, H. "Marriage and the Construction of Reality." In: Corer, R.L., Ed. *The Family: Its Structures and Functions.* New York: St. Martin's, 1974.

120. Pavalko, E.K. Elder, G.H. "World War II and Divorce: A Life-Course Perspective." *American Journal of Sociology,* 1990. 95:1213–1234.

121. Blake, S. *Loving Your Long-Distance Relationship.* New York: Anton, 1996.

122. Blake, S. Bryan, K. *Still Loving Your Long-Distance Relationship.* New York: Anton, 1998.

123. Bryan, K. *Loving Your Long-Distance Relationship for Women.* New York: Anton, 1998.

124. Anonymous. *Long Distance Couples: An Activities Handbook for Strengthening Long Distance Relationships.* Developed by The National Institute for Building Long Distance Relationships. Knoxville, TN: A & E Family Publishers, 2000.

125. Cline, L. Sloan. *Today's Military Wife,* Mechanicsburg, PA: Stackpole Books, 1998.

126. Guldner, G.T. "Long-Distance Relationships and Emergency Medicine Residency." *Annals of Emergency Medicine,* 2001. 37:103–106.

127. Wickersham, J. "Commuter Marriage." *The Hudson Review,* 1989. 42:77–91.

128. Grossenbacher-Boss, P. McCubbin, H. Lester, G. "The Corporate Executive Wife's Coping Patterns in Response to Routine Husband-Father Absence." *Family Process,* 1979. 18:79–86.

129. Allen, I. Wilkie, J. "Commuting Married Faculty Women and the Traditional Academic Community." *Sociological Symposium,* 1976. 17:33–43.

130. Crumley, F.E. Blumenthal, R.S. "Children's Reactions to Temporary Loss of the Father." *American Journal of Psychiatry,* 1973. 130:778–782.

131. Dunkin, P. R. Ending the Commute: Communication Strategies of Couples During Reintegration. PhD Thesis. Department of Speech: University of Oregon, 1990.

132. Michaels, C. S. "So Near Yet So Far: The Non-Resident Father." In: Cath, S.H. Gurwitt, A. Gunsberg, L. Eds. *Fathers and Their Families.* Hillsdale, NJ: The Analytic Press, 1989.

133. Gross, H. "Dual-Career Couples Who Live Apart: Two Types." *Journal of Marriage and the Family,* 1980. 42:567–576.

134. Gerstel, N. Gross, H. "Commuter Marriage: Couples Who Live Apart." In: Macklin, E.D. Rubin, R.H. Eds. *Contemporary Families and Alternative Lifestyles.* Beverly Hills: Sage, 1983.

135. Gerstel, N. Gross, H. "Living Apart: A Comparison of Merchant Marine and Commuter Couples. In: Gerstel, N. Gross, H. Ed. *Commuter Marriage.* New York: Sage, 1984.

136. Vormbrock, J.K. "Attachment Theory as Applied to Wartime and Job-Related Marital Separation." *Psychological Bulletin.* 1993, 114:122–144.

137. Taylor, A.S. Lounsbury, J.W. "Dual-Career Couples and Geographic Transfers: Executives' Reactions to Commuter Marriage and Attitude Toward the Move." *Human Relations.* 1988, 41:407–424.

138. Bloom-Feshbach, J. Bloom-Feshbach, S. *The Psychology of Separation and Loss.* San Francisco: Jossey-Bass, 1987.

139. Baxter, L.A. Wilmot, W.A. "'Secret Tests' Social Strategies for Acquiring Information about the State of the Relationship." *Human Communication Research.* 1984, 11:171–201.

140. Schneller, D.P. "Prisoner's Families." *Criminology.* 1975, 12:402–412.

141. Jupp, J. Mayne, P. "Flying Apart: Separation Distress in Female Flight Attendants." *Australian Psychologist.* 1992, 27:154–158.

142. Helgeson, V. S. "The Effects of Self-Beliefs and Relationship Beliefs on Adjustment to a Relationship Stressor." *Personal Relationships.* 1994, 1:241–258.

143. Lydon, J. Pierce, T. O'Regan, S. "Coping with Moral Commitment to Long-Distance Dating Relationships." *Journal of Personality and Social Psychology.* 1997, 73:104–113.

144. Robinson, D. Owen. "The Medical-Student Spouse Syndrome: Grief Reactions to the Clinical Years." *American Journal of Psychiatry.* 1978, 135:972–974.

145. Westefeld, J. Liddell, D. "Coping with Long-Distance Relationships." *Journal of College Student Personnel.* 1982, 11:550–551.

146. Beckman, K. Marsella, A. Finney, R. "Depression in the Wives of Nuclear Submarine Personnel." *American Journal of Psychiatry.* 1979, 136:524–526.

147. Boynton, K. Pearce, W. Barnett. "Personal Transitions and Interpersonal Communication Among Submariners' Wives." In: Hunter, E. Nice, D. Eds. *Military Families: Adaptation to Change.* New York: Praeger, 1978.

148. Dukes, R. Naylor, J. "Persian Gulf Sojourn: Stereotypes of Family Separation." *Social Science Research.* 1991, 76:29–34.

149. Griffith, C. "The Psychological Adjustments of Returned Servicemen and Their Families." *Marriage and Family Living.* 1944, 6:65–67.

150. Isay, R. "The Submariners' Wives Syndrome." *Psychiatric Quarterly.* 1968, 42:647–652.

151. Lieberman, E.J. "American Families and the Vietnam War." *Journal of Marriage and the Family.* 1971, 33:709–721.

152. McCubbin, H. Dahl, B.B. Lester, G. Ross, B. "The Returned Prisoner of War: Factors in Family Reintegration." *Journal of Marriage and the Family.* 1975, 37:471–478.

153. McCubbin, H. Dahl, B.B. Lester, G. Benson, D. Robertson, M.L. "Coping Repertoires of Families Adapting to Prolonged War-Induced Separations." *Journal of Marriage and the Family.* 1976, 38:461–471.

154. McCubbin, H. Hunter, E. Meters, P.J. "Adaptation of the Family to the POW/MIA Experience: An Overview." In: McCubbin, H. Dahl, B.B. Meters, P.J. Hunter, E. Plag, J.A. Eds. *Family Separation and Reunion: Families of Prisoners of War and Servicemen Missing in Action.* Washington, D.C.: U. S. Government Printing Office, 1974.

155. McCubbin, H. Dahl, B.B. "Prolonged Family Separation in the Military: A Longitudinal Study." In: McCubbin, H. Dahl, B.B. Hunter, E. Eds. *Families in the Military System.* Beverly Hills: Sage, 1976.

156. Nice, D.S. McDonald, B. McMillian, T. "The Families of U.S. Navy Prisoners of War From Vietnam Five Years After Reunion." *Journal of Marriage and the Family.* 1981, 43:431–437.

157. Rosen, L. Durand, D. Westhuis, D.J. Teitelbaum, J.M. "Marital Adjustment of Army Spouses One Year after Operation Desert Storm." *Journal of Applied Social Psychology.* 1995, 25:677–692.

158. Spolyar, L. "The Dynamics of Grief of Wives and Families of Military Personnel Missing in Action." *Medical Service Digest.* 1973, 24:20–24.

159. Schuetz, A. "The Homecomer." *American Journal of Sociology.* 1945. 50:369–376.

160. Short, J.A. *Medium of Communication and Consensus.* London: Communication Studies Group, 1972.

161. Kubler-Ross, E. *On Death and Dying.* New York: Macmillan, 1970.

162. Snyder, A. "Midlife Crisis Among Submariner's Wives." In: Hunter, E. Nice, D. Eds. *Military Families: Adaptation to Change.* New York: Praeger, 1978.

163. Billingham, R. E. Sack, A.R. "Conflict Tactics and the Level of Emotional Commitment Among Unmarrieds." *Human Relations.* 1987, 40:59–74.

164. Roscoe, B. Diana, M.S. Brooks, R.H., III. "Early, Middle, and Late Adolescents' Views on Dating and Factors Influencing Partner Selection." *Adolescence.* 1987, 22:59–68.

165. Lee, J. *The Colors of Love.* Don Mills, Ontario: New Press, 1973.

166. Hendrick, C. Hendrick, S. "Dimensions of Love: A Sociobiological Interpretation." *Journal of Social and Clinical Psychology.* 1991, 10:206–230.

167. Hendrick, C. Hendrick, S. Foote, F.H. Slapion-Foote, M. "Do Men and Women Love Differently?" *Journal of Social and Personal Relationships.* 1984, 1:177–195.

168. Hobart, C.W. "The Incidence of Romanticism During Courtship." *Social Forces.* 1958, 36:362–367.

169. Borys, S. Perlman, D. "Gender Differences in Loneliness." *Personality and Social Psychology Bulletin.* 1985, 11:63–74.

170. Teismann, M.W. Mosher, D.L. "Jealous Conflict in Dating Couples." *Psychological Reports.* 1978, 42:1211–1216.

171. Gryl, F.E. Stith, S.M. Bird, G.W. "Close Dating Relationships Among College Students: Differences by Use of Violence and by Gender." *Journal of Social and Personal Relationships.* 1991, 8:243–264.

172. Baxter, L.A. Wilmot, W.A. "Interaction Characteristics of Disengaging, Stable, and Growing Relationship." In: Gilmour, R. Duck, S. Eds. *The Emerging Field of Personal Relationships.* Hillsdale, NJ: Lawrence Erlbaum Associates, 1985.

173. Lea, M. Spears, R. "Love at First Byte? Building Personal Relationships over Computer Networks." In: Wood, J. Duck, S. Eds. *Understudied Relationships: Off the Beaten Path.* Thousand Oaks, CA: Sage, 1995.

174. Rohlfing, M. "Doesn't Anybody Stay in One Place Anymore? An Exploration of the Under-Studied Phenomenon of Long-Distance Relationships." In: Wood, J. Duck, S. Eds. *Understudied Relationships: Off the Beaten Path.* Thousand Oaks, CA: Sage, 1995.

175. Day, C. *At the Heart of Your Long Distance Relationship.* New York: Writers Club Press, 2002.

176. Timmerman, L.M. *Jealousy Expression in Long-Distance Romantic Relationships.* Doctoral Thesis. University of Texas at Austin. 2001.

177. Bercaw, W.A. *So Close, So Far Away: Understanding Satisfaction in Long-Distance Romantic Relationships.* Doctoral Thesis. Pepperdine University. 2001.

178. Wendel, W.C. "High School Sweethearts: A Study in Separation and Commitment." *Journal of Clinical Child Psychology.* 1975, 4:45–46.

Index